AMBIENT MEDIA

AMBIENT MEDIA

/ JAPANESE ATMOSPHERES OF SELF /

PAUL ROQUET

 University of Minnesota Press
Minneapolis • London

An earlier version of chapter 2 was published as "Ambient Landscapes from Brian Eno to Tetsu Inoue," *Journal of Popular Music Studies* 21, no. 4 (2009): 364–83. Portions of chapters 5 and 6 were previously published as "Ambient Literature and the Aesthetics of Calm: Mood Regulation in Contemporary Japanese Fiction," *Journal of Japanese Studies* 35, no. 1 (Winter 2009): 87–111.

Published by the University of Minnesota Press
111 Third Avenue South, Suite 290
Minneapolis, MN 55401–2520
http://www.upress.umn.edu

Library of Congress Cataloging-in-Publication Data
Roquet, Paul.
Ambient media : Japanese atmospheres of self / Paul Roquet.
   Includes bibliographical references and index.
   ISBN 978-0-8166-9244-6 (hc)
   ISBN 978-0-8166-9246-0 (pb)
1. Mass media—Japan. 2. Mass media—Philosophy. 3. Space and time in mass media. I. Title.
   P92.J3R67   2015
   302.23'0952—dc23   2014046943

Printed in the United States of America on acid-free paper

The University of Minnesota is an equal-opportunity educator and employer.

21 20 19 18 17 16   10 9 8 7 6 5 4 3 2 1

CONTENTS

INTRODUCTION

Jellyfish drift through Tokyo. I had been spending the summer evening watching hundreds of them float down the Sumida River on their way back out to sea. Returning home to my apartment on the other side of the city, I put on an ambient jellyfish DVD I discovered recently in the background video section of a nearby record store. The screen glows blue, and slowly the semitransparent creatures drift into view. They are all breath, floating like disembodied lungs as they quietly push backward across the television.

The jellies' translucent skins begin to glow. Some appear in close-up, some from a distance. Sometimes, multiple jellyfish float by together, a syncopated rhythm emerging between them. At moments a jellyfish will shine with the burst of an electrical charge. Postproduction visual effects add ripples of color across their translucent skin.

Downtempo electronic music emanates from the television speakers, matching the visual shimmer and drift with a pulsing aural flow. The soft textures and gentle throb of the soundtrack provide a rhythmic context for the jellies' periodic contractions. The video is programmed to loop endlessly, so the jellies will drift as long as the DVD continues to spin (Figure 1).

Exhausted from the summer heat, I lie down on the tatami and let the mood continue to grow. I glance over once in a while at the cool shades and transparent forms sliding past. Even without turning to face the screen directly, I feel the blue light as it spreads throughout the room. I absorb the sounds seeping quietly from the television speakers. I get up, work on other things, leave the room, and come back. All the while, I sense the jellies' presence. Without conscious effort my own physical rhythms slowly but steadily attune to their pulse and flow. I am not attending to the video, but it is attending to me.

The DVD is *Jellyfish: Healing Kurage,* a Victor Entertainment release from 2006 (*kurage* is Japanese for jellyfish).[1] These digital jellies may not summon the awe I felt watching hundreds of live jellyfish head down the Sumida, but they can be brought home with no damp, no river stink, and no risk of being stung. What *Jellyfish* presents is not the objective documentation of jellies in the wild but a distillation of the

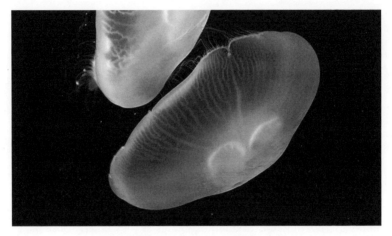

FIGURE 1. Drifting along. Still from *Jellyfish: Healing Kurage.*

subjective drift they afford to the humans who encounter them. The DVD edits the jellyfish experience down to a more portable format and a more specific mood.

Being with the jellies sends my thoughts drifting. The scene at the river had reminded me of Kurosawa Kiyoshi's 2003 film *Bright Future* (*Akarui mirai*), where poisonous jellyfish begin to spread throughout Tokyo's waterways after the main character releases one into the sewer system. I think of a recent news item about a giant jellyfish overturning a Japanese fishing boat in the Pacific and reports of rising numbers of stinging jellyfish lurking in the San Francisco Bay. I wonder about the metaphoric relevance of jellyfish in the twenty-first century: is there something about their transparency, amorphousness, drift, and latent danger that makes them a fitting monster for an age of atmospheric threats like radiation, global warming, and cyberwarfare? My thoughts continue to wander, influenced by the contemplative atmosphere now spread throughout the apartment. I am relaxed, despite these potentially discomforting thoughts. I am not responding to the DVD so much as resonating with it.

My time with *Jellyfish* is an experience of being together with a work of ambient media, of tuning myself through the ambience it provides. The DVD sets a mood, and those within its orbit begin to attune. This focus on mood allows a work of ambient media to afford emotional attunement even when perceived largely through indirect attention, as in the case of ambient music and video. Encountered in isolation, the relaxing stimuli provided by *Jellyfish*—flowing music, soft lighting and colors, gentle movement, slow-paced editing, etc.—may not be sufficient to effectively and dependably produce the promised mood of "healing." Through the repetition and overdetermination of similar affective cues in different aesthetic and sensory registers, however, a strong mood can be established even if audiences are only partially attentive to the on-screen drift. Once cultivated, a mood helps to steer future perceptual orientations, priming the brain to favor sensory cues reinforcing already established feelings.[2] Attuning to ambient media like *Jellyfish* orients the self toward a mix of uncertain calm and drifting reflections, relaxation and wandering thoughts.

AMBIENT SUBJECTIVATION

The idea of ambient media goes back to Isaac Newton, who in his 1704 *Opticks* describes an amorphous and omnipresent "ambient medium" surrounding the human body, coming between it and other objects and serving as a "conveyor of attractive forces" between them. Newton is talking about the air.[3] Air is what makes up the *atmosphere,* in its original meaning of the band of oxygen and nitrogen surrounding the surface of the earth. But air is also the *medium* through which waves of sound and light travel in order to pass from a perceptible object to a sensing body.[4]

Over the next three centuries, the meaning of these words would transform. In an English-language context, the definition of *atmosphere* expanded to refer not just to a pocket of air but to the subjectively felt feeling and tone of a place. The Japanese term for atmosphere, *funiki,* underwent a similar transformation.[5] Meanwhile, *medium* came to refer less to omnipresent substances like air and water and more to "conveyors of attractive forces" invented by humans, from oil on canvas to magnetic discs. While their origins lie close together, atmosphere and media gradually drifted apart. Only in the past half century have they once again come together as the newer media of human invention began to merge with the air itself, filling it with light, sound, and waves of many other frequencies.

In everyday English, *ambience* is a synonym for *atmosphere,* the dispersed and overall tone or feeling of a place. But unlike its more objective sibling, *ambience* always implies a more subjective element of mediation at work: some kind of agency behind the production of mood and a focus on the human body attuning to it. The Latin prefix *ambi-* means "to surround on both sides (left and right)." *Ambience* shares this root with words like *ambivalent, ambiguous, ambidextrous,* and *ambitious,* words that want to have it both ways, to go in two directions at once. Karen Pinkus proposes the "both sides" of *ambience* refers to the binary organization of human hearing and vision.[6] For an ambience to effectively serve as a medium between a human and objects in the surrounding world, it must wrap the eyes and/or ears on both sides of the head. Unlike the more general "in the round" meaning of *atmosphere* (as well as words like *environment* [*kankyō*]), *ambience* emphasizes the mediating role of human sense perception in a person's relationship to the surrounding world. Timothy Morton suggestively notes how the ambient emphasis on embodied perception undermines the Cartesian illusion of a preexisting environment offering itself up to objective and unmediated human perception. Ambience serves to "make strange the idea of environment" by stressing its subjective quality, refusing to equate it with a natural world existing independent of human agency.[7]

The contemporary idea of ambient media as tools of atmospheric self-mediation emerged with British musician and record producer Brian Eno's liner notes to his *Ambient 1: Music for Airports* (1978). In this brief but influential text, Eno proposes "ambient music" as a genre that "provides calm, and a space to think" while maintaining the emotional freedom and subjective interest earlier forms of background music had often sought to erase. Building on the ideas of Erik Satie and John Cage, Eno envisions an ambient style "as ignorable as it is interesting," serving as a tool of atmospheric mood regulation while providing compelling material for open-ended reflection. His idea was quickly taken up in Japan, where by the early 1980s a range of Japanese artists were engaged with producing ambient works in a wide variety of media. As I discuss in the first chapter, while early Japanese accounts of Eno's new genre translated it simply as "environmental music" (*kankyō ongaku*), placing it squarely in the lineage of 1960s environmental art, as the ambient style spread artists and critics began referring to it with a transliterated version of the English term, *anbiento,* more clearly marking out the style from the objective valence of terms like *atmosphere* and *environment.* In this book I use *ambient* to refer to this more specific understanding of atmosphere as something mediated by and for the human senses.

I call this emergence of self with and through ambient media *ambient subjectivation.* As this book explores, ambient subjectivation has become an increasingly common component of everyday life in Japan and other postindustrial societies since the 1970s, emerging as a key technique of contemporary self-care. Earlier twentieth-century modes of atmospheric media focused more explicitly on collective mood manipulation—the "stimulus progression" of Muzak being the most famous example. But the neoliberal emphasis on self-determination demanded more individualistic and autonomous moods. The self, now tasked more than ever with creating a life from scratch, needed an ambience appearing to hand the techniques of atmospheric mood regulation over to the individual, to use as they saw fit.[8]

The notion that new media have become integral to lived experience is now something of a cliché, repeated ad nauseam from the early pronouncements of Marshall McLuhan on the "media environment" to more recent exponents of ubiquitous computing and ambient intelligence.[9] But how did we come to understand atmosphere as a vital component of self-care? The increasing pervasiveness of electronic media certainly has something to do with it, but this is only part of the story. There is more driving the spread of ambient media than simply the push for more immersive, convenient, and integrated technologies. I suggest the rise of ambience is best understood as the neoliberal phase in a shifting relationship between the self and the surrounding air.

My argument builds from Michel Foucault's later work tracing the long and shifting genealogy of *techniques of the self,* practices that "permit individuals to effect by their own means, or with the help of others, a certain number of operations on their own bodies and souls, thoughts, conduct, and way of being, so as to transform themselves in order to attain a certain state of happiness, purity, wisdom, perfection, or immortality."[10] In the historical shift from impersonal Newtonian air to the personalized atmospheres of contemporary media, people began to incorporate ambience as a central technique of self-creation and self-maintenance. In this book I follow Foucault in focusing on subjectivation and not on subjectivity in order not to forget that what later becomes recognized as a "subject" (a Japanese subject, a gendered subject, etc.) is first and foremost a product of particular practices and habits. Foucault ties this back to the two ancient Greek principles of "know thyself" (*gnōthi seauton*) and "care of the self" (*epimeleia heautou*). He notes how somewhere around the "Cartesian moment" of the seventeenth century philosophy began focusing on intellectual cognition alone and for a long time stopped considering issues of embodied practice and habit, at least until phenomenology and twentieth-century thinkers began bringing them back.[11]

Martin Heidegger played an important early role in the return to a more embodied understanding of self, drawing particular attention to the role of atmosphere and mood. Just as Taylorist researchers in the United States were discovering how to improve worker productivity through prerecorded background music, *Being and Time* (1927) set out an argument for the primacy of mood in the shaping of being. Heidegger bases his argument around the German term *Stimmung*. Usually translated into English as *attunement* or *mood*, *Stimmung* also carries overtones of "climate" and "the audition of music and sound." As Hans Ulrich Gumbrecht points out, all of these things involve the experience of being immersed in and influenced by the surrounding world, tuning to the atmosphere whether or not it is consciously attended to.[12] Pushing back against the overintellectualization of being after the Cartesian moment, Heidegger argues *Stimmung* is prior to reflective awareness and a necessary prerequisite to conscious attention: "Mood has always already disclosed being-in-the-world as a whole and first makes possible directing oneself toward something." Mood is "disclosed to itself *before* cognition" and becomes the essential and always present ground of self-awareness. All we can do is substitute one mood for another: "We never master a mood by being free of a mood, but always through a counter mood."[13]

Gumbrecht, drawing on the work of David Wellbery, notes how by asserting *Stimmung* as omnipresent and inescapable, Heidegger was departing from the word's earlier, more limited scope. In Goethe's "Falconet" (1776) and Kant's *Critique of Judgment* (1790), *Stimmung* refers to the pleasant sensation of an "all-encompassing unity and harmony often experienced in altogether commonplace settings." By the end of the century, when Friedrich Hölderlin takes up the concept, it has developed a more romantic tinge, pointing to a harmonious atmosphere lost to the present and available only in retrospect. Heidegger expands the term to serve as a broader and more fundamental determinant of being, incorporating not only joyful and pleasant moods but anxious ones as well.[14]

While helping to establish atmosphere as a fundamental part of subjectivation, Heidegger's conception of *Stimmung* tends to associate it with a preexisting, primordial landscape rather than understanding it as the product of intentional human design. Because of this, readings of atmospheric subjectivation based on his model have tended to fall back into an abstract notion of atmosphere as the total expression of a given time or place. This is true of the work of Japanese philosopher Watsuji Tetsurō, who was among the first to pick up a copy of *Being and Time* when it reached German bookstores in the summer of 1927.[15] Watsuji's own subsequent and still most famous work, *Climate and Culture* (*Fūdo*, 1931), draws heavily on *Being and Time* while arguing against what Watsuji saw as an overemphasis on temporality in Heidegger's text. Seeking to ground Heidegger's notion of a foundational *Stimmung* in specific national spaces, Watsuji's notion of "climate" blends weather and mood with aspects of the social environment like the family, community organizations, and communication technologies.[16]

As with Heidegger's *Stimmung,* Watsuji identifies climate/ atmosphere as the medium through which humans come to understand themselves vis-à-vis the surrounding world: "Climatic phenomena show man how to discover himself as 'standing outside' (i.e., *ex-sistere*). . . . *We discover ourselves, that is, in the atmosphere.*"[17] Watsuji notes how self-understanding is routed through an affective relationship with the larger climate. When people greet each other with "Isn't it a lovely morning?" they locate the source of their own refreshed feelings in the weather by confirming those around them have been similarly affected. Because everyone is shaped by the weather together, Watsuji argues, and (he implies) all shaped *in the same way,* atmosphere can be understood as the original force that ties a nation together. Building on the homogenizing force of Heidegger's *Stimmung,* Watsuji seeks to identify climate as a foundation for the assertion of absolute cultural difference, grounded in nothing less than the weather itself. For Watsuji, being Japanese is not an accident of birth or the result of a historical formation; rather, it is a unilateral collective process of atmospheric subjectivation. Through reference to this totalizing understanding of atmosphere, *Climate and Culture* presents a highly reductive model of environmental determinism, dividing human civilizations into "Monsoon," "Desert," and "Meadow" types and positioning Japan against the "West," China, and India. The seemingly "natural" process of climatic attunement serves as a feint for establishing the authority of the nationalist self.[18]

Watsuji's strategy of locating Japaneseness in the atmosphere went on to become a central pillar of postwar Japanese attempts to secure a unified national character in something other than the vagaries of history.[19] His atmospheric essentialism meshed with a larger cultural emphasis on "reading the air" (*kūki o yomu*) to determine correct behavior. Reading the air was espoused as essential to maintaining a harmonious social mood, what Watsuji describes as the *nakayoshi* (on good terms) imperative foundational to the structure of Japanese society. As Naoki Sakai argues, the way the *nakayoshi* imperative works to govern behavior while disguising the power relations involved makes it an ideology par excellence.[20] Imagining these behavioral imperatives to emerge from the "air" itself naturalizes them even further.

The most famous postwar Japanese critique of the use of air discourse to naturalize social norms is Yamamoto Shichihei's *"Kūki" no kenkyū* (Research on "air," 1977). Yamamoto argues that "reading the air" has been used in Japan since at least World War II as a rhetorical strategy for authority figures to indirectly persuade underlings to acquiesce to the status quo, diverting attention from vertical power structures by shifting blame to the atmosphere instead. The "air" served as a convenient scapegoat when rationalizing objectionable behaviors, explaining them as a response to an invisible and anonymous (and therefore unassailable) climatic influence. In discussions of war crimes, for example, it was much easier to attribute unethical behavior to the wartime atmosphere rather than to name names or assign personal responsibility.[21]

The social imperative to attune to the "air of a place" (*ba no kūki*) has remained prominent in recent decades. A person who misses implicit social cues and expectations is now often labeled someone who "cannot read the air" (*kūki ga yomenai*). The phrase experienced a surge of popularity early in the twenty-first century with an abbreviated version of the term, KY, nominated as one of the most important terms of 2007 in U-Can's widely publicized New Buzzword Competition (*Shingo-ryūkōgo taishō*). As noted in a number of recent self-help books promising to help readers become "air literate," the problem with being KY is that one quickly becomes an annoyance (*meiwaku*) to others, another common Japanese euphemism for those who refuse to bow to the implicit *nakayoshi* norms governing social life.[22]

While these discussions usually assume a proper Japanese subject must avoid being KY at all costs, the prevalence of guidelines on how to properly "read the air" reveals how in recent decades atmospheric cues have gradually come to be recognized as less a "natural" phenomenon than a product of social forces. From around the time of Yamamoto's book, the idea of a collective "Japanese" atmosphere governing all social behavior began to appear less and less convincing, despite continued assertions to the contrary. As the emergence of self-help books for the KY indicate, atmospheric attunement was shifting from a collective imposition to a technology of the self, something people could learn to do on their own. Beginning in the late 1970s, a wide range of artists, designers, journalists, and public intellectuals began pulling atmosphere from the shadows of preordained, primordial weather patterns and approaching it instead as something more personal and open to manipulation. In other words, atmosphere was becoming *ambient.*

TECHNIQUES OF THE NEOLIBERAL SELF

The proliferation of new techniques of ambient subjectivation in the 1970s reflected a shifting understanding of the person: away from forms of collective self-understanding and toward a model rooted in a liberal ideal of autonomy and self-determination.

While the Heidegerrian reading of atmosphere partially broke from Cartesian abstractions by asserting the primacy of mood, the *Stimmung* approach failed to account for how moods themselves are often the product of human involvement and intention and, thus, shaped by the same behavioral norms and inequalities found elsewhere in society.[23] Both Heidegger and Watsuji's emphasis on mood as a "primordial kind of being" too easily falls into imagining the state or nation as an atmospheric social totality, as if a general social atmosphere attuned everyone in the exact same way. There is no room in these atmospheres for the unevenness of social interaction, how the ability to both determine and make use of atmosphere is unevenly distributed across populations, and how moods are increasingly designed and deployed to produce particular kinds of behavior.[24] As I explore in the first chapter, this intentional deployment of mood-regulating media was already happening from early in the twentieth century, though it was not until the 1970s that the practice became more reflexive and personally mediated.

Foucault's work on subjectivation, also emerging in the late 1970s, offers a valuable framework for understanding the environments and practices that come before and shape subjects well below the threshold of self-awareness. Unlike Heidegger's vaguely nostalgic emphasis on "dwelling" and authenticity in relation to *Stimmung,* Foucault's focus on subjectivation emphasizes how people, in their coming into being, are always working through a set of subjective technologies specific to their time and place and deeply entwined with the governance of self and others. Nikolas Rose, one of the chief interpreters of Foucault's "techniques of the self," notes the need to locate beliefs concerning the self not in the "diffuse field of 'culture,' but as embodied in institutional and technical practices—spiritual, medical, political, economic—through which forms of individuality are specified and governed."[25] Following Rose, I work here from the premise that the best way to avoid falling back into vague notions of "culture" (especially, in the present context, "Japanese culture") is to focus on the rise and fall of specific techniques of subjectivation.

As Foucault argued in the late 1970s, the advent of liberalism introduced a key problematic: how could a state effectively govern the behavior of its population while allowing for greater degrees of personal freedom? The solution demanded new forms of *governmentality,* Foucault's term for the way behaviors important for the continued functioning of the state become reimagined as practices of self-care, so much that people often believe they are acting out of their own self-interest rather than in accordance with external social demands. In order for these liberal forms of self-governance to develop, human behavior needed to be mediated by new forms of self-understanding: ways to imagine the self as the product of personal choices, downplaying social influence and collective identities. Rose notes two key forms this new understanding of the self would take: the *psychological* and the *somatic.* While the former imagines the self as an interiority governed by unconscious attachments, habitual beliefs, and repressed memories, the latter understands the self as tied more directly into the surface vitality of the physical body, placing more emphasis on health, physical and sensory disciplines, and preconscious affective responses. The psychological self took hold of popular consciousness over the course of the twentieth century, first in the United States and the United Kingdom and then gradually spreading around the world. The somatic self, meanwhile, is part of the turn to understanding the body as an assemblage of diverse, largely preconscious systems. In recent years the somatic turn has been felt most powerfully in the spread of new biological, information, and surveillance technologies operating at a preconscious, affective, "molecular" level. While psychology envisions a singular consciousness reflecting back upon itself, the somatic self is far more ambient, variable, and dispersed. As Foucault describes in one of his final 1979 lectures on "the birth of biopolitics," this somatic emphasis leads to a "society in which there is an optimization of systems of difference, in which the field is left open to fluctuating processes, in which minority individuals and practices are tolerated, in which action is brought to bear on the rules of the game rather than on the players, and finally in which there is *an environmental type of intervention instead of the internal subjugation of individuals.*"[26] As part of this biopolitical turn, ambient subjectivation works to tune people indirectly, via the atmosphere, rather than more directly demanding the adoption of social norms. At the same time, it lets people feel they are the ones in control of their own somatic fluctuations. The turn from the psychological to the somatic allows more room for self-determination while turning the atmosphere into a site of ever-increasing control and regulation.

This turn toward biopolitics and the somatic self took place in Japan over the course of the twentieth century, intersecting with and in many ways supplanting earlier, often more relational forms of self-understanding. The full story of this complex transition is beyond the scope of this book, but generally speaking, early efforts to govern the population through somatic self-discipline were aligned more directly to the state, such as the Lifestyle Reform Movement (Seikatsu kaizen undō) of the 1930s.[27] Meanwhile, the psychological self entered Japanese medical discourse around the start of the twentieth century and spread widely through the popular imagination in the context of the "national character studies" popularized by American government researchers after World War II.[28] A more liberal understanding of the self also began to emerge, with nascent attempts to assert the value of personal autonomy in and of itself. In this context political philosopher Maruyama Masao was an important midcentury voice, arguing that to build a truly democratic state Japan must learn from the liberal European tradition, particularly John Locke's assertion that in a democracy "the state is mediated through the inner freedom of the individual." While Maruyama still ultimately promoted an understanding of Japan as a harmonious totality (with the emperor system at its center), he sought to carve out, often via reference to Meiji-period thinker Fukuzawa Yukichi, a space for personal autonomy alongside and complementary to this national frame.[29]

During the high economic growth of the 1960s and early 1970s, somatic self-discipline was still largely aligned with the national good, often through the local intermediary of the corporation (for men) and the family (for women). The early stages of postwar consumerism did begin emphasizing more personal comforts as a reward for industriousness (particularly in advertising), but the larger orientation was still to the collective effort for national prosperity.[30] Only after the downturn in the economy (following the 1973 oil shock) and the implosion of the radical politics of the 1960s (especially following the Asama-Sansō hostage incident in 1972) did the wider population begin seeking out more autonomy in governing their lives, often drawing on psychological and somatic techniques of self in the process. As in the United States and elsewhere, this was spurred on in large part by the rapidly expanding consumer culture.

Japanese sociologists identify a large-scale shift from the mass culture (*taishū bunka*) of the 1950s and 1960s to the "micromasses" emerging in the late 1970s, the latter oriented toward a wide range of individual pursuits (a mix of consumerism, health, and more personal and experiential brands of spirituality). From this point on a lifestyle-oriented "therapy culture" based on the American model became more and more prevalent, with an ever-expanding array of techniques of the self on offer.[31] As with discussion surrounding KY, psychological and somatic forms of self-discipline were often presented by journalists, social critics, politicians, and other public figures as personal solutions to social problems. By the end of the century, clinical psychologists turned public intellectuals like Saitō Tamaki and Kayama Rika came to play a leading role, publishing trade paperbacks and often appearing on television to offer advice and commentary. As sociologist Ueno Chizuko famously noted in the late 1980s, the new Japanese pastime was the search for a new "me."[32]

Japanese media producers were in step with these developments, offering personal media as technologies of self-care. With the emergence of the portable audio player, portable video equipment, and other environmental media technologies in the 1970s and 1980s, personal media use could now become a routine accompaniment to everyday life, and background mood regulation could now function as an extension of self-care. As Hosokawa Shūhei recalls, when the Sony Walkman debuted in the spring of 1980 it seemed to announce the arrival of a new era of personal autonomy.[33] In the 1980s consumer electronics companies like Sony, Sharp, and Matsushita (Panasonic) led the world in developing new media formats and new consumer technologies suited to high-density urban living and long train commutes. Financed by the rapid economic growth of the 1960s and 1970s and buttressed by government support, Japan became the leading developer and primary market for new media formats like cassette tape, VHS, laserdisc, CD, VCD, MD, and DVD. These technologies allowed people to choose what media might accompany them through the day. As these media became more affordable, customizable, and portable, the possibilities for their use as ambient media increased accordingly. As Rose puts it, technological developments like these served to "make new areas of life practicable."[34]

Attention to these techniques of the self provides a more grounded way of understanding the transformation of mass culture in postindustrial Japan. Influenced by Jean-François Lyotard and other theorists of the postmodern, critical approaches to contemporary Japan have often focused on the collapse of grand narratives and the turn from "reality" toward mediated simulacra. The increasing focus on background forms of attention, in this context, merely represents an alternative way to reach diverse audiences who no longer have any interest in a unified narrative vision.[35] The problem with these arguments is that narrative has never really gone away, and in recent years even the "grand narratives" of Japanese nationalism have shown themselves highly resilient. I argue the social and cultural shifts beginning in the late 1970s have less to do with the collapse of grand narratives and much more to do with emerging techniques of self-care, somatic techniques that run prior to and in some ways are independent of narrative or even political identification.

There are hints of the somatic turn even among those emphasizing the rise of simulacra. For example, sociologist Miyadai Shinji describes a rising number of "those who used fiction for the homeostasis of the self" in 1980s Japan, as people began using a wide range of media with the specific aim of mood regulation. It is not that fiction has replaced reality but that the reality/fiction distinction ceases to matter in the context of somatic self-discipline: "Reality and fiction have come to be thought of as equivalent insofar as they are material to be utilized for the homeostasis of the self."[36] As this book explores, the turn to somatic self-regulation became a guiding principle for the use and development of personal media around this time, whether focused on "reality" or not. Or to put it another way, a person's somatic condition *is* reality within this new understanding of self.

The significance of this new somatic reality becomes clear within the larger context of postindustrial Japanese biopolitics. Asada Akira famously argued in the 1980s that Japan now constituted a "safe" space where increasingly infantile Japanese could play freely in fictional fantasy worlds, protected by and dependent on a maternal government operating in the shadows.[37] This notion of free play, however, misses the way neoliberal biopolitics pairs personal "freedoms" with intensifying demands for self-discipline and self-restraint (*jishuku*). The emerging private practices of personal mood regulation often, if not always, lined up with larger social demands for healthy, active, emotionally in-control citizens. As Rose writes, the new techniques of governmentality operate "not through the crushing of subjectivity in the interests of control and profit, but by seeking to align political, social, and institutional goals with individual pleasures and desires, and with the happiness and fulfillment of the self. . . . They are, precisely, therapies of freedom."[38] When Japanese turned to media with the aim of regulating their emotional ups and downs, this was never simply a re-treat into the "free play" of fictional worlds. In search of the freedom of self-determination, media users sought to manage their own somatic potentials in relation to an intensifying set of biopolitical pressures and demands.

Michael Bull's anthropological study of the use of iPod playlists in the United Kingdom provides a compelling example of how gov-ernmentality functions on a day-to-day level. Rather than depend on preset radio or television programs, Bull notes how iPod listeners are free to design playlists to help get themselves though the work-day: upbeat music for the morning, a newscast on the way to work, something energizing for the midafternoon, an audiobook for the commute home, and something relaxing for the evening and before bed. Yet the rhythms freely chosen to make life easier largely match the energetic demands of the workday: "Just as users wish to liberate themselves from the oppressive rhythms of daily life, so they appear to sink deeper into them."[39] Personal media use holds out the promise of self-determination, but the technologies also serve as ways for gov-ernments and other social institutions to offload more and more of the labor of subjective maintenance onto an increasingly isolated subject. In Japan, as elsewhere, demands placed on the individual to preserve and develop their own health and social utility rose in direct propor-tion to the dismantling of social services and welfare programs.[40] People were "free" to adjust to these new forms of insecurity, and the new technologies of self served as crucial tools for doing so.

HOW TO READ THE AIR

As many critics have pointed out, neoliberalism as an ideology often depends on sustaining the illusion of an autonomous self—independent of social, environmental, and technological influence—in order to draw attention away from structural inequities and render a person solely responsible for their own successes and failures. What is often overlooked, however, is how atmospheric attunement has come to serve as the necessary background correlate to this foregrounding of the self. As forms of social subjectivation become affectively dispersed into the surrounding environment, they are shielded from critique, naturalized into the air, and cleansed of any association with existing social actors. As film theorist Matsuda Masao proposed in the early 1970s, power was no longer manifesting as a clear struggle between two opposing forces but was increasingly becoming dispersed into the landscape itself, part of the anonymous background infrastructure of everyday life.[41]

As the flip side of this promise of autonomy, neoliberal capitalism also cultivates a desire to *merge* with the atmosphere: subtracting markers of identity and dissolving the self into a stream of sense impressions, letting go of personal responsibility and becoming one with the larger landscape (and in so doing covertly aligning oneself with the power to be found there). This ambient dream of self-dispersal surfaces again and again in the works I examine here. The fantasy of a totally autonomous self and the fantasy of merging with the atmosphere are both essential to neoliberal biopolitics, working to obscure the everyday back-and-forth of ambient subjectivation. This book argues we—neoliberal subjects inside and outside Japan—need to stop disavowing the atmospheric determinations of self and look more closely at how ambient subjectivation does its work. In other words, we need to learn to *read the air* in a way that better recognizes the forces moving through it.

Whereas KY discourse often places the burden of conformity squarely on the shoulders of the person who cannot or will not adapt, reading the air in the sense I pursue here places a large share of the responsibility on those who create, curate, and design a given atmosphere, as well as those who use and sustain it. This more reflexive engagement with ambient subjectivation is the focus and method of this book. While I suggest that the self is far more a product of atmospheric influence than is commonly recognized, I also follow Foucault's later work in focusing on how a person never is simply the passive product of a given environment but can play an active role in shaping her or his own experience of environmental subjectivation. Reading the air means more carefully attending to the ambient determinants of self and realizing there are times when disrupting the given ambience, becoming *meiwaku,* can serve as an important way out from one mood to another.

For helping me learn how to read in this way, I am deeply indebted to the work of feminist and queer theorists of mood, affect, and emotion, including Sara Ahmed, Eve Sedgwick, Lauren Berlant, Arlie Russell Hochschild, Sianne Ngai, and Kathleen Stewart.[42] These writers explore how behavioral and subjective norms operating just below conscious reflection serve to govern and regulate affective encounters and how these norms are embodied and reproduced through materially inscribed forms of social behavior. From this perspective we can see how the label of KY or *meiwaku* marks not just people who fail to pick up atmospheric cues but also those who inhabit the position of an "affect alien," to borrow Ahmed's term for someone who cannot, or *will not,* go with the prevailing mood.[43] Every atmosphere includes a largely imperceptible border demarcating who can move seamlessly within it and who is made to feel uncomfortable, out of place, abject. Learning to trace out these transparent lines is a crucial part of making the air legible.[44]

As the focus shifted to governing the somatic self, media creators also began engaging with a new form of politics—what geographer Nigel Thrift has called the "spatial politics of affect."[45] The politics of affect recognizes that the sensing body doesn't discriminate nearly as much as the rational mind. Everything sensible is affecting, whether consciously attended or not, and all of it plays a role in subjectivation. These affective powers are increasingly instrumentalized, strategically deployed by artistic, business, and political interests alike. As Félix Guattari argues, this impersonal aesthetics of subjectivation is central to contemporary forms of social control, and it is precisely at this level—what he calls the "ethico-aesthetic"—where we must search if we are going to find an alternative.[46]

Learning to read these atmospheres means letting go of the resistance toward mood found in much twentieth-century modernism. As Gumbrecht points out, when twentieth-century avant-garde movements tried to eliminate the mediations of mood and approach "life" more directly, they often paradoxically ended up producing incredibly moody and atmospheric works.[47] Rather than continue to disavow the continuity between a critical aesthetics and the seemingly more compromised, everyday media of personal mood regulation, I suggest we need to more fully attend to the foundational role of mood in shaping the patterns and potentials of subjectivation both inside and outside traditional aesthetic contexts. It is important to emphasize, again following Foucault, that there is no escape from environmental subjectivation, no personal freedom that exists independently of wider techniques of social control. As with mood, the only way out of subjectivation is into another form of subjectivation. But this in itself is reason for hope. Instead of attempting to flee atmospheric influence, we might seek out new forms of agency via atmospheric mediation and think through the ethics of atmospheric design.[48]

Gernot Böhme describes how contemporary life increasingly plays out on a series of specially designed "stages," atmospheric backgrounds for desired lifestyles and their attendant feelings: "Staging has become a basic feature of our society: the staging of politics, of sporting events, of cities, of commodities, of personalities, of ourselves. . . . In general, it can be said that atmospheres are involved whenever something is being staged, wherever design is a factor—and that now means: almost everywhere."[49] This staging of lifestyle is reflected in a growing body of social science research focusing on the use of both public and personal media to design environments for everyday life.[50] While I draw on much of this work in what follows, to note how media are spreading throughout the lived environment is to see only half the picture; we must also attend to how media are becoming more atmospheric at a formal level. The demand for self-care has shifted not just media use but media *aesthetics*. Here, the humanities have the upper hand, and I follow close readers like Gumbrecht, Ngai, Elaine Scarry, and Angus Fletcher in seeking out an understanding of the increasingly environmental and atmospheric dimensions of aesthetic form.[51]

Gumbrecht notes how a reading that tunes itself to the working of atmosphere must pay special attention to matters of nonrepresentational form: "Tones, atmospheres, and *Stimmungen* never exist wholly independent of the material components of works—above all, their prosody. . . . 'Reading for *Stimmung*' always means paying attention to the textual dimensions of the forms that catalyze inner feelings without matters of representation necessarily being involved." The goal of reading the "air" of a text is not to figure out what it *means* but to highlight what it *affords* as a technology of self: "An essay that concentrates on atmospheres and moods will never arrive at the truth located within a text; instead, it seizes the work as a part of life in the present." Gumbrecht proposes, correctly I think, that this orientation toward mood and atmosphere in aesthetic experience is common among general audiences, whether or not they are conscious of the fact.[52] This is all the more true in the era of ambient media, when tuning the self to a mediated mood has increasingly become a reflexive and deliberate form of self-care.

As I explore in this book, the ambient shift in media aesthetics is concentrated at the intersection of therapy culture and more recognizably aesthetic pursuits (music, literature, film, etc.). Inverting the rejection of mood regulation in modern art, proponents of "healing" media often avoid acknowledging the influence of aesthetic form, positioning therapeutic technologies instead as neutral tools for the self-determining subject. Self-help literature, for example, is often at pains to remind readers of their power to determine their own destiny, drawing attention away from the fact that they have just purchased a book to instruct them on how to do so.[53]

The ambient works I present here issue a direct challenge to the notion that aesthetic experience, even at its most challenging, can ever be set apart from more basic processes of subjectivation and self-care. Ambient media fulfill the therapy culture imperative for calming affect, providing a sense of restfulness and relaxation for the humans spending time with them. Unlike more purely utilitarian forms of "healing" media, however, ambient works open up spaces within the overall calm to register a wider range of emotional uncertainty, even anxiety.[54] By affording a calm both effective and indeterminate, ambient media set up the possibility for an equanimous reflection on larger and potentially threatening externalities. At the same time, by pointing toward these unknown horizons, they implicitly cast doubt upon the veracity of their own calming moods. Breaking from more straightforward "new age" or "healing" genres, ambient media hint that therapy culture's mediated provision of calm may ultimately be a fragile cover for larger social landscapes that are anything but relaxing. Yet crucially, they refuse to disavow the importance of affective experience, providing for peaceful moods even amid the encroaching instability of contemporary life.

One of my central conclusions in the following chapters is that the ultimate mood to emerge with ambient media is one of *ambivalent calm,* a form of provisional comfort that nonetheless registers the presence of external threats. In the case of ambient music and video, this often means mixing in unstable, ungrounded, and inharmonic materials that introduce an air of uncertainty into an otherwise relaxing and soporific mix. In other cases, particularly with more narrative media like film and literature, this ambivalence emerges through stories exploring how mediated calm intersects with interpersonal relationships, the search for identity, and the larger sociopolitical realities of life inside neoliberal capitalism. This inclusion of uncertainty allows ambient media to pass as "artistic" in the modernist sense and pay respect to the liberal ideal of emotional autonomy, disavowing their role as utilitarian tools of personal mood regulation. At the same time, there is something undeniably practical about ambivalent calm as a functional mood for venturing out into an uncertain and high-risk future.

Each chapter of the book looks at a specific way music, video, film, and literature from the 1970s onward has incorporated forms of ambient subjectivation. Chapter 1 traces how the ambient emphasis on private, reflective moods developed from the unexpected alignment of postwar Japanese background music and the environmental art of the 1960s avant-garde, converging in the "Erik Satie boom" of the late 1970s and the emergence of ambient music as a genre.

Chapter 2 presents an aesthetic history of how ambient music has sought to enable feelings of ontological security by indirectly situating the self against imaginary acoustic horizons. I trace how the landscapes made sensible by ambient music became increasingly abstract and anonymous moving from the 1980s to the 1990s to the 2000s, in time with shifting social attitudes and new sound reproduction technologies. In the process, I listen closely to key ambient tracks from Hosono Haruomi, Tetsu Inoue, and Hatakeyama Chihei.

Chapter 3 maps out how the atmospheric attunements of ambient video intersect with the spatial rhythms of everyday life in contemporary urban Japan. Drawing on Henri Lefebvre's method of rhythmanalysis, I explore how ambient video positions itself as an intermediary between the impersonal rhythms of Tokyo and the somatic rhythms of the self.

Chapter 4 examines how ambient video stages its own spaces of *shallow depth* between the software layers of image compositing and the aleatory discoveries of found footage, affording both attention restoration and subjective dispersal. Focusing on Ise Shōko's *Swimming in Qualia* (2007), the analysis here builds on the concept of *soft fascination* from environmental psychology, demonstrating how an aesthetic emphasis on mystery and uncertainty may help rather than hinder a work's ability to cultivate a "healing" mood.

Chapter 5 examines the emergence of a "subtractivist" ambience in postindustrial Japan and its implications for interpersonal life. My focus here is on the solitary moods of *Tony Takitani* (2004), a film by Ichikawa Jun based on a short story by Murakami Haruki. I examine the atmospheres generated by Sakamoto Ryūichi's Satie-esque score and the film's ambivalent reflection on the role of aesthetic objects in covering over the sadness of self and others. Considering Tia DeNora's distinction between intersubjectivity and cosubjectivity and the rise of subtractivist lifestyle brand Mujirushi ryōhin (Muji), I explore how Tony's low-affect lifestyle may be well suited to an age of muted fashions and mood-regulating media.

Chapter 6 moves further into Japanese debates over therapy culture and healing media while tracing how literature too can function as a technology of ambient subjectivation. I focus on Kurita Yuki's ambient novel *Hôtel Mole* (2005), a story about what it means to provide affective labor at a hotel designed for the deepest sleep possible. Focusing on the novel's exploration of the aesthetics of calm and the labor involved in providing it, I argue against critiques of mood regulation that see it only as a straightforward form of social pacification. I show how ambient media can lead not only to restful moods but also to a reflection on weakness, care, and healing as core components of self.

By shifting between works of music, video art, film, and literature, I aim to give a sense of how far ambient aesthetics have spread across Japan. Moving between media also allows me to consider a wide range of reception contexts, from private moments of headphone listening and reading on the train to the communal refuges of the art gallery and the movie theater. In order to encompass this breadth of materials, I only briefly touch on the broader history of atmospheric styles in each medium, though I hope this book will prove useful for further research in each of these areas. Similarly, I have largely set aside the many powerfully atmospheric works produced by Japanese artists in ages past, from the delicate soundscapes and wafting scents of *The Tale of Genji* (*Genji monogatari,* circa 1021) to the finely tuned moods of *nō* theater to the self-consciously exotic atmospheres of Kawabata Yasunari's later novels and Mizoguchi Kenji's period films. Some of the concepts I develop here might be useful for approaching these earlier works but would need to be articulated through their very different social, political, and subjective contexts. I have avoided drawing any easy comparisons to earlier moments in Japanese aesthetics, as tempting as this may be, to avoid courting false intimations of an unchanging national character. As we have already seen with Watsuji, atmosphere's appearance of being outside history serves as one of its most powerful obfuscations. This is surely part of why atmosphere and exoticism often run together, whether in Japanese works embraced overseas or foreign works embraced in Japan. To counteract this tendency, this book situates the emergence of ambient media in Japan less as the continuation of an imaginary cultural heritage and more as the historical result of social transformations shared with many other parts of the world.[55]

Many of the musicians, video makers, filmmakers, and writers I consider in this book directly reference ambience and atmosphere in conceptualizing their practice. I also sometimes locate their works' engagement with mood regulation through reviews and other records of the way they have been received. Ultimately, however, I am less interested in following Eno to assert "ambient" as a discreet genre than in developing an understanding of how ambience functions in a wide range of contemporary media environments, whether or not the term is ever used. Rather than seeking to be exhaustive, in building this book's ambient archive I have favored works that best reveal the aesthetic strategies, historical development, and cultural politics of ambient subjectivation.

While mood-regulating media can often simply be coping mechanisms for life under neoliberal capitalism, I nonetheless see hope in the more reflexive understanding of "air" they usher in. While often used simply to ensure productivity, efficiency, docility, and profitability, atmospheric media can just as easily be put to other ends. I am inspired by the wonderfully eclectic uses of background music I have encountered while wandering around Tokyo: the psychedelic guitar rock accompanying the biryani at a local Nepali restaurant, the jaunty noir theme from *The Third Man* (also used in Ebisu beer commercials) that warns of closing train doors at Ebisu Station, the instrumental version of the B-52s' "Rock Lobster" that loops on a small boom box perched above the frozen seafood section of the local grocery. Rather than deploy atmosphere only to increase sales and avoid *meiwaku,* or simply decry it as a threat to the autonomous self, Japanese artists, environmental designers, and shop managers alike have often approached background music as an open-ended experiment in environmental subjectivation. There are plenty of soul-crushing uses of recorded sound in Japan, too, of course, as Nakajima Yoshimichi brilliantly cataloged in his classic polemic *Urusai Nihon no Watashi* (Japan, the noisy, and myself). But these, too, I suggest, should push us not to retreat into fantasies of a quieter, less mediated world—perhaps, ironically, by investing in a pair of noise-canceling headphones—but rather to take a more active role in building the kind of atmospheres we want to live within, alongside, and through.[56]

This is as much a collective question as a personal one. About 70 percent of people living in Japan currently live in cities, and I propose the emphasis on "reading the air" is also in some ways a product of this environment. For city dwellers spending their days surrounded by strangers, often at close proximity, the ambivalent calm and sensory autonomy afforded by ambient media become important personal resources for navigating the information-dense and somatically taxing spaces of urban Japan. At the same time, by smoothing over the rougher edges of everyday life, ambient media often help sustain the same social stressors they set out to soothe. In the chapters that follow, I seek to attune readers to both sides of this predicament and, in the process, imagine other possibilities for the ambient self.

/1/

BACKGROUND MUSIC OF
THE AVANT-GARDE

Just as neoliberalism sought to make social discipline palatable by couching it in the context of freely chosen forms of self-care, ambient music sought to personalize the explicitly instrumental emotions of earlier background music in order to position mood regulation not as an imposition from the outside but as a freely chosen technique of the self. Ironically, in seeking out atmospheres more amenable to personal use, the emerging ambient style would draw heavily from an artistic lineage positioning itself against the earlier forms of communal mood regulation: the environmental avant-garde of the 1960s. Ambient music emerges out of this strange dialectic between Muzak and modernism: a sort of background music of the avant-garde.

In order to get a phenomenological sense of the utilitarian background music against which the avant-garde railed so strongly, I spent a few days immersed in more traditional BGM while staying at a hotel on the southeastern coast of Chiba prefecture, a few hours' bus ride east of Tokyo.[1] The hotel featured perpetual soft piano music piped through speakers in the lobby, the attached café, the hallways, and every guest room. The same piano soundtrack would be playing as I returned to my room each day, wafting down from a gray speaker placed near the center of the vaulted ceiling above the bed. A small knob next to the light switch near the door controlled the volume: from low to very low to inaudible. The music continued automatically until nine in the evening, at which point the piano would fade into silence for the night, only to start back up the following morning.

I left the music playing during my stay, curious if I could experience the sort of productivity enhancement and stress relief touted by so much of the background music promotional literature. The tone of the music was sentimental without ever building to any kind of catharsis, pleasant without allowing for any shade of ambiguity or emotional complexity. Harmonically, the piano never strayed far from consonance, moving through a series of mostly major chords in contin-uously resolving progressions. Occasionally, the melodic line hinted at something more expressive: a jazz improvisation, a distantly familiar tune, a slight deviation from the steady midrange pulse. But these hints never materialized into anything more substantial. While occasionally gesturing at further development, the music would always quickly fall back into the realm of the ignorable, retreating to a series of predict-ably consonant notes.

As I sat and listened for these flickers of expression, I felt a slowly rising frustration. Far from relaxed, I found myself becoming more ir-ritated by the piano with each passing hour. The purposefully limited tonal, dynamic, and emotional range of the music pulled me toward feelings of emotional claustrophobia. I felt my range of possible re-sponses narrowing to a thin selection of noncommittal pleasantries. The lack of musical ambiguity and complexity left no room to enter the music and move around in it. The more I tried to find a place for my-self to emerge within these sounds, the more frustrated I became. The music allowed no gap between audience and sonic mood that might allow a relationship to develop between the two. I was being pushed into an emotional dynamic I was not ready to reciprocate, leading to discomfort and emotional alienation. I was at the hotel by myself but felt haunted by the unsettling sensation the feelings occupying the room were not my own.

Looking back, I was trying to be a good neoliberal subject, responsi-ble for and in control of my own emotions independent of environmen-tal influence. Yet the music would not let me, interrupting my ability to make my own choices about how I was going to feel. I came to the hotel hoping to find a quiet space to write alone and undisturbed. But really, I was alone only if the single kind of being-with that counted was being with other humans. At the hotel I was together with the music, or rather, the music wouldn't leave me alone. I was becoming the type of subject the music allowed me to be, but in this case, it didn't match my own desire for self-determination, my preference for a music leaving me to determine how I wanted to feel yet serving as a willing tool to help me get there. But this more pushy, more explicit form of atmospheric mood regulation wasn't frustrating me just because it wasn't respecting my demands for self-determination. What made it particularly annoying—and what I think has long made this kind of music an affront to anyone with aspirations to self-determination—was it forced me to confront the fact I was never really as independent as I wanted to believe. All music was going to help determine me in one way or another. The difference between traditional BGM and the ambient music I might voluntarily listen to was the ambient music helped sustain my illusions, letting me carry on believing I was ultimately the one in control.

Fueled by a similar antipathy to being told how to feel, critical responses to background music have for a long time focused on resisting emotional manipulation, promoting instead a supposedly more neutral set of emotional cues. From this perspective, a less mediated reality is out there for the sensing, but BGM undermines this objectivity with its inauthentic and calculated moods. BGM critics from the 1930s to the 1960s regularly portrayed urban space as a battleground between the inauthentic mood regulation of corporate and governmental interests and the independent, objective sensory needs of the autonomous modern subject. This distrust of mood regulation is understandable considering the history of corporate and governmental mood music. When Japanese artists and composers turned to the "environmental arts" (*kankyō geijutsu*) in the 1960s, they began to acknowledge the impact of atmospheric design on human behavior but remained suspicious of attempts to use it to manipulate human emotion. But while they were caught up in the question of how to replace moods governed by corporate and government interests with the more emotionally ambiguous atmospheres of the avant-garde, their experiments in fact opened up a path for the ambivalent calm of ambient styles. In what follows I trace this strange historical crossfade, from utilitarian BGM to ambient subjectivation, by way of the environmental avant-garde and one long-dead French composer of "furnishing music" by the name of Erik Satie.

THE BIRTH OF MODERN BGM

For the most part, the early history of environmental media is a history built on attempts to regulate the behavior of others. The workplace was the first site where background music was put to practical use. Music to accompany and ease the burden of work has probably been around as long as music itself. But starting in the late nineteenth century, work music began to move to increasingly rationalized, utilitarian, and prerecorded rhythms. The earliest documented uses of background music in a business setting were in the United States, where a Chicago automobile plant was experimenting with it as early as 1886. The practice spread as the American push for worksite productivity enhancement grew to a frenzy around the turn of the century, under the influence of Frederick Taylor's "scientific management" theories and the larger flourishing of efficiency studies and managerial psychology.[2]

Japanese manufacturers were inspired to try similar experiments in the following decades. In 1932 the Imperial Silk factory in Yamanashi prefecture began spinning records to increase efficiency. Another factory serenade accompanied the mostly teenage girls working to package candies at the Glico bagging facility in Osaka. Factory managers studied the girls and found playing popular music over the speaker system increased productivity by as much as 10 percent.[3]

On the retail side of the equation, in-store mood music began with live performances in high-end establishments before gradually shifting to more affordable and easily deployed recorded forms. Philadelphia's John Wanamaker Store, one of the first department stores in the United States, introduced an organ player in 1876 to provide "store music" and hired a group of singers performing as a "store chorus." Japan's first department store, Mitsukoshi, began a similar practice in 1907 at their Nihonbashi, Tokyo, location, hiring a youth ensemble to perform in the style of a Scottish band. In 1930 the store installed a pipe organ as well to serenade shoppers.[4] While itinerant vendors had long called out to advertise their wares and traveling bands of *chindon'ya* musicians could be hired to play in front of a shop to lure customers from late in the nineteenth century, this was the first time music was deployed in Japan to set the background mood for indoor retail.

These proved to be rather isolated experiments, however, and up through the 1950s most workplaces and retail establishments in Japan remained BGM-free. The silence was particularly conspicuous during the Pacific War. The wartime government outlawed music not oriented toward the national cause, and skeptics insisted much of the acceptably patriotic Japanese song repertoire was too languid to contribute much toward increased productivity anyhow. This was in stark contrast with the enthusiastic embrace of workplace music for wartime manufacturing in the United States, where it played to workers at thousands of factories and weapons manufacturers.

Meanwhile, outside the context of workplace productivity, radio stations across Japan were commanded by the government to play patriotic music at set hours of the day. Japan's first national attempt at musical mood regulation thus emerged in the service of war—though it is not clear how many people actually tuned in.

Pioneering science fiction author Unno Jūza's 1937 short story "The Music Bath at 1800 Hours" (Jūhachi jikan no ongaku yoku) is an early, incisive satire of the use of music as social mood control and a direct critique of the patriotic music the Japanese government was forcing radio stations to play. The story describes a future society on a fictional planet where all citizens are forced to take a "music bath" every day at six in the evening. The music is scientifically engineered to make citizens both hyperproductive and absolute believers in government propaganda. Everything is running along smoothly until a threat from a neighboring race emerges, a military coup takes place, and the new ruler decides to play the music twenty-four hours a day in the hopes of creating an even more productive citizenry. At this sustained intensity, however, the music bath proves toxic to the human body, melting everyone's brain and leaving the planet wide open to invasion.

"The Music Bath" points precisely to emotional manipulation through background music as the moment where science loses its conscience and slips toward fascism. For Unno, as for the later environmental artists of the 1960s, science is wonderful when it stays dry and objective but becomes dangerous the moment it begins to manipulate human feeling.[5]

MUZAK IN JAPAN

Background music fully emerged in Japan in commercial contexts in the aftermath of the war, spurred on by the American occupation (1945–52). George Thomas Forester, an American who first came to Tokyo with the American forces, teamed up with the British company Readytune in 1957 to form the first company in Japan specializing in background music, the Japan Music Distribution Corporation (Nihon ongaku haikyū kabushiki gaisha). Other companies soon followed: Tōyō Music Broadcasting (Tōyō ongaku hōsō), an affiliate of the American company Altphonic; the Tokyo Radio Service, another affiliate of Readytune based on a public-broadcasting model; and Asahi Broadcasting (Asahi hōsō), affiliated with the American company National Musitime. Around 1963 these providers consolidated into the Key Corporation, which emerged as Japan's primary provider of "sound conditioning" to consumer environments like banks, restaurants, and shopping arcades (shōtengai).[6]

In 1964 the most famous elevator music of all arrived in Japan. Mainichi Broadcasting (Mainichi hōsō), with the cooperation of Nichimen Jitsugyō, signed a contract with the American Muzak Corporation to form the exclusive Japanese Muzak affiliate, the Mainichi Music System (Mainichi myūjikku shisutemu, now the Mainichi eizō onkyō shisutemu). Muzak was at the height of its commercial and cultural influence in the United States, having been piped into the White House by Dwight D. Eisenhower and included to accompany astronauts on NASA space missions.[7]

Mainichi's Nagamatsu Akira introduced the term "environmental music" (*kankyō ongaku*) as the preferred Japanese translation of Muzak, probably to distinguish it from the more common abbreviation for background music, BGM.[8] The company published a book of the same name in 1966, explaining the history of Muzak and laying out the research demonstrating its efficacy. The text is stuffed full of graphs and charts documenting the benefits of Muzak's patented mood regulation systems and proclaiming their greater rationality over ordinary background music.[9] As the Muzak corporate literature put it at the time, "music is art, but Muzak is science."

Despite its infamy as a ubiquitous purveyor of "elevator music," however, Muzak's global market share began to shrink rapidly in subsequent decades, amid changing musical tastes and an increased preference for original artists over "canned" backgrounds. In 1984, after being purchased by Seattle's Yesco, Muzak shifted their focus from productivity enhancement to corporate branding, with background music selections now sourced directly from existing artists in their original "foreground" arrangements.

In the switch from productivity to atmospheric branding, Muzak was catching up with global developments in environmental design spurred on by Philip Kotler's landmark 1973 paper "Atmospherics as a Marketing Tool." Here, Kotler introduced the term "atmospherics" to describe "the effort to design buying environments to produce specific emotional effects that enhance purchase probability."[10] Numerous studies soon followed investigating the impact of different varieties of in-store music on sales. This evolved into a push for "sensory branding," the creation of synesthetic atmospheres providing specialized moods for target demographics, with the aim of indirectly making customers more likely to make a purchase.

Muzak vice president and creative director Alvin Collis describes the approach as one of staging emotion as a marketable good:

> I walked into a store and understood: this is just like a movie. The company has built a set, and they've hired actors and given them costumes and taught them their lines, and every day they open their doors and say, "Let's put on a show." It was retail theatre. And I realized then that Muzak's business wasn't really about selling music. It was

about selling emotion—about finding the soundtrack that would make this store or that restaurant feel like something, rather than being just an intellectual proposition.[11]

Muzak's new role was to mix playlists to capture as precisely as possible a store's target audience, working toward a "personal audio imaging profile."

At the time of Muzak's rebranding, however, just one regional affiliate petitioned Muzak not to completely abandon stimulus progression: Japan's Mainichi. Among all the new foreground styles on offer, Muzak still maintains at least one program of traditional Muzak in order to keep Japanese programmers happy. In interviews Muzak executives in the United States appear rather baffled at their Japanese client's continued preference for the "stimulus progression" style of Muzak. One former Muzak executive in the United States was quoted as recently as 2006 as remarking (with thinly veiled condescension) "the Japanese think they love it, but they actually don't. They'll get over it soon."[12] And yet even in 2010, Mainichi presented their services primarily in terms of background stimulus, using the same graphs and charts from decades before. Japan is currently one of the few places where "elevator music" of the older style is still regularly encountered, albeit most often in older establishments clearly behind the times in more ways than one.[13] Even at Mainichi, stimulus progression is now only one option alongside others like "stylish," "classical," "jazz," "healing/relax," "Modern Japanese," "lounge," and the new BGM standard bearer, "bossa nova." This more flexible list of channels (which, with satellite technology, expands into the hundreds) provides a much wider palette of possible in-store moods, each with their own set of atmospheric affordances.

These more individually tailored backgrounds appear in a sequel to *Environmental Music* published in 1992, featuring new contributions from Japanese sound researchers from across the country. In the book's introduction, psychologist Osaka Ryōji notes how background music has gone from being a rather obscure idea in Japan when the book was first published in 1966 to something almost entirely taken for granted in the 1990s.

The book provides a long list of the various objectives driving the deployment of background music over the intervening decades. Part of the list includes older productivity-oriented goals, such as "reducing the amount of time spent resting one's hands," "reducing the amount of idle chatter," and "controlling the monotonous feeling of work." There are also some nods to the newer sensory branding emphasis on using in-store music as a way to "improve company image" by associating it with a desired musical demographic. But above all, the emphasis is on mood regulation for calm and comfort at a somatic level: "reducing feelings of tension and strain," "eliminating emotional variability and anxiety," and "contributing to the construction of comfortable spaces."[14] Japanese environmental designers eagerly embraced this ever-expanding list of atmospheric objectives starting in the 1970s, and by the 1980s the country was at the forefront of sensory branding.

ENVIRONMENTAL MUSIC

Let's jump back now to when BGM was first spreading through Japan in the 1950s and 1960s. Many artists and social critics were growing uncomfortable with this use of aesthetic conditioning to regulate public space and began seeking out other aesthetic approaches to the shared environment. A wide range of Japanese artists began developing alternative environmental aesthetics in the 1960s and 1970s, including a range of experiments in what, despite Mainichi's claim to the term, also came to be called "environmental music" (kankyō ongaku). Part of a larger movement toward "environmental art" (kankyō geijutsu), the avant-garde environmental music of the period sought to critically respond to the larger transformation and rationalization of the urban Japanese soundscape.

The most well-known of the environmental art groups to emerge in Japan was the short-lived Environment Society (Enbairamento no kai), based in Tokyo. The Environment Society consisted of a group of thirty-eight artists in a wide variety of disciplines, including music, painting, sculpture, design, photography, and criticism. The group is best known for *From Space to Environment* (Kūkan kara kankyō e), a 1966 exhibition at the Matsuya Department Store Galley with an accompanying performance event at the Sōgetsu Art Center, both in Tokyo.

As expressed in a statement presented for the show, the Environment Society sought to create "works that are not autonomous and complete by themselves but . . . become open to the external world by involving viewers in their environment."[15] In this the group was closely aligned with the happenings and performance art presented by people like Allan Kaprow and John Cage in New York—a scene with which at least two society members, Akiyama Kuniharu and Ay-O, had been involved immediately before returning to Tokyo to start the group. The Environment Society drew on the widely discussed ideas of Marshall

McLuhan, who wrote of the "new environmental communication of the electronic age," and on the "correalism" of Romanian theater designer and architect Frederick John Kiesler.[16] More fundamental than these distant influences, however, was the Environment Society's desire to directly respond to large-scale transformations in the city they called home. Tokyo had been radically transformed in the lead up to the 1964 Tokyo Olympic Games, with massive raised highways built across the city and large tracts of land cleared and rebuilt. On a more intimate scale, environmental conditioning of all kinds had emerged as a powerful rationalizing force on urban Japanese life, providing calculated comforts that, from the perspective of Environment Society artists, threatened to have a numbing influence on everyday life. If Mainichi's background music promised an environment conducive to productivity, marketability, and comfort, the Environment Society pushed back with environments built around the classic avant-garde principles of play, experimentation, and the creative potential of discomfort.

In her study of the *From Space to Environment* exhibition, Midori Yoshimoto provides two brief examples of what this meant in practice. Music critic and composer Akiyama Kuniharu's work for the exhibition, *Environmental Mechanical Orchestra No. 1,* uses sounds picked up from transistors aimed at the surface of a basin of water presented in the gallery space, as well as microphones picking up the voices and footsteps of exhibition visitors. The work literally takes the mundane sounds of the given "space" and mediates them into an immersive but unpredictable sound "environment," which subsequently generates its own responsive actions from gallery visitors. Another piece envisioning a more volatile environment was a performance by Fukuda Shigeo, Awazu Kiyoshi, Tōno Yoshiaki, Ay-O, and Ichiyanagi Toshi, based on a composition by Ichiyanagi simply entitled *Environmental Music (Kankyō ongaku).* Moving beyond the strictly auditory, the score instructs performers to "incline your body on a chair as slowly as possible to an unbearable position."[17]

For the Environment Society, the creation of more open and unstable environments like these served as a means of defending against the increasingly rationalized and predictable spaces emerging all around them. From a broader perspective, however, these artists were themselves generating new approaches to urban environmental design. Like the creators of Muzak, the Environment Society introduced mediated atmospheres into a communal space and allowed audiences to physically attune to these environmental affordances. While the types of behavior the two groups hoped to cultivate in their audiences were ideologically opposed, the aesthetic "stages" created by both Mainichi and the Environment Society came together on a more basic premise: the use of environmental media to shift audiences' engagement with the everyday spaces of urban Japanese life.

Where the two groups differed was not simply the degree of environmental volatility desired but also their attitudes toward the role of emotion. Commercial background music early on embraced mood as a core component of environmental mediation, recognizing how powerfully feeling inflects human behavior. In contrast, the Environment Society, like Unno before them, remained suspicious of emotional manipulation, downplaying its role by assuming a posture of detached, quasi-scientific objectivity in their work.

This resistance to emotional control was an attitude common to avant-garde expression in postwar Japan, based on a view of emotion as an irrational force easily susceptible to ideological manipulation. We might suppose the recent experience of highly emotional propaganda during the Pacific War made this danger a salient one for Japanese artists in the 1960s, and this shaped the environmental artists' attitudes to background music and other forms of environmental design. But this resistance to feeling would soon be eclipsed in the following decade.

EXPO '70

While the environmental artists were busy pushing people out of their chairs, comfort (*kaitekisa*) was steadily securing its place as a central affective priority of postindustrial Japanese society.[18] This emerged as part of a larger transnational move toward "amenity culture," a major focus of key 1970s environmental design texts like Jay Appleton's *The Experience of Landscape* (1975).

For environmental designers, factoring out individual particularities and focusing as much as possible on preconscious, predictable somatic responses allowed for the creation of environments able to appeal to as wide and diverse a population as possible. This prioritization of somatic comfort over semantic meaning marked an important shift in postindustrial design, toward an increasing reliance on aesthetics aiming to trigger affective responses before they could begin to be colored by personal reflection and memory. Unlike earlier approaches to landscape, which focused more on what a place represented to a particular group or culture, the newly rationalized environments of postindustrial Japan began to focus instead on providing impersonal amenities to a rapidly diversifying consumer population.[19]

The gap between the 1960s avant-garde environmental volatility and the emerging orientation toward engineered comfort came out in vivid relief on the grounds of the 1970 World Exposition in Osaka. While the expo was commercially successful, drawing over 83 million visitors in the 183 days it was open, its emphasis on high-tech corporate-sponsored pavilions symbolized for many artists in Japan the death of the avant-garde and the advent of a new era of consumerism. In this context the participants in Expo '70, including many of the members of the Environment Society, were on the side of the coming corporate takeover. Protests in print and in person greeted the opening of the expo and have done much to shape the subsequent narrative of the event's larger cultural impact.[20] But there was also an aesthetic and ideological rift within rather than around the Expo '70 grounds. This rift was between the more challenging musical environments presented by many of the participating Japanese artists and the more harmonious, comfortable environments sought out by many expo visitors.

The tension between these two orientations is evident in the contrasting coverage of Expo '70 in two large tomes dedicated to the history of electronic music in Japan, Kawasaki Kōji's *Japanese Electronic Music* (*Nihon no denshi ongaku*) and Tanaka Yūji's *Electronic Music in Japan* (*Denshi ongaku in Japan*). While the former approaches the topic from the perspective of the electronic avant-garde, emphasizing the Expo '70 works as a culmination of many of the musical experiments of earlier decades,[21] the latter opens by presenting the expo as the last gasp of an overly theoretical and out-of-touch art music, one about to give way to the more popular electronic music of the coming decades. The latter book blames this on the abstract dissonance favored by many of the Expo '70 works—including those curated by ex–Environment Society members like Akiyama. Tanaka writes:

> With the boom in science fiction following the television broadcast of *Astro Boy* in 1963, along with the reverberations of the success of the Apollo moon landing, there ought to have been a lot of interest in the electronic music flowing out of the various Expo pavilions. It should have given new expression to these dreams of the future.
>
> However, most of the electronic music played at the corporate pavilions was the kind sounding like *piiiii, garigari-gari,* or *puuuuuun* ... difficult to understand modern music with no melody. If you listen to the few recordings still available from the pavilions ... you soon understand why

this music left the average visitor with no fond memories (as opposed to, for example, the moon rock on view at the American Pavilion).

NHK's Satō Shigeru recounts an episode where one female attendant at the Japan Pavilion complained of suddenly having irregular menstrual cycles. According to the doctor called to examine her, the reason was likely the dissonant electronic music playing nonstop as BGM within the pavilion. Of course, the staff were quite disturbed by these unprecedented "incidents."

The German Pavilion, featuring a live performance of electronic music by Karlheinz Stockhausen, apparently had many visitors there simply to enjoy the air conditioning and escape from the disappointing chaos of the other pavilions. One heard stories of old couples, tired from walking around and finally sitting down to take a rest, who nonetheless had to quickly flee once the *garigarigari bakyuuun* of Stockhausen's music began.[22]

Tanaka reads the unpopularity of the expo's electronic music as evidence of a disconnect between the participants' modernist notions of "environmental music" and the type of sounds the Expo '70 audience might appreciate in their environment. There were, undoubtedly, visitors who enjoyed the music itself. But for audiences looking for a comfortable environment in which to spend some time, however, all the *garigarigari* in the world was no match for a quiet space with good air conditioning.

These scenes from Expo '70 underline the tension between the atmospheric priorities of the emerging amenity culture—comfort, calm, refreshment, relaxation—and the more unwieldy alternatives offered by the avant-garde and its emphasis on complexity, surprise, and contingency. Among those pieces from the expo still available to audition, the most compelling works capture this tension between comforting and discomforting design in their own internal structure. For example, Ichiyanagi Toshi's *Music for Living Space* (*Seikatsu kūkan no tame no ongaku*) starts with a background layer of flowing Gregorian chant, a soft modal music with mood to spare. On top of this calm foundation, however, Ichiyanagi presents a metallic electronic voice reciting a text by metabolist architect Kurokawa Kishō on the future design of everyday life. The harsh, angular voice was synthesized entirely by computer (a familiar sound now but a difficult technological feat in 1970).

The work was installed in the "Future" section inside the upper part of Okamoto Tarō's massive *Tower of the Sun* sculpture, the seventy-meter-tall visual centerpiece of the Expo '70 grounds. Listening to it now, the contrast between the monks' flowing chant and the harsh, inhuman voice in Ichiyanagi's piece seems to sound out the tension between the hard-edged resistance of the avant-garde and the comfortably designed "living spaces" rapidly spreading across urban Japan.[23]

AGAINST DESIGNER MUSIC

A key figure in curating the expo's environmental music, Akiyama Kuniharu (1929–96), was also the central critic of Japanese avant-garde music during this period. He was one of the founding members of the influential Jikken Kōbō (Experimental Workshop) in 1951 and in the early sixties participated in the Fluxus movement in New York before returning to Tokyo middecade to help start the Environment Society. Akiyama repeatedly published essays in the 1950s and 1960s warning against the dangers of emotional manipulation in commercial background music, which for him represented a threat to both art and culture.

Akiyama makes his most elaborate anti-BGM argument in a 1966 essay published in *Dezain hihyō* (Design criticism) entitled "Dezain suru ongaku" (Music that designs).[24] He begins by emphasizing his general disdain for design as a field of activity and the way it has—in recent decades at least—functioned mainly as a tool of commercialism. For Akiyama design, in its obsession with functionality, has become powerless as a form of artistic expression. Yet he admits design, along with the rise of consumer electronics, has became the main venue where the aesthetics of ordinary experience are forged. Music was earliest among all the existing art fields to become absorbed into a design context, as background music rapidly expanded to fill the spaces of everyday life.

Akiyama notes he has been warning against this "music for design" since the mid-1950s and sees it as a major threat to the integrity of music as an art form. Not only does BGM reduce music to serving as a tool of commerce, but musically it tends toward pale imitations of earlier musical genres. BGM arbitrarily loots music of the past, creating a shoddy mixture of classical and popular (foreign) music styles. Tapping into a fear of miscegenation, Akiyama argues background music, unlike "pure" music, flattens all genres into a "mixed-blood" amalgam of stitched-together musical cues. He frets many composers in Japan are already moonlighting as producers of commercial BGM and warns this can be a slippery slope into mediocrity. Without realizing it, a composer's entire musical output becomes contaminated by these side jobs selling their music as a functional backdrop for someone else's product line.

Up to this point in the essay, Akiyama's argument reads as a reactionary plea against the mixing of music and design, of the contamination of "pure" expression with practical utility. After rehearsing this familiar art-versus-design complaint, however, the essay swerves to propose something else: a more purely scientific BGM.

First, Akiyama acknowledges the absurdity of his earlier idea of artistic or musical "purity," noting music composed for background use has a long and surprisingly distinguished lineage: Mozart made music for the dinner table, and Bach's *Goldberg Variations* (1741) were written as a kind of insomnia medication for sleepless royalty.[25] Second, he admits contemporary background music does in its own way reflect the same aspects of modernity with which so much twentieth-century art music has grappled: the disappearance of shared social investments and the increasing isolation and atomization of the person against ever more rationalized and anonymous urban environments.

Akiyama's issue with BGM is not that it fails to respond to these contemporary social conditions but that its response is incomplete, still laced with vestiges of an earlier humanism based on romantic ideals of unmediated expression. The problem Akiyama has with background music is its focus on atmospheric mood creation (*funiki mūdo zukuri*), whereas, he proposes, a truly "contemporary" background music would not get lost in such sentimentality.[26] He pursues this point by proposing a hypothetical compositional challenge: the design of BGM to accompany astronauts on their voyage to outer space (a remarkably prophetic proposal, given Muzak would in fact accompany the Apollo astronauts to the moon just three years later):

> It goes without saying that thinking [of BGM as mood creation] leads to all kinds of random makeshift designs. For example, from this perspective, it would make sense for there to also be mood music installed inside a space shuttle. However, in such a narrow and solitary space, mood music would be a completely useless form of BGM for the astronaut. To the contrary, it might even be dangerous. . . .
>
> Why is mood music inappropriate here? Because mood music is someone else's music [*tanin no ongaku*]. In providing a virtual existence to accompany the astronaut, it at first seems like it might be of use. But in an isolated context like

this where connections with other people have been thoroughly severed, mood music cannot provide anything like comfort. For it to be comforting, the astronaut would have to be an extreme optimist, or at least sentimental.

Mood music, from the first instant you hear it, already does not belong to you. And precisely because it is someone else's music, there is no responsibility involved. Even as you acknowledge its existence, you also fail to hear it. It is a kind of irresponsible music within the crowd.[27]

Akiyama argues most BGM seeks only to shallowly represent the feelings of abstracted "other people." It doesn't engage with the listener's personal psychology, so in an isolated environment like the space shuttle, it quickly begins to irritate. For Akiyama, background mood regulation makes sense only in the context of an anonymous crowd. It becomes a way to establish an impersonal relationship between isolated selves without demanding any personal responsibility for the collective situation. Listened to in isolation, as an inauthentic echo of the self, this same impersonality becomes unbearable.

After my frustrating experience alone with the sentimental piano at the Chiba hotel, I could understand what Akiyama means when he describes Muzak-style BGM as "other people's music." The narrow emotional range of Muzak is easier to tolerate in a public setting like a café or a shopping arcade. There, the simplified emotions of the music match the shallow emotional façades deployed when interacting or co-existing with strangers in the city. Muzak, to borrow Ngai's apt phrasing, "runs on a feeling that no one actually feels."[28] The lightweight, narrow emotionality of the music diffuses the potential threat of being in close proximity to so many strangers. The music in these impersonal situations contours the relations between people, rather than serving as an expression of any single one of them. Often, it is not clear who is responsible for choosing the music, making it belong to no one but the space itself (and difficult to lodge a complaint against it).

When listening alone, however, there is nowhere to situate this emotional narrowing except the space of one's own reflective identity, and there it can feel only narrow and constricting, an ill match for anyone seeking to understand the self as an independent subject in full control of its feelings.

As an alternative to this "irresponsible" music of the sentimental crowd, Akiyama proposes a space shuttle music directly seeking to counter the isolation and atomization of the astronaut. This demands a more unemotional, scientific approach, with frequencies tuned to the specific physical and mental needs of the astronaut. "More than 'music,' this would be a 'sound' prepared specially for the inside of the space shuttle, the manufactured sonic equivalent of space food." Akiyama contrasts these hypothetical research-based sound compositions with the cold and spacey electronic music most often heard in TV commercials and science fiction dramas, concluding "we shouldn't call it 'design' if it just appeals to a private pathos or mood."[29]

Akiyama's discomfort with emotion regulation emerges from within his semifacetious argument for a hyperrational space music. By proclaiming the need for an even more rationalist BGM completely devoid of sentimentality, Akiyama seeks, in part, to reassert a clear distinction between music for listening and music for design. His essay is indicative of a more general approach to the new media landscape among the environmental avant-garde, one seeking out emotionally "dry" forms of mediation capable of overcoming the manipulative sentimentality of the commercial mass media.

While insightfully diagnosing the incompatibility of BGM sentimentality with the lonely space crusader, Akiyama replaces it with an ambivalent proposal to do away with emotional considerations entirely. While for Akiyama and many of his circle this lack of sentimentality was key to the music of the future, for many would-be listeners—including visitors to Expo '70 a few years later—the lack of attention to human feeling made the new music just as off-putting as the older forms of BGM, if not more so.

In this respect both traditional BGM and the environmental avant-garde were out of sync with the contemporary turn toward using music as a technology of the self. What the new listeners wanted, above all, was an environmental music reflecting their own feelings, desires, and physical needs while *also* acknowledging the isolation and atomization of the individual within the emerging consumer culture. They would find their personal soundtrack in neither BGM nor the Japanese avant-garde but in the work of long-dead French *gymnopédiste* Erik Satie (1866–1925).

THE QUIET BOOM OF ERIK SATIE

In the 1970s and early 1980s, Satie's work became central to the Japanese avant-garde's ongoing fascination with environmental listening, impersonal repetition, and intermedia performance. But at the same time, his softer music played a pivotal role in establishing an audience for moods of comforting autonomy, priming listeners for the subsequent emergence of ambient music and other related genres including new age, "healing" music, and the more atmospheric side of the 1980s "world music" boom (featuring, among other things, a lot of Gregorian chant).[30]

Unlike the corporate creators of Muzak and other affiliated background music, Satie's image as an idiosyncratic and solitary genius from Montmartre allowed him to serve as an ideal ancestor for later generations of ambient musicians attempting to envision a more artistic and independent heritage for atmospheric music. His *musique d'ameublement* ("furniture music," or more literally, "furnishing music"), while a minor part of Satie's total oeuvre, became a key reference point for ambient music when it emerged later in the 1970s.

Satie first introduced the furniture music concept in a 1917 collaborative concert with Darius Milhaud. The program states:

> We are presenting today for the first time a creation of Messieurs Erik Satie and Darius Milhaud, directed by M. Delgrange, the "musique d'ameublement" which will be played during the intermissions. We urge you to take no notice of it and to behave during the intervals as if it did not exist. This music . . . claims to make a contribution to life in the same way as a private conversation, a painting in a gallery, or the chair in which you may or may not be seated.[31]

Satie later writes:

> We must bring about a music which is like furniture, a music, that is, which will be part of the noises of the environment, will take them into consideration. I think of it as melodious, softening the noises of the knives and forks, not dominating them, not imposing itself. It would fill up those heavy silences that sometimes fall between friends dining together. It would spare them the trouble of paying attention to their own banal remarks. And at the same time it would neutralize the street noises which so indiscreetly enter into the play of conversation. To make such a noise would respond to a need.[32]

Satie's emphasis on furnishing music as a way to "fill up those heavy silences" and "neutralize the street noises" strongly parallels the emotional and cognitive orientation of the commercial BGM to come.

Crucially, however, his plea to treat music as if it were a chair "in which you may or may not be seated" is delivered in a playful and ironic tone. Presented by Satie, environmental music sounds like a lighthearted experiment with everyday life rather than a deadening pursuit of increased productivity and managed moods. Furniture music hints at environmental mood regulation, but only while ironically distancing itself from its own instrumentality. The idea of a music for playfully furnishing everyday life appealed not only to the postwar avant-garde but also to those pursuing the new self-mediated designer lifestyles on offer in 1970s Japan. By middecade Satie had emerged as an important icon for a new era of atmospheric mood regulation and self-care (Figure 2).

Like John Cage in the United States, Japan had its own tireless Satie champion in the form of none other than Akiyama Kuniharu. Akiyama first encountered Satie as a second-year student in middle school through reading Sakaguchi Ango's translations of Jean Cocteau and, later, by finding his music at a used record shop in Kanda, Tokyo. This was before John Cage discovered Satie and began championing his work in the United States.[33] At the time, the composer was largely unknown in Japan outside the new music community and a few literary salons.[34] This all changed following the Japanese premier of Louie Malle's 1963 film *Will o' the Wisp* (*Le feu follet,* also known as *The Fire Within*). Malle's film included much of what would come to be Satie's most well-known compositions, including the *Gymnopédies* and the *Gnossiennes*. Not long after the film's appearance, the same pieces started popping up in Japanese theater productions, films, and television commercials.[35]

This popularity grew over the next decade, and in September 1975 Akiyama began the *Complete Works of Erik Satie* concert series at Jean-Jean in Shibuya, Tokyo, timed to mark the fiftieth anniversary of Satie's death. The concerts featured Akiyama's wife, Takahashi Aki, and her brother, Takahashi Yūji, on piano, along with a wealth of other musicians, dancers, and artists; poetry readings; a lecture on Dada by critic Nakahara Yūsuke; and a screening of René Clair's short experimental film *Entr'acte* (1924), with its Satie score and cameo appearance. The series was a smash hit and ran for over two years, at which point a full-scale Satie revival was well under way. The *Yomiuri* newspaper dubbed this swelling interest in Satie a "quiet boom."[36]

The many Satie concerts following this initial outing are remarkable not only for their quantity but also for their multimedia character, as if the Japanese avant-garde's earlier interest in "intermedia"

音楽の手帖

サティ

Erik Satie

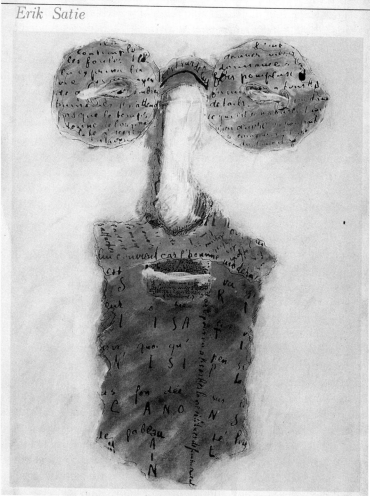

FIGURE 2. Cover of the Satie volume of the *Ongaku no techō* (Music note-book) series, released in 1981 at the height of the Satie boom. Includes texts by Akiyama, Takahashi Aki, Takahashi Yūji, and others, as well as key Satie texts in Japanese translation, an original score by Takemitsu Tōru, and "Satiricollages" by Akiyama. Image based on a calligram by Guillaume Apollinaire.

environments was finding itself reflected in Satie's turn-of-the-century works for theater, cinema, dance, music hall, offices, and living rooms.[37]

Reviews of the Satie events often note with some surprise how the enthusiastic audiences at these concerts were not the usual classical music crowds. In an *Asahi* newspaper review of one of the 1977 Satie concerts, composer Shibata Minao notes how Satie's accessible avant-garde sensibility had drawn many new young listeners to attend a classical music concert for the first time.[38]

The more classically trained, academically researched, experimentally minded participants in these concerts greeted Satie's newfound popularity among the general public with both excitement and consternation. There was a clear recognition early on the younger Japanese attending the concerts were not regular classical (or even avant-garde) music listeners and there was something different in their relationship to the music. In his comprehensive 1990 study of Satie's work, Akiyama recalls the eager anticipation and packed crowds greeting each event (a memory I have often heard echoed in speaking with others who were in attendance). Recalling the first *Complete Works* concerts, he writes:

> Each time there was a feverish response from the packed
> audience of young people. I think this was a period where
> we were starting to see, alongside an empathy with Satie's
> music, a new transformation in the audience itself. At
> the time I really felt this was the birth of a newly active
> (rather than passive) audience, one eager to participate
> in the music they had chosen for themselves. This was
> still an age with no relation to what came to be called the
> "Satie boom."[39]

Here, Akiyama reveals his hope the new audiences were more "active" and ready to pursue the music "they had chosen for themselves," unlike an earlier classical music crowd—or, implicitly, "passive" listeners of standard BGM. At the same time, Akiyama, with his roots in both Fluxus and Jikken Kōbō, was often at pains to emphasize Satie's more avant-garde side. As the "Satie boom" progressed, he became increasingly chagrined at how his favorite composer became known only for the relaxing melodies of early compositions like the *Gymnopédies, Gnossiennes,* and *Nocturnes* and not the absurdist provocation of a piece like *Vexations* or the ironically upbeat moods of the furnishing music works.[40]

At the same time, even early on Akiyama recognized Satie's popular appeal had much to do with his music's softness and its compatibility with contemporary lifestyles. Akiyama explores this idea in a 1977 article in the *Yomiuri* newspaper, where he ponders why Satie has become so popular among a younger generation of Japanese listeners. He proposes much of Satie's music—which he describes as "naked music, white music, pure music, poetic music"—is now in "metaphysical alignment" with the "everyday gentleness" aspired to by a younger generation of Japanese listeners. In this it outdoes even pop and folk music. Satie's work seems to directly soothe the struggles of contemporary life. Akiyama urges, though, the harder edges of Satie's "acerbic critical spirit" not be forgotten, including the works born from the composer's personal and financial struggles and his later work as part of the Dada movement.[41] Eight years later, in an interview connected with her 1985 Satie recital, pianist Kamiya Ikuyo sounds a similar note, telling the *Yomiuri* Satie was no minor composer and that despite the strange titles his music has deep feeling. She pleads, "Don't listen to it as BGM, okay?"[42]

In an essay reflecting back on the Satie boom, Takahashi Aki gives a somewhat different perspective on the composer's popularity, one more accepting of his position in Japanese popular culture:

> These simple and quiet melodies that seemed to wrap up and heal the tired soul were soft and beautiful—and sad. Satie's music didn't bother with imagery or story, but turned drama into the creation of atmosphere. At the same time, it was polished until there was almost nothing left, leaving a musical structure made of few sounds, a wafting aroma with beauty hard like a diamond.[43]

After Takahashi released a string of popular recordings of Satie's music, as she describes, strangers often approached to thank her, saying things like, "Even when I am tired, when I listen to Satie my mind goes blank, my spirit relaxes, and I can go on working." Takahashi describes being glad to hear this from her listeners, as she feels it is a realization of Satie's original ideal of furniture music: "Music like a chair, or wallpaper, or other furniture, that can comfort and relax people even when they are not focusing on it."[44]

A SOUNDTRACK FOR THE PRIVATIZED SELF

The Satie boom reveals the increasing priority on comforting mood regulation from the 1970s on, in stark contrast with both BGM and the hard-edged experimentation of the previous decade. But it also maintained ties to the more ambivalent atmospherics rooted in Satie's original furnishing music. By providing moods simultaneously soft, sad, and healing, Satie's work sounded an advance echo of not just the ideals of neoliberal autonomy and therapy culture but the isolation and uncertainty of the emerging social situation. This emphasis on ambivalent yet relaxing moods made Satie's music an important model for ambient music to follow. Unlike commercial BGM or the environmental avant-garde, the ambiguous comforts of Satie's music respected Japanese listeners' desire for self-determination while acknowledging the flip side of this autonomy in its moods of isolation and loneliness.

Satie's most well-known piece, *Gymnopedie No. 1,* sounds out this delicate balance in the contrast between the crisp contour of the right-hand melody and the much more dispersed background of the sustained chords of the left hand. Takahashi captures this duality in her description of Satie's work as "a wafting aroma with a beauty hard like a diamond."[45] While this piece was written almost nine decades earlier, the sculptural way the piece dissolves the hard edge into the foggy background allowed it to serve as a catalyst for the 1970s shift from using atmosphere as a tool of productivity and provocation to a more autonomous and slightly sad style of subjective drift.

Key to the ability of Satie's music to allow for more open forms of subjectivation is its refusal of forward-moving harmonic series in favor of giving the listener more freedom in choosing how to relate to the music. John Cage notes how rather than relying on harmonic progressions to organize a composition, Satie's work defines structure through discrete blocks of time.[46] This freer approach to duration refuses forward momentum, replacing regimented pulses and teleological harmonic progressions with a more static, sculptural creation of time-space. As Constant Lambert writes:

> By [Satie's] abstention from the usual forms of development and by his unusual employment of what might be called interrupted and overlapping recapitulations, which causes the piece to fold in on itself, as it were, he completely abolishes the element of rhetorical argument and even succeeds in abolishing as far as possible our time sense. We do not feel that the emotional significance of a phrase is dependent on its being placed at the beginning or end of a particular section.[47]

Lambert goes on to emphasize the unique spatial properties of Satie's works, noting how the three *Gymnopédies* were conceived as three different versions of the same piece—a radical idea at the time:

> Satie's habit of writing his pieces in groups of three was not just a mannerism. It took place in his art of dramatic development, and was part of his peculiarly sculpturesque views of music. When we pass from the first to the second *Gymnopédie* . . . we do not feel that we are passing from one object to another. It is as though we were moving slowly round a piece of sculpture and examining it from a different point of view. . . . It does not matter which way you walk around a statue and it does not matter in which order you play the three *Gymnopédies*.[48]

For Satie's new audience in 1970s Japan, this more open use of time modeled a music that did not, to borrow Morton Feldman's famous phrase, "push the sounds around."[49] But just as important, the music didn't push listeners around either. Rather than being forced to respond to the music, as with the BGM at the Chiba hotel or the electronic squelching of the Expo '70 pavilions, the *Gymnopédies* allow listeners to approach the sounds on their own time and in their own space, choosing when and how to situate themselves in relation to the music's more ambiguous atmospheres.

Satie's *Gymnopédies* served as a model for an ambient music reflecting the new autonomy even as it soothed it. It is not difficult to imagine how these Satie soundtracks, wafting stylish solitude, minimal yet poignant, were eagerly taken up as preferred listening for those attempting to tune themselves to the emerging postindustrial society. Satie's music allowed for the molding of a disciplined emotional self while hinting at both the allure and uncertainty of unknown mysteries lying just below the surface. This is perhaps the source of the remarkable ubiquity of the first *Gymnopédie*, used to sell a wide range of products, serenade shoppers and urban strollers, and lend mood to all manner of visuals from the 1970s onward, making it one of the most frequently heard classical compositions of late twentieth-century Japan. Satie's music allowed Japanese to feel better and, also, better about themselves—whether fantasizing in front of one of the many Satie-scored luxury car commercials, picturing themselves driving free and easy across the countryside, or watching Kitano Takeshi's film *Violent Cop (Sono otoko, kyōbō ni tsuki*, 1989), in which a wayward police officer lumbers down the street socially isolated but accompanied by Kume Daisaku's version of Satie's first *Gnossienne*. Satie's music modeled a form of subjectivation where this new autonomy felt not threatening but relaxing, playful, and free, if always a little bit sad. [50]

THE POST-SATIE AMBIENCE

Ambient media would come to take up this task of affording moods of reflective calm with a hint of deeper mysteries within. Brian Eno's 1978 essay introducing his conception of ambient music (packaged with *Ambient 1: Music for Airports*) reached Japan at the height of the Satie boom. The type of listening Eno called for soon converged with Satie's work in the minds of Japanese listeners.[51]

In the oft-quoted liner notes, Eno describes ambient music as an attempt to expand the attunement possibilities of BGM by moving beyond its purely instrumentalist orientation. After declaring his desire to rehabilitate environmental music from the taint of Muzak, Eno goes on to specify exactly where ambient music departs from commercial BGM:

> Whereas the extant canned music companies proceed from the basis of regularizing environments by blanketing their acoustic and atmospheric idiosyncrasies, Ambient Music is intended to enhance these. Whereas conventional background music is produced by stripping away all sense of doubt and uncertainty (and thus all genuine interest) from the music, Ambient Music retains these qualities. And whereas their intention is to "brighten" the environment by adding stimulus to it (thus supposedly alleviating the tedium of routine tasks and leveling out the natural ups and downs of the body rhythms), Ambient Music is intended to induce calm and a space to think. Ambient Music must be able to accommodate many levels of listening attention without enforcing one in particular; it must be as ignorable as it is interesting.[52]

Here, Eno provides a succinct articulation of how ambient music sets out to synthesize BGM and the environmental avant-garde, cultivating a calm and thoughtful mood for the listener while promising to stay out of the way and make room for a listener's personal rhythms and preferred level of attention. Eno's essay gives a precise name and definition to the aesthetic space Satie's music helped carve out for an alternative BGM, one playing more directly into new cultural demands for both autonomy and self-care.

When Eno's idea of "ambient music" arrived in Japan, it was quickly taken up as a useful term to mark a transformation in listening already well under way.[53] The first Sony Walkman came on the market just months after *Music for Airports,* setting off a radical transformation in the experience of recorded music. By the 1980s recorded music was no longer tethered to living rooms and bulky stereos but could be carried on a person's body as they made their way through the city. People could now wrap their ears with their chosen audio accompaniment and quickly learned how different music might influence their movement through public space. The primary purpose of music was gradually shifting to become, as Böhme succinctly puts it, "a modification of space as it is perceived by the body."[54] Ambient music and the new portable audio technology made an excellent pair. When Sony Japan set out to release their new Compact Disc format in 1984, they commissioned Eno to produce the sixty-one-minute ambient track *Thursday Afternoon* to demonstrate the long-playing background potential of the new technology.

As the next chapter explores, the Japanese ambient music of the following decades followed Satie and Eno in seeking to sculpt sound as a spatial object. The emerging ambient composers smoothed sonic contours by stretching out attack and decay. They avoided hard edges in favor of gradual transitions between different background layers. They implied vast open spaces through lush echo, reverb, and delay effects. They worked toward a mood of calm uncertainty by basing drones around the fifth of a chord rather than the tonic or by keeping tonality consonant but always slightly ambiguous or by repeating a basic pattern in constantly shifting permutations. Steady rhythms would give way to a slow pulse, a gradual ebb and flow.[55] In the ambivalent space carved out between environmental art and designer moods, in drifted the ambient.

/2/

THE SOUND OF EMBODIED SECURITY

While writing this book, I was living close to Shuto Route 3, one of the elevated highways crisscrossing Tokyo. Route 3 begins in Shibuya and runs to the southwest through Setagaya Ward, forming the first leg of the road to Nagoya. The highway was built around the time of the 1964 Tokyo Olympics to bring traffic quickly in and out of the city.[1] The location was convenient, but walking on the street underneath the raised highway was far from pleasant. Despite the noise-dampening sidewalls, the sounds of heavy traffic above readily bounced off the tall buildings on either side of the highway, blending with the engine sounds of the equally busy road down below (Figure 3). To be under Route 3 was to be sunk into a flood of traffic noise. This automobile roar masked the presence of both myself and others. It was difficult to hear oncoming bicycles, nearby conversation, and even the sound of my own footsteps. While these elements of the soundscape usually play an important role in helping to situate the self in relation to the surrounding space and the other people in it, under the weight of the highway noise this acoustic horizon was effectively obliterated.[2]

When I first moved to the area, this massive roar of noise from above felt heavy and oppressive. When walking in the neighborhood, I took side streets to avoid Route 3 as much as possible, although since many of the major train stations and facilities in the area were along the main road this was not always feasible. Then, one day, I happened to walk down the busy street while listening to ambient music on a pair of headphones. I had the music turned low so as not to be completely oblivious to the sounds around me, including the frequent bicyclists swerving around pedestrians on the sidewalk. After about forty minutes of walking, I was surprised to discover I had arrived at Shibuya faster than expected and without the usual fatigue from spending time on the noisy road.

What had happened? I realized the music, even at low volume, had

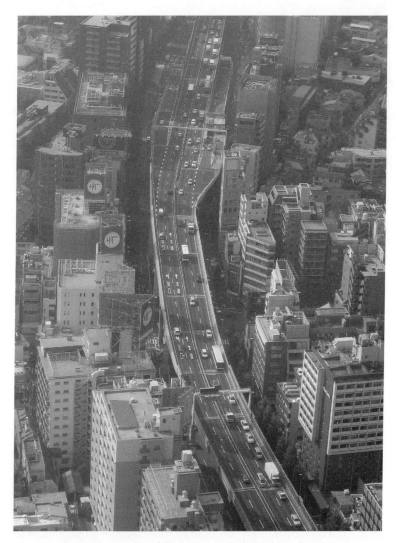

FIGURE 3. The noise corridor of Shuto Route 3, Tokyo, as seen from Roppongi Hills. Image by itoshin87/Wikimedia Commons (public domain).

effectively transformed my relation to the existing environment, regularizing its rhythms and softening its contours by sifting it through the music streaming at low volume through my headphones. As John-Paul Thibaud writes in his ethnography of the Walkman, headphone listening in urban space serves to filter other parts of the soundscape: "The

walking listener uses it not only to protect himself from the sonic ag-
gressions of the city but also to filter and enhance events. . . . The sound
volume of the Walkman is used in order to listen to or mask conversations, bells ringing, children's screams, traffic noise, and so forth."
With the help of the music, listeners can selectively ignore particular
parts of the existing soundscape, shifting foreground elements into the
background.[3]

Under the music's influence, I could hear the highway not as an endless roar of combustion engines and scraping tires but as something
closer to the relaxing sound of waves breaking on the seashore—a
sound acoustically similar to the indirect echoes of the raised highway
but with emotional associations far more calming in effect. The ambient mediation eased my habitual antipathy toward the traffic noise,
turning it instead into something almost peaceful. Paired with ambient
music, my walks under the raised highway were almost—almost but
not quite—enjoyable.

An earlier generation of acoustic ecologists would argue I was
merely coping with the stresses of living in a too-noisy city, placating
myself with an artificial sonic supplement rather than confronting the
unlivable aspects of urban space.[4] I understand these concerns, but at
the same time, it is misleading to make a firm distinction between the
"real" soundscape existing outside the body and the personal soundscapes unfolding in a more circumscribed space between the ears.
Sounds generated by engines and reflecting off nearby walls are not
necessarily more meaningful than sounds generated by small speakers vibrating as instructed by an electronic device. Seemingly more
situated environmental sounds like the engine noise and the highway
architecture are also the products of design, after all. There are some
elements in the soundscape, however, with more immediate personal
relevance: that oncoming bicyclist I need to dodge, for example, or
someone yelling to get my attention before a billboard falls on my head.
The music might keep me from noticing these things before it is too
late. It might also, though, put me in the right frame of mind to stay
observant and give me the rhythm to not lose my footing as I step out
of the way.

Whereas the next chapter focuses on how ambient media modulates
the rhythms of the city, this chapter focuses on a more basic process
of ontological attunement: how ambient media provide *imaginary
sensory landscapes* to *filter, unify,* and *stabilize* existing environments,
much in the way I experienced while walking down Route 3. Following
Gilles Deleuze and Félix Guattari, I suggest one of the key functions

of ambient media is to provide an *absolute background,* or a unified, coherent, and stable sensory surround. The absolute background provides people with a ready-made framework for grounding their sense of ontological security. This ground is more stable than most precisely because it rests in the background of awareness, often just below the level of conscious attention. As this chapter traces, the aesthetic form of these imaginary landscapes has shifted over time, becoming gradually more abstracted as part of an ongoing struggle to remain unmarked and unnoticed.

In the chapter "The Smooth and the Striated" in *A Thousand Plateaus,* Deleuze and Guattari describe ambience as an "encompassing element" rendering diverse environments homogenous: "an ambient space in which the multiplicity would be immersed and which would make distances invariant."[5] While ambience itself would seem at first to be on the side of the smooth and the flexible, in practice this slipperiness allows it to serve as a powerful mechanism for providing spatial cohesion, using atmosphere to provide a ubiquitous "interlinkage by immersion in an ambient milieu." In other words, ambience, like neoliberalism more generally, creates a space striated at such a fine grain that it appears (and feels) smooth. Ambience ties everything together in a way that feels organic, and this feeling comes to serve as the absolute background against which all other points in space can be located:

> The absolute is now the horizon or background, in other words the Encompassing Element without which nothing would be global or englobed. . . . The desert, sky, or sea, the Ocean, the Unlimited, first plays the role of an encompassing element, and tends to become a horizon: the earth is thus surrounded, globalized, "grounded" by this element, which holds it in immobile equilibrium and makes Form possible.[6]

This absolute background provides an organizing horizon all the more effective because it rests just outside conscious attention, providing the *sense* of cohesion without claiming it more directly. As Joe Milutis notes, the imagined location of this "Encompassing Element" has shifted over time, particularly as science has steadily eroded the mystery of what were once distant horizons. The frontier, the oceans, and eventually outer space all served as unknown horizons to bound more local territories, though as these too became colonized their utility as absolute backgrounds began to wane. Milutis traces a history of the gradual loss of this fantasy of a pristine frontier, leading humans to work ever harder to imagine an uncontaminated and secure horizon of cohesion still beyond their reach.[7]

In this chapter, I suggest one important role ambient media has played is as an aesthetic replacement for this absolute background, lending a sense of sensory cohesion to existing environments that might otherwise have little holding them together. At the same time, the history of ambient music's imaginary landscapes also registers the ever-receding horizon of the unknown and unmarked. This chapter reads the shifting landscapes of ambient music's sound and imagery as part of this ongoing quest for an absolute background to serve as a stable ground of embodied security.[8]

ENTRAINMENT

In *Music in Everyday Life,* Tia DeNora describes the various ways listeners use recorded music as an "entrainment" device. Not only can specific works call up particular memories and emotions within listeners, but music also provides a spatial and temporal framework for bodies to move through. Humans naturally align themselves to environmental rhythms, a practice going back to the alignment of the unborn child with its mother's heartbeat. Developers of background music have long studied the impact of various rhythms on listening bodies, whether aimed at increased productivity or increased sales. In recent decades the practice has extended into more personal domains of self-care. DeNora describes a group aerobics class in which the rhythms provided by the steady pulse of electronic dance music aid exercisers in making it through the workout, the beats pulling their bodies into sync and buoying them through time. The book describes how contemporary listeners are increasingly turning to music for the affordances it offers in their daily lives—usually as a background stimulus to underlie an activity (exercise, study, work, relaxation) rather than as an isolated and focused listening experience.[9]

DeNora writes of the ways music can provide a sense of *embodied security* by mediating a person's relationship with the surrounding world:

> Bodily awareness of environmental properties would
> appear to be a pragmatic, semi-conscious, matter. It need
> not involve any reflection or articulation as propositional
> "knowledge," though at times it also may do so. . . . The

creaturely ability to locate and anticipate environmental
features engenders a kind of corporeal or embodied security, by which I mean the "fitting in" or attunement with
environmental patterns, fostered by a being's embodied
awareness of the materials and properties that characterize
his or her environment. Embodied *insecurity,* by contrast, is
what happens when one is unable to locate and appropriate
such materials . . . unable to locate resources with or against
which to "gather oneself" into some kind of organized and
stable state. Embodied security involves one's ability to *fit in,*
or situate oneself, bodily, with an ergonomic environment.[10]

This perspective sees "bodily states and forms of embodied agency as
produced through the body's interaction with and abilities to appropriate environmental materials—materials that can perhaps best be
understood as resources for the constitution of particular states over
time and social space."[11] This mediated sensory interface between body
and surrounding space emerges as a contested site in the quest for ontological security.

EVACUATED LANDSCAPES

As I experienced while using headphones on my walk under Route 3,
ambient music can provide sonic landscapes for listeners to deploy as
immersive environments of embodied security. References to landscape abound in writing and images surrounding the style.

   Eno offers some hints about the relationship between landscape
and ambient music in the liner notes to *Ambient 4: On Land* (1982),
in which he begins using "landscape" as a figure for ambient music itself. In ambient music "the landscape has ceased to be a backdrop for
something else to happen in front of; instead, everything that happens
is a part of the landscape. There is no longer a sharp distinction between foreground and background."[12] Unlike the sharp foreground/
background distinction maintained in BGM (as Akiyama discusses
in chapter 1), ambient media seeks to undermine this kind of subject/
environment duality by dissolving the subject into the surrounding
space. These imaginary landscapes are, by and large, devoid of people.
Eno later notes:

> An aspect of this landscape concern is to do with the re-
> moval of personality from the picture. You know how differ-

ent a landscape painting is when there is a figure in it. Even
if the figure is small, it automatically becomes the focus—all
questions of scale and depth are related to it. When I stopped
writing songs I took the figure out of the landscape.[13]

By eliminating all forms of figural focus, ambient landscapes can better
serve as impersonal topographies for listeners' anonymous drift.

This desire for music to serve as an evacuated environment of ambient subjectivation is closely tied to the increasing mobility of contemporary listeners. Eno writes of his personal use of recorded music
while living the peripatetic life of an artist constantly traveling from
place to place:

> I realized while I was living this nomadic life, the one thing
> that was really keeping me in place, or giving me a sense
> of place, was music. . . . We can use recordings to insert a
> sense of place in the various locations we end up in. They
> repeat identically each time—they're reliable portable
> experiences.[14]

As noted in chapter 1, this type of ambient subjectivation differs from
earlier forms of BGM in not only providing embodied security but registering the precarity of contemporary lifestyles within the textures of
the music itself. Eno makes this connection explicit in his comments
on creating *Ambient 1*. He recalls thinking a music for airports

> has to have something to do with where you are and what
> you're there for—flying, floating, and, secretly, flirting with
> death. I thought, "I want to make a kind of music that pre-
> pares you for dying—that doesn't get all bright and cheerful
> and pretend you're not a little apprehensive, but which
> makes you say to yourself, 'Actually, it's not that big a deal
> if I die.'"[15]

Eno here provides a classic example of how the absolute background
incorporates uncertainty by rendering it calm: the music doesn't pretend to have removed any of the actual risk of flying but is nonetheless
reassuring precisely because it both acknowledges this fear and orients
it toward a more impersonal and equanimous sensory horizon. Ambient music models a form of ambivalent calm not only appropriate but
advantageous for a less grounded time.

THE GRADUAL ABSTRACTION OF AMBIENT STYLE

At the same time, the ambient landscape has a history of its own. In what follows I trace how the content of these imaginary landscapes has shifted in subsequent decades. Starting from a fantasy of blissful solitude, over the years ambient styles have shaded toward the ambivalently peaceful, imbuing their absolute backgrounds with a more pervasive sense of risk and insecurity even as they have strived to keep an underlying calm.

The August 2008 "Ambient & Chill Out" special issue of Japanese music magazine *Studio Voice*—the seed of what would become the first of the three ambient discographies released by Japanese publishers in the past several years—puts forth a rough framework for the past three decades of ambient music worldwide.[16] Beginning with *Music for Airports,* the editors divide ambient music history into three periods. The first is the Classic Ambient Era (1978–87), when Eno and others carved out a new genre of atmospheric music in the space between popular music and the avant-garde. In the second period, the Club Culture Era (1988–97), ambient music joined the thriving rave and club scenes, becoming the "chill-out" partner to trance, house, and other forms of electronic dance music. Finally, the editors frame 1998 to the time of publication in 2008 as the Electronica/Drone Era, in which ambient music followed the emergent electronica scene out of the club and into a context of intensive and sustained home listening. In the process ambient became more aligned with independent experimental music and its small-scale, more personalized circuits of exchange. It might be argued this tripartite division is too schematic—exceptions can easily be found in each period—but it does provide a loose structure for understanding how ambient music has reimagined its role and its landscapes over time. Building on this model and linking it to larger social transformations, I present one key ambient musician from each of these periods, showing how the ambient approach to embodied security has over time become more abstract, deterritorialized, and insecure.

Hosono Haruomi, Ambient Tourist

Hosono Haruomi (1947–) was the first Japanese artist to begin exploring ambient music as a genre. Well versed in exotica and folk music after collaborations with Van Dyke Parks and others in the late 1970s, Hosono was the first to recognize the relationship between ambient music's imaginary landscapes and the international relaxation tourism on the rise in Japan at the time. Hosono is best known for his

California-styled folk rock project Happy End (Happii endo, 1969–72) and his highly innovative electropop trio with Sakamoto Ryūichi and Takahashi Yukihiro, Yellow Magic Orchestra (YMO, 1978–83).[17] What is less well known is his instrumental role in introducing ambient music to Japan, serving as its primary Japanese exponent throughout the 1980s.

Hosono was introduced to Eno's Obscure Records label (including his early 1975 protoambient release *Discreet Music*) by graphic artist Yokoo Tadanori, his collaborator on the India-themed psychedelic synthesizer album *Cochin Moon* (1978).[18] He first began seriously listening to ambient music under YMO bandmate Sakamoto's influence at the beginning of the 1980s. While Sakamoto had long been steeped in contemporary classical music, Hosono describes the early 1980s as the point where even a "pop music person" like himself began to listen to people like John Cage and Steve Reich in earnest.[19] Yellow Magic Orchestra's subsequent fourth album, *BGM* (1981), marked a shift to a more ambient sound. Hosono notes this was in part due to criticism of the band's lightweight "cuteness" and partly out of a desire to embrace the new sounds coming out of Europe at the time. He looks back on the album as one of the band's most important, a move away from their earlier Kraftwerk-style technopop and toward something more abstract and subtle.[20] *BGM* is still a pop album, but the more abstract electronic touches running throughout mark a more atmospheric dimension to the band's sound, particularly on "Happy End" and "Loom." The latter track closes the album with three minutes of soft echoing synth chords and distantly dripping water that would not be out of place on one of Eno's *Ambient* albums from the time.[21]

For Hosono the "extremely free time" (*hijō ni jiyū na jikan*) of Eno's music made it an important part of his own musical self-care regimen in the early 1980s:

> When the *Ambient* series came out, the music had a very psychological, healing effect on me, sort of like a tranquilizer. At that time YMO was doing really complicated, noisy songs, but when I came home and listened to music, I would only listen to ambient. From that point on I suddenly started going much more in that direction, playing the synthesizer on my own and going to a very private place. . . . I would put the *Ambient* series on auto play and let it run all day. I really listened to it as ambient music. It was incredibly refreshing. At the same time, among the so-called New Wave in

London, there was a lot of this kind of thing, with musicians like Michael Nyman and the Flying Lizards. I was really influenced by this type of style. While on the one hand this was contemporary classical music through a pop filter, it also had a strong psychological pull. For me it was a really mysterious music, and other styles just couldn't compete.[22]

Hosono came to ambient music as a way to afford peaceful moods in both listeners and in himself. As science writer Yoshinari Mayumi proposes in a 1984 discussion with Hosono, in the ancient past music probably first emerged as a form of therapy, a way to create spaces where people could come and feel better. In response Hosono claims the most interesting aspect of recent electronic music is the rediscovery of music's role as an environmental healer.[23]

In a Euro-American context, Eno is often noted for his role in developing the music studio as a tool for creating atmospheric recordings (an approach following from the early 1970s studio experiments of Jamaican dub producers like Lee "Scratch" Perry). Hosono played an equivalent role in Japan.[24] He describes the nonlinear studio production process as what allowed him to step outside the pop music scene and produce layered instrumental music as a solo artist. Hosono approached composing with a computer as a form of private "collaboration" with the machine, as the technological complexity introduced surprises into his usual compositional habits. For both Eno and Hosono, it was precisely the sculptural nonlinearity of studio composition and electronic technologies that allowed for the creation of a more private and atmospheric sound.[25]

In 1984, soon after Yellow Magic Orchestra disbanded, Hosono launched a series of recordings and books under the names Non-Standard and Monad (both as sublabels of Teichiku records). The Monad series became his ambient label, on which, paralleling Eno, he released a series of four ambient works: *Mercuric Dance, Coincidental Music, The Endless Talking,* and *Paradise View* (all 1985). The first is a score for an ambient video by Arai Tadayoshi; the second, a collection of Hosono's music for television commercials; the third, music for an installation in Genova, Italy; and the fourth, a soundtrack to the eponymous film by Takamine Gō, part of the "new Okinawan cinema." Hosono's diverse ambient styles on these and later albums include psychedelic synth improvisations based on alchemical concepts, atmospheres inflected by traditional musics (particularly gamelan, north Indian classical music, Okinawan folk, and early Japanese music), minimalist arpeggio workouts, atmospheric dub, and field recording–based collage.

Hosono mixes Eno's ambient influence with the exoticism of his 1970s work and infuses it with his own interest in the work of Carlos Castaneda and a wide range of indigenous cultures.[26] In the book Hosono produced to announce the new labels, *Globule* (1984), he introduces his aspirations: "Non-standard . . . develops the ambient music started by Brian Eno to a global level and to converse with and respond to a dispatch from the earth."[27] Hosono introduces the term *kankō ongaku* (sightseeing music) to describe his ambient works, a pun on *kankyō ongaku* (environmental music)—the phrase most often used at the time to translate Eno's "ambient music" into Japanese. With this nod to global ecotourism, Hosono strategically brought ambient music into dialogue with the emergent genre of "world music" and the larger boom in international tourism occurring in Japan in the mid-1980s. This image of the global (or "globule") in Hosono's mid-1980s work serves not just as a marker of ecological awareness but as an "encompassing element" of embodied security based on a planetary horizon (one striving to leave the more local insecurities of Japanese identity behind).

Marilyn Ivy has documented the rising interest in rural sites in Tōhoku (northeastern Japan) like Tōnō and Mount Osore in the 1970s, all part of a larger desire for horizons of primal mystery and folk cultures resistant to the rationalizations of modernity. The empty rural landscapes featured in Dentsū's long-running Discover Japan domestic travel campaign transformed into more explicitly otherworldly sites with the introduction in 1984 of the Exotic Japan campaign, focused on esoteric destinations like Mount Kōya, the secluded Shingon Buddhist temple complex. Travel beyond Japan's borders was also increasingly available as a means to engage these exotic realms. New tourist infrastructures and increasing purchasing power in the 1970s and 1980s allowed unprecedented numbers of Japanese to leave the country and explore. The mass media was eager to show the way, as in NHK's popular Kitaro-scored series *The Silk Road* (1980–84, 1988–89). Hosono had just completed his own more literal forms of spiritual tourism, traveling around Japan to various religious sites as part of a project with religious studies scholar Nakazawa Shinichi (published as *Kankō* [Sightseeing], 1984).[28] The landscapes on offer in Hosono's ambient works move from the hazy metropoles and marshes of Eno's early ambient recordings to embrace this "paradise view" of global tourism, offering up the imaginary atmospheres of exotic cultures for affective consumption by the urban listener.

In 1978, the same year Eno's *Ambient 1: Music for Airports* was released, Hosono collaborated with graphic artist Yokoo Tadanori on two landmark albums, the tropicalia-styled *Paraiso* (Alfa) and the aforementioned electro-exotica experiment *Cochin Moon* (King Records). The latter was the product of a trip Hosono and Yokoo made together to India, and the covers feature Yokoo's signature collage aesthetic. The *Paraiso* cover (Figure 4) imagines a coastline where hula dancers, floating Buddhas, the Taj Mahal, the Manhattan skyline, a Polynesian choir, Mt. Fuji, palm trees, and cherry blossoms all come together in a single landscape. This cultural composite assumes a totality of representation, reaching all the way to the horizon. Like Eno's *Ambient* series covers, these covers are cartographic in a way, but they map cultural rather than physical spaces, using images drawn from exotica, movie posters, and religion. Unlike Eno's quasi-scientific anonymity, Yokoo's maps draw freely from popular culture and the rapidly developing global tourism industry.

The self-consciously exoticizing approach of his 1970s tropicalia albums continued in Hosono's subsequent ambient invocations of other cultures—particularly his use of images and sounds from Okinawan, Caribbean, Pacific Islander, South and Southeast Asian, and Native American cultures. In typically ambivalent Hosono style, this embrace of the exotic is often performed with a wink to the audience. As with Satie's description of furnishing music (described in chapter 1), it is difficult to know how seriously Hosono intends his "sightseeing music" to be taken and how much he is simply playing with his audience.[29] Like Satie and later ambient innovators the KLF (but unlike Eno), Hosono's ambience is often tinted with a subtle sense of the parodic, noting the ridiculousness of the "paradise view" while performing it with relish. Building from the self-consciously artificial exotica of artists like Martin Denny, Hosono's "sightseeing music" acknowledges how with global tourism and "world music" the planet has become affectively mapped, with certain locations deemed more calm and atmospheric than others. In this respect Hosono's sightseeing music ironically foreshadows the later cultural appropriations of major-label "world music" releases of the 1990s such as Enigma's *MCMXC a.D.* (1990) and Deep Forest's self-titled debut (1993).[30]

At the same time, Hosono was serious in seeking out an ecological perspective within ambient music. In a recent discussion with Nakazawa, Hosono looks back on his 1980s ambient music as a precursor to contemporary environmentalist movements, noting how the genre presented a more integrated perspective on a unified earth. In 1986

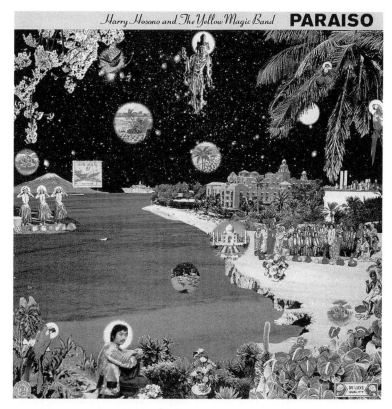

FIGURE 4. Hosono's tongue-in-cheek exoticism first appeared in earlier albums like *Paraiso* (Alfa, 1978). Cover by Yokoo Tadanori.

Hosono released his own environmental manifesto, the *F.O.E. Manual,* based on Stewart Brand's *Whole Earth* catalogs in the late 1960s and early 1970s. F.O.E. stands for Friends of Earth, one of Hosono's ecologically themed ambient music side projects of the mid-1980s. This 1980s ambience, Nakazawa points out, sought out a form of spirituality and religion not tied to any particular tradition, seeking instead to bring everyone together through an ambient orientation to this planetary horizon.[31]

A central track on *Mercuric Dance,* "Fossil of Flame—Fifty Bell Trees" is exemplary of Hosono's ambient music in this calming planetary mode. As with all of *Mercuric Dance,* the track is composed largely of an analog synthesizer voice rich with harmonic warmth and soft in contour. The individual notes have a long decay, expansive reverb, and a gently wavering pitch. The tempo starts off slow and soon grows slower, with indulgent pauses between each phrase. The simple melody rises for four notes and then drifts back down the octave with a more restful and dispersed energy. Translated into somatic terms, these unhurried melodic lines take the form of a steady inhalation followed by an exhalation increasingly slow and deep.

With each cycling of the melody, supplemental notes appear on the descent, making the exhalation more textured and profound. After two and a half minutes, sharper sawtooth synthesizer tones bubble up at the fringes of the descending phrase. The texture grows gradually richer but maintains a harmonic simplicity drawing listeners into a more sedate and focused frame of mind. The music repeatedly falls back into near silence, only to resume again with the melody reaching toward higher and more sustained tones.

Around the seven-minute mark, this sonic focus widens to take in an expanded range of sounds, with the jangle of what sounds like a Tibetan singing bowl and the distant cry of a crow now softly audible in the distance. The crow caws as the synthesizer drones gradually peel away and the track falls silent.

The hints of traditional musics (in both instrumentation and rhythm) sprinkled across Hosono's ambient works situate the synthesizer less as a novel technology and more as an organic extension of the "world music" growing popular at the time. The track's title, described in the liner notes as a synthesis of the elemental forces of fire and wood, pictures an exotic landscape both unfamiliar and organic, combustible but timeless and ritualistic: a fossil of flame, fifty bell trees.

For all its exotic trimmings, however, Hosono's evolving theory of ambiance eventually came to understand these esoteric landscapes as expressive of an imaginary rather than an existing space. As Hosono argues in his essay collection *The Ambient Driver* (*Anbiento doraivā*), "Ambience is less a particular style of music, and more a word designating a certain mental state."[32] In a 1998 panel discussion on neoshamanism at the NTT InterCommunication Center in Tokyo, Hosono revises his earlier approach to ambient music, repositioning it away from a mimetic role representing the earth and toward a more private interior space:

> Since the beginning of the 1980s I had been doing mostly
> ambient music, which was like an ocean of music to me.
> The people from the younger generations of the pop music

world began creating their music from an "oceanic feeling" sensibility from the beginning of the '90s. Ambient was originally associated with a more ecological context, but this was mistaken. Ambient is the musical form with the greatest reach, or periphery of attraction—in short, from the expanses of one's deeper interior. And in making ambient music I came to the realization that it is definitely not an external environment, but rather the internal ambience that has this "oceanic feeling."[33]

Here, Hosono comes close to admitting the exotic landscapes adorning his "sightseeing music" from the 1980s primarily served as affective resources for his own (and his listeners') inner feelings of reflective calm. The simple, rippling blue of the *Mercuric Dance* album cover reflects the ambiguity of this oceanic feeling: does it depict a sea turned on its side or simply the curves of a window shade softly insulating the listener from the outside world? (Figure 5).

Tetsu Inoue, Ambiant Otaku

In the 1990s ambient styles began spreading into the electronic dance music scenes, partly in response to the KLF's seminal album *Chill Out* in 1990 (packaged with a sticker reading "file under ambient"). As home electronic music production became more affordable later in the decade, however, the main locus of ambient music production shifted away from the chill-out rooms of the dance clubs. Aphex Twin, Autechre, the Black Dog, Boards of Canada, and other British electronic music producers inspired a migration toward a more complex strand of rhythm-oriented electronic music, incorporating unusual meters, modes, and compositional structures. Ambient music production followed these shifts into more conceptual territory.

A central figure in this transition to a more cerebral ambience was Japanese ambient music producer Tetsu Inoue, who moved from Kyushu to San Francisco and then to New York in the mid-1980s after being turned on to ambient music via the progressive psychedelia of Pink Floyd, the synthesized classical music of Tomita Isao, and the compositional experiments of Yellow Magic Orchestra. Inoue recalls becoming gradually frustrated with the drugged-out audiences at his club performances, leading him to seek out a more focused and meaningful relationship with his listeners. The ideal listening environment became, for Inoue, a quiet domestic space, with lights off and

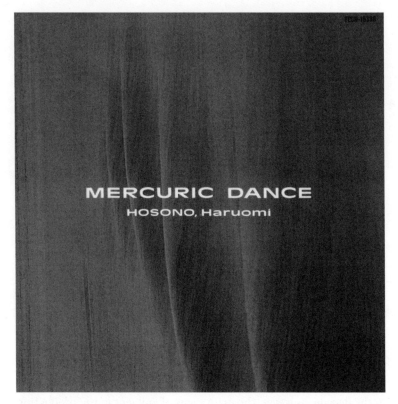

FIGURE 5. Oceanic feelings. Hosono Haruomi, *Mercuric Dance* (cover).

headphones on. By the end of the century, ambient music would increasingly focus on this type of "bedroom listening."[34]

In contrast to Hosono's exotic elsewheres, the ambient music of the
1990s moved further from a mimetic relationship with existing landscapes, seeking out more abstract imaginary horizons instead. Inoue
describes the motivation behind his 1996 album *World Receiver* as a
purely mental environment: "I have a landscape in my mind that I had
to express."[35] The weightless sounds and anonymous images scaffold-
ing Inoue's ambient spaces make a marked contrast with the more specific horizons of Hosono's exotic cultural itinerary. As a representative
example, consider the title track to Inoue's debut album, *Ambiant
Otaku* (1994).[36]

"Ambiant Otaku" is based on three loops: a short, descending five-
note pattern in a middle register repeating roughly every two seconds,

a higher three-note pattern intersecting it on a similar rhythm, and a lower note pulsing, Morse code–like, also roughly once every two seconds. There is a slight difference in duration between the first two and the last of these three patterns, however, so they offset each other in shifting syncopation as the loops continue to cycle. The amplitude of their reverberations slowly grows as they continue to loop across the first few minutes of the piece. Around the one-minute mark, another element appears: a synth tone sliding up and down playfully through the lower-mid frequencies. The contour of the slides recalls the shape of whale song, swimming up and down in a smooth arc through a re-verberant ocean. This continues throughout almost the entirety of the piece. In contrast to the tightly structured loops, this voice has a gestural and improvisational quality, a freedom playing across the shifting pulse of the more patterned layers. About a minute and a half into the track, an even higher-pitched cluster of fluttering tones en-ters, shimmering and bright as they slide over one another. Around the three-minute mark, something resembling a more traditional rhythm appears—an occasional thumping bass drum. These thumps, together with the offset rhythms of the ongoing loops, often appear to be on the verge of coalescing into a steady beat. Instead, they continue to slide across one another without ever falling into sync.

At nearly five minutes, a contrasting three-note loop comes in louder in a lower register, responding to the patterns that opened the work. This complex assemblage of sliding loops and shimmering layers continues until near the end of the piece, almost eleven minutes after it began. Different voices continue to emerge and drop out as the music progresses. The original two loops gradually disappear about halfway through, only to reappear in the final two minutes to take the track to its concluding fade. As is evident here, Inoue's ambient style had ab-sorbed a great deal from the new electronic music (and the minimalist music before it), particularly its emphasis on interlocking looped pat-terns and the building up and breaking down of textures layer by layer across the length of a piece.[37]

The emphasis in "Ambiant Otaku" is on high-frequency shimmer-ing textures. Along with the whale song and the expansive reverb, my impression as a listener is one of drifting inside the ocean, looking up at the light flickering off the surface of the water above as a variety of sea creatures slowly swim by. I am perhaps influenced by the image of a large stingray floating across the sea floor in the booklet to Inoue's next album, *Slow and Low* (1995). The deep seas often come to mind listening to Inoue's resonant textures—or, if not the ocean, then the depths of space. Unlike the more culturally specific topographies of Hosono's ambient works, Inoue's absolute backgrounds are weightless, ambiguous, and pulsing with abstract patterns. The spaces to which they refer are oriented more toward floating than walking, standing, or sitting—more zero gravity than earthbound.

This shift from potentially inhabitable imaginary landscapes toward more abstract horizons is evident in the artwork accompanying the albums. Unlike the quasi-cartographic images adorning Eno's *Ambient* series, the simple designs and hand-drawn sketches of Hosono's *Monad* quartet, and Yokoo's exotic collages, Inoue's FAX +49-69/450464 label releases all feature highly symmetrical covers, with circular images organized in empty black fields. The mandala on the cover of *Ambiant Otaku* (Figure 6) is characteristic of the music's conceptual organization: a highly detailed geography, but one without reference to any human-scale landscape. Rather, the mandala offers a simultaneous guide through the mind and the universe as a whole— the macrocosm and the microcosm together. On the reverse sleeve is a striking image of a fetus wired into a microchip. Here, Inoue hints at the kind of psychedelic mood regulation producing these abstract patterns and oceanic feelings. Are we drifting under the sea or tucked away inside an electronic womb? The title of the album similarly riffs playfully on the image of the Japanese *otaku,* devotees of various subcultures who strive for encyclopedic expertise in their chosen field, even if it leaves them out of touch with the wider world. While the valence of the term has shifted in subsequent years, the stereotype of the otaku in the mid-1990s imagined them as isolated at home, surrounded by and in some sense surviving off electronic media: a state parodied by the circuit-board fetus pictured here.[38] Inoue playfully invokes the otaku to imagine a different kind of ambient listener, one who approaches this ostensibly "background" genre with an obsessive attention to detail.

While Eno focused on music for airports and Hosono imagined travels through distant cultures, Inoue's ambient otaku might never desire to leave the house at all. This increasing interest in more private, listener-controlled atmospheres becomes clearer when looking at the production context for Inoue's work. While Eno and Hosono were known for studio-based production techniques, Inoue's music was part of a larger shift toward the autonomy offered by home-based recording.

Pete Namlook's FAX +49-69/450464 came to serve as the premier otaku-style ambient music label of the 1990s. Founded in Germany in

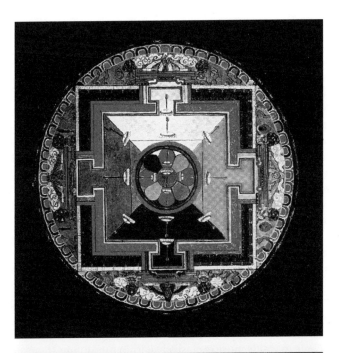

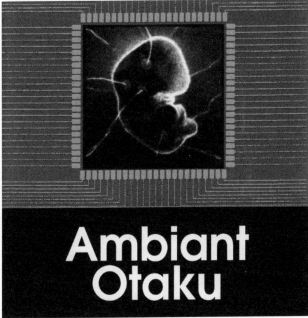

Ambiant Otaku

FIGURE 6. Mandala and electronic fetus. Tetsu Inoue, *Ambiant Otaku* (cover and inside sleeve).

1993, the label was known for its highly systematic packaging (where different icons and colors denoted minutely differentiated subgenres), highly limited editions (usually from five hundred to two thousand copies per release; *Ambient Otaku* was first released in an edition of five hundred), and prolific output (at its height in the mid- to late 1990s, the label was releasing one album every two weeks). FAX +49-69/450464 was successful in developing a small, dedicated audience of devoted ambient listeners, some even taking out a subscription to the label to ensure they did not miss a single release.

The image of the "world" and, more specifically, the planet Earth appears repeatedly in Inoue's work. The cover designs for the first three volumes of *2350 Broadway* (1993–96), an ambient collaboration between Inoue and Namlook, pair circular photographs of New York street scenes with an image of Earth. Both images float in a larger circle of empty black space.[39] Unlike Hosono's "Globule," however, this Earth is firmly detached from any specific culture, serving as an abstract terrain for the listener to drift alongside.

In this way, the "landscapes" produced by ambient music in the 1990s came to reside more exclusively within the albums themselves—and between the ears of the listeners floating within them. This is not to say those making or listening to this kind of music were socially withdrawn. Collaboration between artists is a regular feature of both Hosono's and Inoue's discographies and, indeed, of ambient music as a whole. Ambient music in the 1990s was also becoming increasingly transnational, as mapped out in the title of a release by the ambient "supergroup" HAT (Hosono Haruomi, Atom Heart, and Tetsu Inoue): *Tokyo Frankfurt New York* (Daisyworld, 1996). Collaborations across continents became a regular practice, as technology allowed for an easy exchange of musical material, first through the mail and later over the Internet.

Inoue describes the value of collaborative work precisely in terms of his interaction with other musicians: "Collaboration is more like vibration and feedback. . . . I get bored sometimes working by myself, because there's no feedback."[40] Inoue's comment hints one impulse for an otaku-style turn toward more private forms of music is a dissatisfaction with the modes of interaction available in contemporary social environments and a desire for the more significant person-to-person exchanges available within subculture groups formed around particular hobbies and interests. This dissatisfaction with the given landscape is reflected in the texts accompanying Inoue's FAX projects. The liner notes to *2350 Broadway* describe the albums as "music for a city that is unlivable."

While rejecting the larger social landscape, the FAX +49-69/450464 label demonstrated a renewed interest in fostering accessibility and direct communication at a more personal level. Namlook's actual fax number was included in the label name for easy reference, and 2350 Broadway was the address of Inoue's apartment in New York, where the music was produced. The (sometimes controversially) limited print runs of FAX +49-69/450464 releases allowed Namlook to grant artists more control over their releases and facilitated contact between a small community of artists and listeners. Inoue's recognition of the facile sociality of public listening in the club environment, paradoxically, entailed a return to private spaces, capable of sustaining potentially more satisfying interpersonal and artistic interactions.

In the 1990s ambient music aligned itself closer to the neoliberal focus on personal autonomy, from the solo "bedroom" producer to the solitary headphone listener. The more abstract, imaginary landscapes on offer allowed more room for audiences to mix the recordings with their own personal horizons, allowing ambient music to function more effectively not just as music for airports and chill-out rooms but as a more private technology of the self. Finding the given landscapes unlivable, ambient producers and listeners in the 1990s increasingly decided to invent their own.

Hatakeyama Chihei, Ambient Isolationist

Approaching the turn of the century, darker textures began to emerge as the "encompassing element" of this abstracted ambient sound. In a 1995 *Artforum* essay, music critic Simon Reynolds notes a shift from a warm and fuzzy ambient style toward what he calls, borrowing the name of an influential 1994 ambient compilation, "isolationism."[41] While isolationism maintained the general ambient emphasis on slow-changing textures and timbres, the style introduced a more explicit feeling of unease. Following David Toop, Reynolds describes an isolationist focus on "nonspecific dread," the flip side to the earlier ambient styles' tendency toward "nonspecific bliss":

> With isolationism, the absence of narrative signifies not utopia but entropy, paralysis. But there's still a neurotic jouissance to be gleaned from this music; it's a victory over what Brian Massumi calls "ambient fear," the omnipresent low-level anxiety of the late-20th-century mediascape. By immersing yourself in the phobic, you make it your element.[42]

As Reynolds goes on to argue, isolationism was based on the allure of dystopian calm, an empty space where all signifiers of social life had been evacuated. He cites literary critic John Carey on the modernist fantasy of apocalypse, which Carey sees as a response to overpopulation. Reynolds reads isolationism as "a kind of estheticized death wish," a "near-monastic impulse" to flee the endless turnover of pop culture, turning away from an already weakened social solidarity to "revert to an inanimate, inorganic state, free of the irritation of fleshly, animal desire." This emerging form of ambience was a curious sort of anesthetic affording calm at the same time as it registered the painful loss of what had to be erased in order to create such empty horizons. But this "neurotic jouissance" did serve a purpose: isolationist ambience offered affective entrainments for a calm confrontation with loss and uncertainty.

Miyadai Shinji makes a similar argument in the Japanese context in *Owari naki nichijō o ikiro* (Live the endless everyday), written in the wake of the Kobe earthquake in January 1995 and the release of sarin gas onto the Tokyo subway system by the doomsday cult Aum Shinrikyō two months later. Miyadai notes the prevalence in 1980s Japanese popular culture (particularly in anime and manga) of a psychological desire to transcend the routine boredom of the postindustrial everyday by destroying the existing world and living in a heightened state of postapocalyptic awareness. Miyadai proposes this as a way to understand the motivations of apocalyptic cults like Aum Shinrikyō as well as the "disaster volunteer" boom in the wake of the 1995 Kobe earthquake. He reads this desire for apocalypse as a desire for the clutter and crowds to be swept away in order to usher in an evacuated and oceanic space granting freedom of movement and an escape from existing social identities. The intensity of this cathartic upheaval is followed by the absolute background of a world made cohesive through complete desolation. In music a similar boom and bust can be heard, for example, in the general shift from the noise music of the 1980s and 1990s, with its emphasis on sensory overload, to the more reductionist and "lowercase" sounds of the new century.[43]

While already quiet to begin with, Japanese ambient music in the 2000s made a similar shift toward postapocalyptic isolationism. The new ambience began to set aside the fantasy of floating freely over large expanses and instead stuck close to the materiality of sounds embedded in more diminutive and constrained spaces. Where earlier styles stimulated feelings of movement and drift, ambient music in the new century often sounded like it was doing its best just to hold still. The tones were darker, and the compositions often hinted at fatigue even when they did their best to stay bright and open. Compared with the ambient music of earlier decades, compositions became more fractured and partial, with no image of global wholeness, no oceanic feeling without registering the sinking pull of the undertow. The absolute background was becoming less absolute, even as it still strove to provide a sense of cohesion on the somatic, sensory level.

This shift was again paired with shifts in music production technology. The computer music of the 1980s and early 1990s was heavily based around synthesizers and samplers and depended on the MIDI interface to allow these electronic controllers to communicate with one another. By the turn of the century, however, computers had developed enough processing power to perform more advanced signal processing using onboard software. With the spread of digital audio processing tools like Max/MSP in the late 1990s, ambient music production shifted away from its origins in analog knob twiddling and moved toward a more malleable palette of digital signal processing (DSP). The new digital audio interfaces allowed for the easier manipulation of microsounds (sounds less than one-tenth of a second in duration) as well as more extreme variations in frequency range and sonic contour. Early experiments in digital ambience (such as Inoue's 2000 release *Fragment Dots*) tended toward the digitally pristine and informationally dense. By the mid-2000s, however, artists were beginning to grow fatigued with purely electronic signal manipulation and began seeking out ways to integrate the tonal richness of traditional acoustic instruments with the new textural possibilities of DSP.[44]

Hatakeyama Chihei (1978–) is one of the most active of this younger generation of ambient musicians in Japan, releasing over a dozen albums under his own name, recording and performing with Date Tomoyoshi as the ambient duo Opitope, and (like Hosono) sidelining as a soundtrack composer and record producer. His first solo album, *Minima Moralia,* appeared on the trendsetting Chicago independent music label Kranky in 2006. The album focuses on recordings of guitar and vibraphone reworked through digital processing, exploring the properties of both acoustic and software-affected sustained tones. On some tracks the sound of the original instrumentation comes through relatively unmanipulated; more often, though, it comes through mostly effaced, with the sounds containing only a vague memory of their original source.

Unlike ambient producers of the 1980s and 1990s, Hatakeyama and others of this younger generation often create music rooted in recordings of acoustic instruments and the gradual decay and transformation of these signals.[45] The music returns to the emotional directness of acoustic instrumental performance, but not without simultaneously hinting at a hollowing out of the affective promise it once held. It is as if the capacity for digital audio manipulation at the microsound level has undone the integrity of individual musical notes, and yet these fractured remains are the only emotional material left to work with. As with postapocalyptic isolationism more generally, this is a music stitching together a new type of absolute background from the fragments and residues of an earlier, less mediated age.

Minima Moralia's seven tracks each reference a particular space in their titles, from small cinematic scenes ("Swaying Curtain in a Window," "Beside a Well") to digital weather patterns ("Granular Haze") to intimate Bachelardian spaces ("Inside of the Pocket"). The intrigue in many of these tracks comes from listening for traces of the original guitar and vibraphone signals as they emerge distorted to various degrees through filters, time manipulations, and digital effects. Many tracks build to a counterpoint briefly established between a relatively recognizable guitar picking and a more abstract set of sounds obliquely referencing the original acoustic recordings. The melodic quality of the unmanipulated guitar, nodding toward the sentimental at times, is continually undermined by the destabilizing patterns of the squeezed and stretched textures surrounding it. In this way the music stays local and intimate, even as it hints at the anonymous and uncertain. As envisioned in their track titles, Hatakeyama's compositions appear to reference highly atmospheric locations but make it difficult to imagine these scenes against any stable horizon. Refusing to blot out the uncertainty engulfing these quiet moments, the compositions warmly lure the listener in while hinting at a larger threat.

"Beside a Well," the last and longest track on the album, begins with a set of fluttering drones: one sharp and mid- to high frequency, the other a low-end wobble. In between these two more constant textures, vibraphone chords echo and swell at regular intervals. The layering gradually intensifies over the first five minutes of the piece, with the bass drone growing stronger and the high end coalescing into a piercing static haze. The individual drones begin to bleed into one another, reflecting and refracting the other sounds as they rise and fall in amplitude.

Soon after the five-minute mark, these textures fall away, and a more recognizable guitar picking enters and loops, drenched in reverb and with upper harmonics amplified. This more gestural picking in the middle registers remains audible but is gradually submerged in a more active

set of glitchy textures and sine tones in the high end, just as the vibraphone begins responding indirectly to the pluck of the guitar strings.
Around eight minutes into the piece, these sustained loops begin to give
way to a more all-consuming flood of soft static, with glassy harmonics
emerging in the high frequencies. By the ten-minute mark, this wash of
noise and a rising electric guitar squall have completely taken over. The
low-end drone from the beginning of the piece again starts to lumber,
contorting slowly within the fuzz. This mix continues looping, eventually fading into silence at the eleven-and-a-half-minute mark.

"Beside a Well" is organized into a three-act structure common to
ambient drone works, with a loosely looping intro, a somewhat more
defined and melodic central section, and a final sequence where the
individual elements begin to dissolve into a wash of noise. Despite
all the wobbling and throbbing textures, "Beside a Well" carefully
avoids a regular pulse. The drones and the guitar picking lumber forward with an asymmetric gait, raising their heads above the fuzz only
to eventually be pushed back under amid the quietly swirling mass
of sounds. As with earlier ambient music, most changes are gradual,
allowing a listener's concentration to wander elsewhere. Compared
with Hosono and Inoue's work, however, Hatakeyama's textures are
far noisier, with digital static and wayward frequencies often making
for a relatively rougher mix.

The album is named after Theodore Adorno's classic book of short
essays and aphorisms *Minima Moralia: Reflections from Damaged Life*.
Written while Adorno was in exile in the United States in the late 1940s,
the book attempts to rethink morality in the face of both the stultifying
effects of popular culture and the horrors of the early twentieth century.
Hatakeyama, who regularly structures albums around ideas from philosophy as well as classical Japanese literature, denies any deeper meaning in his use of the title beyond a personal admiration for the book.[46]
In the context of ambient music history, however, the invocation of
Adorno's "damaged life" is an apt one. Ambience in the new century operates in a situation where sound has lost its structural and semantic integrity, where minute digital manipulations have ripped apart the once
reassuring confines of stable instrumentation and acoustic resonance.
The fractured materiality of sound, in turn, echoes the deepening social
instability of Japanese life in the new century.

Ambient fear—which Brian Massumi described in 1993 as a low-
level "background radiation saturating existence"—was a real presence
as Japan moved into the twenty-first century and worries over the nation's future continued to deepen.[47] The popular media had plenty to

fret over: global economic trends brought home the increasing vulnerability of the local economy even as the recession continued; the rise of China threatened to place Japan in the position of an also-ran Asian neighbor; North Korea continued to threaten missile strikes; a long string of ineffectual and short-lived political administrations did little to inspire confidence; and confusion reigned about Japan's global role in an age of oil wars, the post-9/11 "war on terror," the rise of Silicon Valley–style capitalism, and ever-looming ecological catastrophes. Meanwhile, more deeply rooted social problems were proving increasingly difficult to ignore: the low birthrate and rapidly growing ranks of elderly in need of care, relatively little progress in the push for gender equality and work–life balance, and an increasingly insular workforce relatively ill equipped to operate in the international arena. After the most recent natural disaster and nuclear meltdown in March 2011, national discussion again centered on whether Japan would find a way forward, even as much of the political maneuvering surrounding these events seemed only to evidence further stalling. While it is worth questioning who stands to gain from painting such a bleak picture, it is fair to say these various threats have often combined to generate an ambiguous if palpable mood of anxiety and uncertainty.[48]

The Japanese ambient music of the new century has often sought to provide atmospheres suitable for this more precarious time. Rather than blurring out the larger landscape to feel safe in a drifting cocoon, ambient music increasingly renders audible the fraught relation between its local affordances of mediated calm and the deeply troubling developments in the middle and far distance.

The abstract ikebana on the cover of *Minima Moralia* (Figure 7) portrays exactly this: the ambivalent rest of a beleaguered object in an uncertain setting. A single blackened flower with a bent stem sticks up out of a simple curved white vase, barely distinguishable against an empty white background. The flower appears dried out and fragile but is nonetheless rooted to this uncertain ground, holding on and trying to hold steady.

Taken together, Hosono, Inoue, and Hatakeyama model three ways ambient music has sought to foster feelings of embodied security through attunement to imaginary landscapes. Hosono's 1980s listeners were dissolved within a far-flung global exoticism, albeit not without a sense of ambivalence and irony. Inoue provided, as the liner notes to his *Slow and Low* album put it, "Muzak for random sculptures and Mixmedia mood swing." Ambience in the 1990s retreated to a more

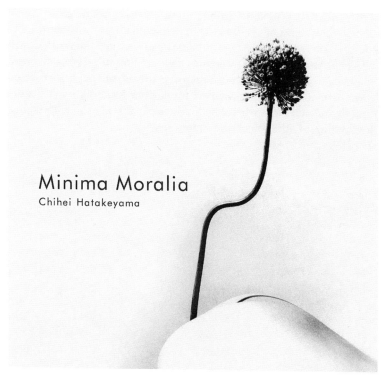

Minima Moralia
Chihei Hatakeyama

FIGURE 7. Overexposed to the atmosphere. Hatakeyama Chihei, *Minima Moralia* (cover).

imaginary and internalized setting, but in its own way reintroduced the possibility of more personalized and interactive landscapes. Hatakeyama's work in the new century has allowed for a more expressive acoustics to enter into the picture, but situated within a far more uncertain sonic territory. While ambience of all three types continues to be produced even now, an increasing number of ambient musicians has sought to organize their work around an absolute background resonating with, rather than resolving, the larger anxieties of twenty-first-century life. This incorporation of uncertainty might be understood as an even more effective way of affording calm: rather than providing alternative fantasy landscapes, the more porous and ambivalent backgrounds of recent ambient music mesh more easily with the uneven flows of everyday life, whether you are walking under the noisy highway or stuck in traffic yourself.

The next chapter shifts from a focus on the absolute background to look more closely at how ambient media help us move with these complex rhythms of the city. Whereas this chapter focused on how ambience works at the far horizon of perception to serve as an absolute background of ontological security, the next chapter focuses on how ambient media can provide a framework for mobility at a more directly somatic level, where the rhythms of the body come up against the rhythms of other objects in shared space.

MOVING WITH THE RHYTHMS OF THE CITY

Alongside establishing an absolute background, the attunement patterns of ambient media also serve as an interface between the rhythms of the body and the pulse of the surrounding city. This chapter moves into a closer analysis of the rhythmic aspects of ambient entrainment. Before examining how ambient media filter the rhythms of the everyday, I first consider how complex the patterning of urban life has become by tracking the rhythms accompanying a trip to Nakano, a neighborhood in western Tokyo a few stops outside Shinjuku. I then turn to the work of Henri Lefebvre for a model of different ways rhythms can align and what these ways imply for social relationships. The remainder of the chapter looks at how ambient video artists have negotiated the relationship between video and the existing rhythms of the city. Although the turn to personal mediation has long been read as a retreat from social engagement and the outside world, I suggest the ambient use of media can also be understood as an adaptive way to align the somatic self with the fluctuating rhythms of the city.

Nakano, like most urban Japanese neighborhoods, is arranged around a central train station. Nakano Station services around 125,000 passengers a day via the Chūō, Chūō-Sōbu, and Tōzai lines. Nakano's rhythms are oriented, first, around the Japan Railways and Tokyo Metro trains stopping briefly at the Nakano Station platforms on their journey between central Tokyo and the western suburbs. From the first train in the morning (around five a.m.) to the last train deep into the evening, regular and express trains arrive at frequent intervals to more than a half-dozen platforms. Prerecorded voices announce upcoming trains every minute or two.

After a train arrives with a blast of air and the doors automatically open, a spontaneous choreography emerges: those in line to board take their places perpendicular to the boarding zones, timing their entry to the moment the train car has finally disgorged all its disembarking passengers. A melody plays on the loudspeakers, warning the doors are about to close. This melody is enough to trigger an immediate bodily response—for example, an increased heart rate while watching someone rush to cross the train car's threshold before the doors slide shut.[1] By the time the latecomer catches his or her breath, the train is already moving out of the platform and picking up speed. The standing and sitting passengers onboard adjust their bodies to the rocking of the carriage as it speeds away along the tracks.

The same scene repeats every two to seven minutes. Above, overhead speakers play looped recordings of the soft sound of chirping birds. Set against the urgency of the other platform noise, the bird recordings introduce a slower, more relaxed temporality amid the trains' swift arrival and departure. Whatever daily and yearly rhythms these birds may have originally had—dawn choruses and rainy-day retreats—are eliminated in favor of ensuring the calming affordances of their perpetual chirping presence.

Paired with these auditory cues, visual and tactile rhythms help orchestrate the flow of people. Rapidly updated train arrival information appears on overhead displays in the station and over the doors inside the trains themselves, sharing space with the advertising and advisory posters placed at regular intervals inside the trains and around the station. Ubiquitous bumpy yellow lines mark the edge of each platform and form a walking path for the visually impaired, while color-coded horizontal bars on platform edges serve as guides on where to cue for each arriving train.

The trains are divided into numbered cars, each with a set of numbered doors. As the train slides into the platform, these doors lock into alignment with the horizontal bars marked on the platform and the parallel lines of waiting passengers assembled behind them. Posted on a nearby pillar is a vertical chart of stations the train will subsequently stop at and the exact number of minutes needed to reach each. This diagram maps out the choreography awaiting passengers as they line up in spaced intervals synchronized to their chosen length of train. Recently, graphic scores have appeared on JR train platforms marking the location of exits and elevators at each subsequent station, allowing passengers to choose which train car to board with a thought to their trajectory at the other end of the line.

Nakano station disgorges its users through two sets of gates, again setting up a transient rhythmic ritual as people cue, swipe, tap, or insert proof of payment and slide through the now opened gates (another set of doors about to close). Outside the exits a circle of taxis and several lines of busses edge forward length by length, their automatic doors opening and closing to allow passengers to board. To the north, past the daily lottery stand and the seasonal vendors, an island of smokers gathers around the designated area, their time there measured by the length of the burning sticks between their fingers. Off to the side, there is likely some busking—perhaps the tap dancer, the jazz band, or the teenage girl playing a Casio keyboard and serenading her older male audience with the theme song from *Neon Genesis Evangelion*.

Past this group near the entrance to the main covered shopping arcade, Nakano Sun Road, two or three people hand out advertisements and tissues and repeat their marketing entreaties to passersby, only to be mostly ignored. Once into Sun Road, the pedestrians usually maintain a brisk tempo while walking up through the rows of brightly lit shops. Pacing this procession is music played on overhead speakers throughout the shopping arcade, an unpredictable (though usually weather-appropriate) mix of dramatic motion picture soundtracks, Miles Davis's *Kind of Blue,* steel drums, and the occasional selection of easy-listening hits for sitar. On both left and right, the automated doors of each storefront slide open and closed at irregular intervals, triggered by the passing movement of bodies up and through the arcade and in and out of the stores.

The intensity, density, and tempo of this procession shifts across the course of the day, peaking during the morning and evening rush. It also shifts across the week, with the weekend leisure crowd bringing an entirely different energy than the weekday commuters. Holidays pull even more people to Nakano, while rainy weather diverts those who prefer the quieter side streets in toward the covered shopping arcade. Immediately to the east, narrow alleys crowded with bars and small restaurants follow a slower rhythm—more attuned to lingering over small plates and the evening ritual of alcohol consumption—while on the larger streets to the west and north traffic lights punctuate a much faster flow of automobile traffic.

These midlevel rhythms of transportation, work, consumption, and leisure have the most immediately visible impact on the space in and around the station, but they are in constant interaction with patterns of larger and smaller scale. On the scale of the person, individual rhythms abound, beginning from the diverse range of walking styles in evidence (more quick and determined among the suited businesspeople, more relaxed along the fringes where the children and the elderly trod along). Within the body even more localized biorhythms help shape the action: digestion, heartbeat, energy levels, speech, and the habits of thought.

At longer wavelengths are fluctuations of the weather, the seasons, and the local economy. Then there are the vicissitudes of local history: the consolidation of the area's twelve villages into two in the late nineteenth century, the transformation of the region from farmland to residential suburb in the wake of migrations following the 1923 Kanto earthquake, the destruction of nearly half the neighborhood after the American bombing raids of 1944, and the more recent influx of people from other parts of Asia—not to mention the disappearance of the forests that covered the area when humans first arrived around 23,000 years earlier.

This brief tour of Nakano's rhythms barely begins to describe the interwoven patterns of people and objects as they move through and around the station. But it gives a sense of how much movement through the city depends on navigating a multitude of temporal and spatial meters. Navigating these complex urban spaces demands continual negotiation with the rhythms traversing them.

The challenge here is to find a way to align all these rhythms and move between them in a way that allows them to work together rather than cancel each other out. Crucially, this does not demand a person's complete submission to the already established rhythms of the city. As a passenger the coming and going of trains may be largely out of my control, but inside and around them, I am constantly enacting my own small compositional choices with and through the rhythms I encounter. Do I swerve or stop, take the escalator or take the stairs, stand or sit, keep near the doors or move further into the train, look around or pretend to sleep? Once settled in my spot within the train car, do I watch the short, silent advertisements looping endlessly from the video screens above the train doors, or do I try to resist their call and gaze out the window at the swiftly passing scenery? There is something enjoyable in all of these choices, despite the monotony of the daily commute.

For Henri Lefebvre this complex set of interlocking patterns is what structures city life: the rhythms of the stars and the seasons, the rhythms of the workweek and broadcast media, the individual rhythms of daily life, and on down to the physiological rhythms of the body and its biological cycles. In *Rhythmanalysis* Lefebvre proposes four ways these overlaid rhythms can come together: (1) *polyrhythmia* refers to diverse rhythms occurring simultaneously without synthesis or interaction; (2) *eurhythmia,* in contrast, finds multiple rhythms sliding together in a kind of loosely syncopated assembly; (3) *isorhythmia* occurs when one single isolated rhythm imposes itself on all the others; and (4) *arrhythmia* refers to the opposite extreme, where individual cycles remain isolated and the larger environment dissolves into cacophony.[2]

These forms of rhythmic interaction each imply a particular form of social organization. Isorhythmia characterizes totalitarian attempts to bring diversity under the sway of a single authority, whereas a poly-rhythmic society separates people into discreet channels with little influence on one another. An arrhythmic society has fallen out of sync and dissolves into chaos. Eurhythmia, meanwhile, envisions a society where individuals and groups can come together in shared space without eliding the differences between them.

In addition to these four different rhythmic relations, Lefebvre identifies two overall modes of urban temporality: the cyclical and the linear. Linear time is characterized by uniform repetition, the ongoing and endless ticking of the clock. This is the classic temporality of modernity, always pitched forward from past into future. But Lefebvre notes how cyclical time persists in many places, doing a different kind of work. We can find it, for example, in the hands of the analog station clocks circling around and around, in the shops and gates and doors opening and closing, and in the leisurely looping of the Nakano Station's recorded birdsong.

Lefebvre notes how linear time can be transformed into cyclical time by giving it a meter and thus making it rhythmic: "Cycles invigorate repetition by cutting through it."[3] Rhythm makes repetition meaningful by introducing the capacity to move through it in various ways—literally opening up the aesthetic potential to dance alongside and within it. Cyclicality connects rationalized urban time with the rhythms of the body, the weather, and the patterns of a drifting consciousness. This introduction of rhythm results in the release of pleasurable energy in excess of the directed movement needed to get from point A to point B.[4] In this way, Lefebvre writes, rhythms help compensate for the linearity of everyday modern life. Instead of everyone falling mechanically into isorhythmic lockstep or falling out of line into isolated polyrhythms or the chaos of arrhythmia, a spontaneous choreography emerges at the interstices of the city's layered patterns, raising the possibility for individuated rhythms to prosper within a flexible overall orchestration. A eurhythmia of difference.

STAYING OPEN TO OTHER RHYTHMS

As they negotiate Nakano's meters, no two persons move in the same way. Moving fluidly through the city demands an improvisational ability to open oneself to the diverse rhythms traversing the self. The navigation of interlocking rhythms provides a framework for coexistence among the millions of people, other creatures (crows, cockroaches, jellyfish), and other objects (trains, phones, sliding doors) sharing the tight spaces of urban Japan. This rhythmic conception of sociality makes little distinction between humans and other "more or less animate" bodies (including media objects). Everything engaging with rhythm participates in this shared environmental orchestration.[5]

Ambient subjectivation in this urban context consists of attunement to both the larger flows of the metropolis and the smaller flows moving within, without, above, and below the body. This is where ambient media comes in. By recasting urban rhythms in ambient forms more focused on biorhythmic attunement, ambient media serve as a training in how to sense and sway to the syncopated cycles emerging with every new mixture of people and place. Ambient media bring urban rhythms into circulation with aesthetic materials and through this blending locate points of attunement between them. To find a way to dance here amid the crowds is to resist falling back into the isorhythm of a sedimented social identity (of the state, of the company, of the family) and to resist tripping forward into the isorhythm of the isolated body, a form of social withdrawal radically severed from other cycles of life.

The arrival of more atomized, autonomous lifestyles was accompanied by a set of new media technologies both responding to and furthering these concerns. We have already considered the arrival of the Sony Walkman and the age of autonomous listening. Alongside the privatization of audio, however, came a concurrent privatization of the moving image with the rise of video. Portable video technology (beginning with the first Sony Portapak in 1967) allowed for a newly intimate relationship between body, camera, and screen.[6] As the size of cameras and screens continued to shrink in subsequent decades, video came to slip ever more seamlessly into the routines of everyday life.

For some theorists this in itself symbolized a retreat from more pressing social issues. Video art was quickly identified as a practice tending toward "the aesthetics of narcissism," as Rosalind Krauss described it in her influential early essay. Krauss describes video as providing a real-time, closed-circuit loop between the body of the artist and/or audience and the image of their self-regard.[7] In this reading, video provides a way to turn the moving image away from the social and toward the self, recording the personal concerns of everyday life in isolation from any immediate impulse to communicate with others. In Japan, similarly, the rise of video has often been associated with a turn away from the social politics of the 1960s and toward an over-riding concern with the self, particularly the everyday life and private struggles of the person behind the camera. Abé Mark Nornes notes a "retreat from the world" and a "turn to the self" in Japanese documentary beginning in the mid-1970s, in tandem with but generally even more apolitical than similar developments in Europe and America. For him and other critics, this marked the start of a "steady decline" in the state of Japanese cinema.[8]

We could point here to the counterexample of the early video collectives of the 1970s, which pushed for using video as a tool of collective social intervention in the model set out in Michael Shamberg's *Guerilla Television* (1971). This call was taken up in Japan in Nakaya Fujiko's *Friends of Minamata Victims: A Video Diary* (1972) and other works from the Video Hiroba (Video Commons) group. I want to suggest, however, there might also be a socially adaptive side to the use of video as a technology of the self. In this chapter I focus on the ambient use of video as a way of interfacing with the larger urban environment through personal, embodied rhythms. I suggest the rhythmic video interface serves as a different form of sociality, less discursive perhaps but no less important or necessary. Rather than a retreat from the world, my rhythmic approach understands the turn to ambient video as a practical way to tune the self within an urban sea of intersecting rhythms.

There is a socially adaptive side to ambient subjectivation: it atmospherically affords engagement with a wider range of environments and people, enabling movement through a diverse and complex world. Anxious commentary on social withdrawal in Japan often skips over this practical side of self-care, as if people were faced with a stark choice between identifying with the local community and culture or rejecting society and turning inward. But the guiding desire of ambient self-care is not to reject more traditional forms of belonging but to find other, more flexible modes of engaging the everyday, moving past the pressures and confines of a discreet identity and attuning to more impersonal flows. This freedom, for many part of the appeal of an impersonal metropolis like Tokyo, is not simply an illusion.

Commentary tends to focus, perhaps understandably, on cases where this desire for personal autonomy has gone to the extreme, past the loosening of social bonds and toward their complete dissolution. In response, prominent voices in Japan proclaim the need to unite around political and historical issues, whereas others call for the strengthening of local and national identities—both of which risk merely substituting one form of isorhythm for another. Reading a focus on the somatic as merely a slide into social withdrawal misunderstands the desire held by many to move beyond what might be oppressively narrow cultural norms and expectations, to find a way to move differently while still moving together.

This desire deserves to be taken seriously, for alongside its considerable risks, it simultaneously reaches toward an expanded circle of engagement, beyond the boundaries of family, nation, and species toward a more inclusive model of coexistence. I do not mean to suggest the serious issue of social withdrawal in Japan can be solved through somatic attunements alone—only that the ambient dimensions of subjectivity need to be taken into account when seeking to understand contemporary forms of urban sociality (or a lack thereof). Attending to rhythmic alignment is essential to any project hoping to enable communication and cooperation between disparate and diverse populations without collapsing their differences into a form of greater or lesser adherence to the local standard. Understanding ambient subjectivation demands attending to the complex dynamics of movement, rhythm, sensation, proprioception—the many ways material bodies encounter one another through space and time in ways irreducible to reflective forms of human identity and sociality.

Certainly, this dance is full of dangers, not only of inhibiting more direct forms of dialogue but also, as a number of critiques of multiculturalism have established, of overlooking how the capacity for physical belonging is itself dispersed across populations in highly uneven ways. As queer and disability theorists have described, social environments come already shaped by social norms, and those for whom an environment has been designed are going to have a much easier time moving through it. It is important not to idealize drift and movement in itself, as early ambient styles were wont to do. As Ahmed asks, "Is the subject who chooses homelessness and a nomadic lifestyle, or a nomadic way of thinking, one that can do so, because the world is already constituted as its home?"[9] To put this a different way, does a *Music for Airports* belong only to the jet-set crowd? Further, as critics of neoliberalism often point out, the type of loose rhythmic alignment characteristic of the contemporary city is central to the just-in-time delivery structures of global capitalism.[10] Sometimes, the hardest thing, as it often is in public space in Tokyo, is to just stay put.

The impersonality involved in ambient subjectivation also courts the danger of complete depersonalization: giving oneself over to larger social flows always at the same time raises the risk of losing the self in the process. The aspiration for impersonal mobility, over greater and greater areas, brings with it the risk of spreading oneself too thin, courting subjective collapse.[11] The more complex and stratified a society becomes, the more difficult it is to reconcile personal rhythms with wider social flows.

As noted, the risk of falling outside society entirely has become a major concern in contemporary Japan, a reminder of just how difficult and emotionally taxing the constant navigation of these complex environments can become. Increasing numbers of people in Japan are unable to manage, falling into various degrees of social withdrawal. In the now widely publicized scenario of someone living isolated in their room, only the barest of external temporalities enters in—the abstracted time of the Internet and, if they are lucky, the rhythm of food being regularly deposited at their door by a relative or a delivery service. Even these cycles may break down, leading to the near absolute isorhythmia of those who die alone in their homes and are not found for weeks or even months—their participation in social rhythms already so curtailed their silence barely registers.[12] The rising number of such cases in Japan reminds us of the cruel fate awaiting those who will not or cannot follow the demand to keep moving along.

This struggle for rhythmic alignment is precisely where ambient media seek to intervene. As Anna McCarthy notes in her work on the placement of television screens in urban space, a screen always encounters preexisting "webs of signification and material practice" at the same time as it "activates and embodies" heterogeneous forces of its own. The rhythmic approach I pursue here echoes McCarthy's observations on how the placement of urban screens is always deeply political but also supports a great deal of "ideological flexibility." Urban screens are "an apparatus capable of linking everyday locations and their subjects to wider, abstracted realms of commerce, culture, and control in any number of ways."[13]

Without forgetting how ambience, itself, is subject to these heterogeneous forces, I want to draw attention to the adaptive side of rhythmic attunement in urban space, how mediated entrainment can help people navigate the speeds and slownesses of life in the city. Instead of denouncing the turn to the self and looking back wistfully to an earlier cultural moment (a common tendency in recent studies of postwar Japan), I propose a more pragmatic understanding of the mediated atmospheres of recent decades. The techniques of self-tuning described here remain an important part of the struggle to not fall back into more stratified rhythms, where the only choices are to fall in step with dominant social beats or not to join the dance at all.

ATTUNING TO AMBIENT VIDEO

The embodied social landscape of rhythmic sociality is precisely where ambient video intervenes. The rest of this chapter looks more closely at how ambient video mediates between the rhythms of the city and the rhythms of the body, opening up an aesthetic space for a flexible eurythmic interplay between them. If in the introduction I focused on the "air" as a social force, here I focus on the (audiovisual) waveforms moving through it and setting it in motion.

Experimental filmmakers have grappled with how to integrate urban rhythms into visual form as far back as the "city symphony" films of the 1920s.[14] In Japan the immediate postwar decades saw filmmakers going out into the streets in greater numbers, as in documentaries produced by Iwanami Productions in the 1950s and independent features produced by the Art Theatre Guild in the 1960s. These efforts were aided by the arrival of lighter and more portable cameras and audio equipment. Meanwhile, the long history of "visual music" in experimental animation established many precedents for the use of visual materials to achieve rhythmic musical effects. Ambient video artists in Japan could also look to the strategies of seminal experimental landscape films like Andy Warhol's *Empire* (1964) and, more locally, Hagiwara Sakumi's *Kiri* (Mist, 1972).[15]

Opportunities to present audiovisual materials also continued to diversify, from the public television viewing stations (*gaitō terebi*) of early postwar Japan to the expanded cinema movements of the 1960s and 1970s (themselves closely tied to the environmental art and intermedia movements described in chapter 1).[16] By the late 1970s, major railroad conglomerates like Tōkyū, Tōbu, and Seibu began installing the first jumbo outdoor video screens outside their flagship department stores in high-traffic Tokyo hubs like Shibuya, Ikebukuro, and Roppongi. As screens continued to shrink in weight and cost while diversifying in size, video gradually became a familiar presence on public transportation and in restaurants, nightclubs, live houses, and other public spaces.[17]

Following the Japanese turn to ambience in the wake of the Eric Satie boom, new video genres emerged seeking to work directly on the atmospheres of everyday life. Commercial video producers quickly embraced the new genre of background video, or BGV, as a new tool of environmental mood regulation. A steady stream of BGV releases began appearing on VHS and laserdisc in the early 1980s and the flow has yet to cease. BGV producers continue to be early adopters of new video formats like DVD and Blu-Ray, in an eagerness to promise ever higher-resolution audiovisual moods. Common subjects include tropical islands, the Tokyo skyline at night, cherry blossoms, waterfalls, the moon and the stars, and creature-specific titles like Synforest's *Hitsuji ga suki* (I like sheep, 2009) and the "healing jellyfish" described earlier.[18] Taking their cues from commercial BGM, these works often present themselves as utilitarian tools of mood regulation, focused largely on relaxation and stress relief but also on providing atmospheres appropriate to show on screens in venues like upscale restaurants, hotels, and shopping malls.

Just as ambient music responded to more traditional forms of BGM by incorporating more ambiguity and ambivalence, video artists produced an ambient response to BGV. Drawing on the lineage of visual music and environmental cinema, the new ambient video sought out more flexible ways of tuning physical rhythms through the mediation of existing environments. As with ambient music, this allowed ambient video to synchronize more closely with the autonomous ideals of contemporary urban audiences.

The first proponents of ambient video in Japan were often visiting artists from abroad. Bill Viola lived in Japan for a year and half from 1980 to 1981 on a cultural exchange fellowship, spending time as the first artist in residence at Sony's laboratory in Atsugi, Japan, and producing his landmark environmental video *Hatsu-yume/First Dream* (1981). Brian Eno came to Japan in the summer of 1983 to present *Brian Eno: A World of Video Art and Environmental Music,* a much discussed installation of ambient video and music at the newly built Laforet Museum, in the Laforet department store in Akasaka, Tokyo. This was followed by the release of Eno's Sony-commissioned ambient video on VHS, the eighty-two-minute *Thursday Afternoon* (1984).[19]

Japanese video artist, painter and sculptor Yamaguchi Katsuhiro (1928–) began producing large-scale ambient video installations in Tokyo around the same time. Like Akiyama Kuniharu (discussed in chapter 1), Yamaguchi was a former member of the Experimental Workshop and the Environment Society. He was also a key member of Video Hiroba in the early 1970s. Following on the heels of Eno's ambient video exhibition at Laforet, Yamaguchi began a series of what he called "artificial gardens" including *Future Garden* (1983) and *Galaxy Garden* (1986), each subtitled *A Yamaguchi Katsuhiro Video Spectacle.* The gardens were composed of numerous video monitors, later adding holography and lasers as well.[20]

Thanks to video, audiovisuals could increasingly be installed in an

environment at low cost and, with the more recent advent of smartphones and tablet screens, carried directly on the body as well. As a result, audiovisual media is now woven through Japanese cities as never
before, setting the stage for an increasingly ambient relationship with
the moving image. Rather than assuming a viewer would sit down to
face a screen for a fixed length of time, the ever-expanding range of
video genres in the 1990s and 2000s began to favor more dispersed and
flexible forms of attention: videos for urban screens and public transportation networks; short-form videos designed to stream over smartphones; and video art for hanging in galleries, filling store windows,
and projecting outdoors onto the sides of buildings.[21] Moving images
could now mesh more finely with other rhythms of everyday life, opening up new possibilities for urban attunement. These new contexts
often lent themselves to ambient forms of engagement, shifting fluidly
between foreground and background forms of attention.

I now turn to examine a set of Japanese videos focusing on this interface between the rhythms of the body and the rhythms of contemporary urban life. Rather than consider the position of screens in urban
space (a question well mapped in McCarthy's *Ambient Television*), my
focus here is on the rhythmic attunements produced *within* specific
works of ambient video and how these patterns situate themselves in
relation to the type of urban syncopations I have described.

Kick the World

A key example of early video art addressing Japan's shifting rhythms is
Kick the World, a 1974 video by Kawanaka Nobuhiro (1941–). Kawanaka
was a member of Video Hiroba and an active proponent of experimental
film and video in the 1970s. He went on to found what would become the
main resource center for experimental film and video in Japan, Image
Forum. *Kick the World* is his best-known work and has recently been
featured in several retrospectives of early Japanese video art.[22] The video
consists of the artist holding a video camera with his hands and shooting
his feet as he kicks an empty Coca-Cola can around a park full of scale
replicas of famous international monuments. Kawanaka claims to have
made the video in order to explore the newfound ability to record syn-
chronous sound and video with a single machine—a technical capacity
he exploits by recording the crunch of the tin can as his sandaled feet
send it hurtling around the puddle-strewn park (Figure 8).

Over the course of the video's twenty minutes, the sound of Kawanaka's kicking frequently competes with the sound of a woman's voice

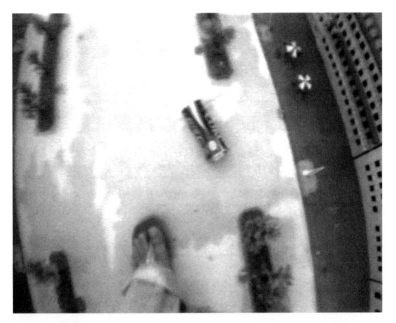

FIGURE 8. Kicking back against the acoustic horizon. Still from Kawanaka Nobuhiro, *Kick the World.*

making announcements about the monuments on view, broadcast loudly across the park through a closed-circuit public address system. The video structurally documents the relationship between this solitary man with a camera, grunting as he aggressively if ineffectually kicks an empty aluminum corporate logo around a bunch of concrete monuments to power, and this faceless but composed female speaker, blanketing the space with official instructions for how this global simulacra should be approached. *Kick the World* stages this unequal dialogue between the female announcer, positioned as an invisible but aggressive reminder of who owns the space, and the man with the video camera, flailing in his attempt to register the sound of his own bodily attack upon the acoustic horizon of this corporatized world.

Electroacoustic composer Barry Truax, one of the original researchers behind the World Soundscape Project in the 1970s, defines the acoustic horizon as "the most distant sounds that may be heard in a soundscape."[23] He draws particular attention to whether an environment is quiet enough for sounds made by the listener's own body to be audible. If it is not, the acoustic horizon can be said to have shrunk below the size of the listener's body, resulting in a sensory estrangement from the physical self. In this regard, we can understand Kawanaka's repeated kicking as a way to try and reestablish the acoustic horizon of his own physical agency against the blanketing isorhythm of the public address system.

Visually, the work also sets up conditions for Kawanaka to register his physical impact upon the surrounding "world": the camera in his hands follows the impact of his body as it comes into contact with the can, launching it into the wider world and the image's depth of field. In this way, Kawanaka's performance seeks out a place for his own physical rhythms within the louder sonic disciplining of this heavily regulated space. But his efforts result only in a failure of syncopation. The stumbling rhythm of Kawanaka's kicks cannot connect with the impartial announcements emerging from the loudspeakers, and his roving camera cannot soften the cold concrete of the miniature monuments on view.

The Age of Ambient Video

A less oppositional approach to environmental attunement is taken by Arai Man (1946–), a prize-winning novelist; a producer for the leading Japanese advertising company, Dentsū; a singer-songwriter of nostalgic easy-listening pop songs; and one of the most active early proponents of ambient video in the 1980s. Arai began producing ambient video after ten years as a producer of television commercials in a message-dense visual style he describes as "the informational equivalent of condensed milk." He convinced Dentsū to let him produce a series of what he called *kankyō bideo* (literally "environmental video") works, which the company released on VHS, videodisc, and laserdisc.[24] *Kankyō bideo* might also justifiably be translated as "ambient video," given *kankyō ongaku* (environmental music) was the then-current translation of Eno's "ambient music" and Arai directly acknowledges Eno's influence. Arai's dozen or so ambient video releases focus on Japanese nature scenes, including Mt. Fuji, cherry blossoms at Lake Biwa, waterfalls in Minowa, and cedars in Wakayama, as well as settings outside Japan like an early morning on Tiananmen Square, the Grand Canyon, the shores of the Ganges in Benares, and a coral reef in Micronesia. In his 1990 book promoting the style, *Kankyō bideo no jidai* (The age of ambient video), he describes it as "a friend always by your side and easy to get along with; a new media for people living in the city" (29).

Arai recalls background video puzzling Japanese viewers at first but notes how before long BGV could be found in many locations, including department stores, airports, museums, hospital waiting rooms, bank lobbies, cafés, and bars. What unites all these places, Arai argues, is that the people visiting them do not have time for storytelling. The nonnarrative, unstructured time of environmental video functions regardless of length of stay. It works well in retail settings, he notes, allowing shopkeepers to casually establish an atmosphere while folding newcomers easily into the already established mood (28–29).

Arai's ambient videos from the 1980s are unique in their structuralist austerity, bringing what could have been rather straightforward BGV into the more affectively ambiguous realm of the ambient. Arai's ambient works are governed by a strict set of rules he set for himself. Each landscape must be captured in real time. No camera movement is allowed, and the final product must consist of one extended take. If possible, the soundtrack should contain only synch environmental sound. There should be no humans in the shot and no major changes in the image from beginning to end. Anything overtly dramatic should be avoided (13–14). This elimination of dramatic interest is strategically oriented toward a particular type of viewing experience. Arai writes:

> BGV doesn't demand to be seen or heard. In most cases, it has no beginning or end, and only rarely does a figure appear. If we were to compare it to something, it is close to furniture that sits quietly in a room. We could say it resembles curtains, flooring, or wallpaper. Ultimately it erases your own appearance, dissolving you into the atmosphere— this is what BGV does. (8)

Here, Arai echoes Erik Satie's notion of furniture music, envisioning video "furnishings" effortlessly blending with the visual landscapes of everyday life, easing viewers' self-consciousness and masking lulls in the dinner conversation. While he references BGV in general here, it is clear by Arai's references to Satie and Eno and his austere working methods he wishes to push background video in a more ambient direction.

Arai refers to his works as "video hanging scrolls," or "twenty-first-century landscape paintings" (*21-seiki no sansuiga*), associating ambient video with the nature paintings traditionally hung in the alcove (*toko no ma*) of Japanese homes. He describes living with a video and gradually attuning to its rhythms:

> Sometimes I let one of my BGV of Japanese landscapes play
> all day. Once in a while I look over at it. Sometimes I do
> something else. When I get tired of that I start watching it
> again. . . . There is no need to stare at it for an hour or two
> at a stretch. Just like there is no one who would sit and stare
> at a hanging scroll, there is no need to watch BGV continu-
> ously. If you did, it might actually be a little dangerous. . . .
> Just try letting some BGV run. Live with it like a Japanese
> landscape painting hanging somewhere in your room. Once
> in awhile you look at it, at other times you don't. But as you
> live your life, you feel it somewhere there in the back of your
> mind. If you do this, I think you will achieve a balanced
> mind and body. You might call it one way to provide a sense
> of equilibrium. (18)

Arai writes of the ability of his largely unaltered long takes to reunite
time and space, even when not consciously attended to. The various
rhythms of everyday life are collected and organized through the continuous time of the video as its audiovisual rhythms spread through and
tune the surrounding atmosphere (a variation on the "absolute background" described in chapter 2). By affording an open rhythmic interplay between the discontinuous attention of the viewer and the slowly
changing video environment, Arai's ambient videos work toward eurythmic attunement between audiences' psychosomatic rhythms and
the mediated atmospheres within which they dwell.

+*Intersection*

In the new century an increasing number of Japanese video artists are
producing ambient works for gallery and museum display as well as for
use in advertising, in-store displays, music videos, and concert background visuals. Ise Shōko (1969–), for example, began her solo art practice in 1998, producing album designs and photography for Speedometer,
Takayama Jun's solo ambient electronic music project.[25] She went on in
the early 2000s to branch out into music videos and motion graphics
backgrounds, first for the clothing brand Carhartt and later for a wide
range of bands, including Yellow Magic Orchestra and associated projects like HASYMO and Pupa. She continues to produce both photography and design work alongside her video productions, and these still
formats often become source material for the video works.

Ise can be understood as part of the most recent generation of *eizō sakka* (moving image creators), whose software-based video work increasingly overlaps with the fields of motion graphics, video art, animation, and computer-aided design.[26] Whereas Arai's ambient videos took a hands-off approach to the slowly changing landscapes in front of the camera, ambient video in recent decades works more toward the gradual transformation of the digitally composited image. This younger generation of ambient video artists uses software effects to build new rhythms into the existing environments captured by the camera, reinterpreting found rhythms and introducing new movement possibilities. Through these software interventions, the works open up a creative space in between the rapidly fluctuating patterns of urban life and the parallel rhythms of human physiology and mood.

Negotiating these flows is the central focus of Ise's +*Intersection,* an installation curated by Hatanaka Minoru for Pepper's Loft Gallery in Ginza, Tokyo (December 2002).[27] The multichannel work features a series of urban landscapes in motion, including railroad tracks viewed from a moving train, overhead highways and streetlights viewed looking up from an (unseen) moving vehicle, flamingos mingling at the local zoo, views of windblown pine tree branches and cloudy skies, and the occasional bridge and building seen from a boat passing below them. Five English-language phrases repeat as superimposed titles throughout the series, outlining the relation of the videos to the everyday rhythms they engage:

> world in the other side of daily life
> relationship between the unrelated thing
> energy in the tedious repetition
> crossing point of air and mind
> memory, oblivion, and imagination

Taken together, these five statements outline the ways Ise's work mediates between the audiovisual rhythms of the city and the routine flows of everyday existence. The urban landscapes visible in the series document the banal repetition of contemporary urban life while working to transform this same tedium into a source of energy (Figure 9). Paired with Speedometer's downtempo beats, the videos generate a looser ambient relation to these familiar urban rhythms, allowing a more eurythmic "world" to come into view.

Much of Ise's work begins with her videotaping movement and visual patterns discovered in environments near her home city of Takarazuka (near Osaka): urban infrastructure, animals at the zoo, forests full

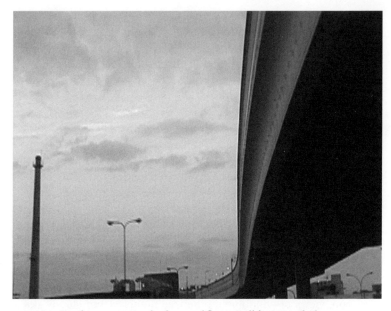

FIGURE 9. Looking up at city rhythms and flows. Still from Ise Shōko, +*Intersection*.

of fog. As with many in her generation of ambient video artists, Ise's process begins on location with a kind of videographic rhythmanalysis: she seeks out spontaneous patterns created by automobiles, animals, machines, and pedestrians while moving in and around her immediate environment. This use of the video camera has close parallels not only to on-location filmmaking but also to street photography and "found sound" musical composition.[28] As noted earlier, this type of on-location engagement soon became possible for video artists as well, with the development of smaller, lighter, and more discreet video cameras.

Ambient video like Ise's bring to this tradition an increased focus on mood and an emphasis on the affective potentials of attunement with found rhythms. Both the music and the editing of +*Intersection* are structured around the loop and the repeated gesture. Most segments are built around a pulsing rhythm and a gradual ebb and flow. Sonically, the beats tend toward a slow tempo, often 70 bpm or lower. These rhythms organize a looser flow of vocal samples and synthesizer textures. Visually, the pacing is calm without losing forward momentum.

Speedometer's beats often fall away just as the images shift toward the ethereal, as concrete roads give way to an expansive view of the sky.

The relation of these edited rhythms to the existing rhythms of the city is more subtle than simply opposing "slowness" to "speed," however. As Lefebvre emphasizes, humans always register rhythms in relation to other rhythms, particularly the rhythms of the human body:

> A rhythm is only slow or fast in relation to other rhythms with which it finds itself associated in a more or less vast unity. . . . Every more or less animate body and *a fortiori* every gathering of bodies is consequently polyrhythmic, which is to say composed of diverse rhythms, with each part, each organ or function having its own in a perpetual interaction which constitutes a set (*ensemble*) or a whole (*un tout*).[29]

Ise organizes the edited rhythms of the videos around the rhythms visible in her footage of found movement: water rippling, windmills rotating, elevators rising and falling, automobiles rolling smoothly along raised highways. This ensemble of rhythms, both found and fabricated, serves to syncopate the landscapes of everyday life with the rhythms of the viewing body, adding energy to the "tedious repetition."

Summer Afternoon

Ise's *Summer Afternoon* (2001) demonstrates this process of ambient rejuvenation with great clarity. The visuals consist of a series of partial views of a large, green urban park, with clues here and there in the sky and foliage that a summer storm is approaching. The text (presented in English, subtitled in Japanese) describes a leisurely summer day in the life of someone living with a cat in an apartment near the park. The narrator—never on-screen and present only through the superimposed titles—ponders various topics, walks to the store to buy a few things, encounters random passersby, and considers the day's news. The titles also provide a series of lists, including what the narrator purchased and how much it cost:

> Razor ¥560, shaving cream ¥700,
> two packets of cigarettes ¥500,
> five cans of cat food ¥900.

Later, there is a similar list of the narrator's wandering thoughts and the time spent on each:

- Convenience store robber shouldn't pay compare to its risk. (5 min.)
- That record shop is too noisy with loud music to chose records taking time. (30 sec.)
- About the internal organ transplantation. (2 min.)
- About equality of men and women. (4 sec.)

This is followed by some thoughts on how "this country is deeply in debt" and yet "people go to the rock music festival paying ¥80,000 for the ticket in this country."[30] Passing thoughts float by—a world made up equally of slow elevators, cat food, weather patterns, and social trends (Figure 10). This is not a dramatic world, but neither is it an unpleasant one. The series of images of the park (uninhabited except for a few out-of-focus humans seen at a distance) provides a relaxed, lush setting for these wandering thoughts. The narrator's mention of various smells and sensations (water, the potential for rain, the heat) infuses the ordered yet abundant greenery of the images.

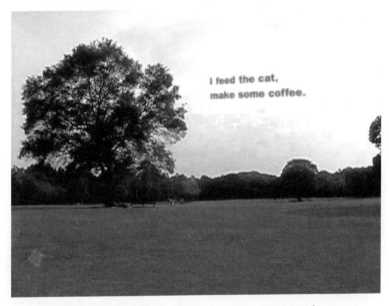

I feed the cat, make some coffee.

FIGURE 10. Ordinary landscapes. Still from Ise Shōko, *Summer Afternoon*.

Paired with these visuals is Speedometer's easygoing downtempo instrumental hip-hop, matching these drifting thoughts with a relaxed, head-nodding beat. The rhythm gives this summer afternoon its bounce. Late in the piece, a sample of a local southern Japanese weather report surfaces, tying the soundtrack to the rainy-season storm gathering on-screen.

As with most ambient video, the world presented in *Summer Afternoon* is largely a solitary one, to the extent it is inhabited at all. The narrator remains unseen, and the only social exchange (indirectly recalled) is a brief encounter with a tattooed man in the elevator of the narrator's apartment building. The rest of the world is mediated through the radio and newspaper headlines. The world of the video consists of a cat, a park, a bridge or two—a world along the lines of Wallace Stevens's "two or three hills and a cloud." The only tension here is the lingering tension before a summer rainstorm, made pleasurable through the breezy downtempo mood of the music. The world of the video seems circumscribed, and yet, by interweaving these different encounters, the work opens onto a wider landscape registering the interplay between distant news, weather patterns, organ transplants, gender equality, and the physiological rhythms of humans and cats. Everything is woven together in a summertime ambience, and this atmosphere moves through the gallery to shape viewers' bodies in turn.

Apoptosis

Ambient video continued to develop new ways of mediating the city in tandem with the transition toward software-based media production. As the power and accessibility of motion graphics software like Adobe's After Effects continued to increase, both the visual and auditory rhythms of urban space were further opened to digital reconstruction, resulting in both new forms of ambient mediation and expanded phenomenological horizons.

Like Ise, Tsuchiya Takafumi (1979–) is a contemporary *eizō sakka* working in a wide range of contexts simultaneously. Tsuchiya's *Apoptosis* (2008) is an ambient music video produced for Japanese electronic music producer Caelum (Tsukahara Kōtaro). The visuals are based on a simple but ingenious effect of wrapping the horizontal axis of a set of found landscapes around itself, collapsing the horizon into a point in the center of the screen. When the footage is set in motion, the now circular image creates a kaleidoscopic effect. These rotating landscapes are accelerated and decelerated, slipping and transforming as they spin, generating the impression of different horizons alternately being sucked into and pushed out from the center of the frame (Figure 11).

At times, these landscapes appear to be pouring forth from the screen itself and, at other times, to be literally going down the drain. This allows audiences only an ambivalent connection to each fleeting environment. The pace shifts over the course of the piece, allowing glimpses of a more subdued natural environment slipping away while letting loose a more accelerated whirlpool of electrified cityscapes. As with the phenomenon of apoptosis in biology, the process of cell death occurring as part of an organism's growth and development, the landscapes here slip away only to give rise to new horizons in turn. The movement within each environment matches up with the rhythms of the software-controlled spinning and compositing, filtering the different visual patterns together into an open and affectively ambiguous mix.

Caelum's music matches the ambivalent mood of this environmental death and rebirth. Appearing on his 2008 album *Weather Report,* the track is characteristic of Japanese electronica from the mid-2000s: somber piano chords pedaling slowly under an effervescent flurry of glitchy percussion in the higher registers. While the restless arpeggios, skidding loops, and frothy feedback layers provide a brightly enthralling foreground, tickling the ears with lots of microsonic detail, the much slower cycling of the low end underpins this activity with a far more subdued foundation. As with Tsuchiya's visuals, the frenetic foreground motion is set against a somber atmospheric background—an unresolved tension characteristic of recent ambient media's ambivalent feelings toward the ongoing transformation of the urban landscape. *Apoptosis* hints at nostalgia for a slower-paced environment at the same time as it indulges in a headlong rush toward new sensations. The video attempts to integrate these contrary desires by allowing the shape of the video itself to be the ambiguous point around which everything revolves. The encompassing horizon has become the vanishing point.

rheo: 5 horizons

The digital remediation of urban rhythms is taken even further by Kurokawa Ryōichi's *rheo: 5 horizons* (2010), this chapter's final example of ways ambient video rethinks the physical encounter between self and environment. Kurokawa is known for his installations and concert performances in which abstract audiovisual materials are subject to digital transformation. He often crosses sound and video signals so

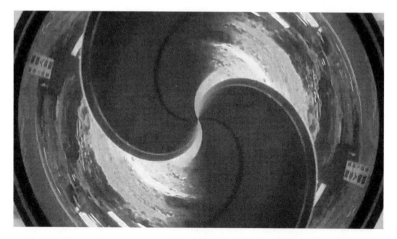

FIGURE 11. Wrapping the horizon. Still from Takafumi Tsuchiya, *Apoptosis*.

visual image data help sculpt the soundtrack and sound waves guide what transpires on-screen. The *rheo* "time sculpture" was shown in a dark room with five large-screen plasma displays at the Japan Media Arts Festival at the National Art Center in Tokyo in 2011, and there is also a three-channel concert version. The title, *rheo,* means "to flow" or "to stream" in Greek.

Rheo won the Golden Nica prize for Digital Music and Sound Art at the 2010 ARS Electronic Festival in Austria, the most important international competition for media art. In his acceptance speech for the prize, Kurokawa describes attempting with this work to enhance his audience's ability to spatially locate objects through sound by synchronizing audio input with moving visual cues.[31] The bending of the horizons on-screen directly echoes the contours of the soundtrack, creating a powerful synesthetic effect (Figure 12). This complexity is underpinned by the droning sound of the *shō*, the Japanese mouth organ used in *gagaku* and a range of contemporary music. Here, the shō provides a droning foundation for fluctuating layers of digital noise. Both the shō and the noise move in synesthetic unison with the shifting visual horizons.

Mapping the visual landscape onto the "flowing" properties of digital sound produces new sensory possibilities for rhythmic orientation. While the sonic mapping of cities has been an object of research ever since the World Soundscape Project began mapping Vancouver

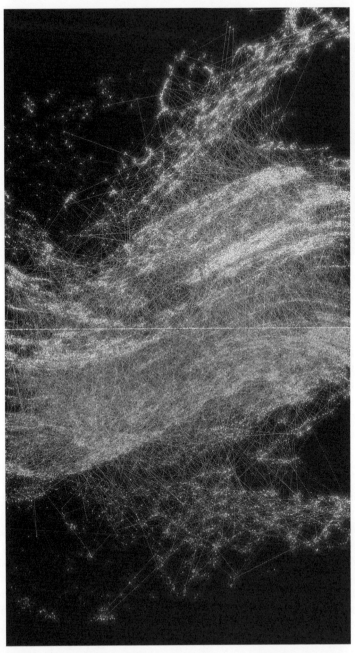

FIGURE 12. Synesthetic horizons. Still from one channel of Kurokawa Ryōichi, *rheo: 5 horizons* (five-channel digital video installation). Courtesy of the artist.

"soundmarks" in the 1970s, little attention has been paid to sound as an alternate means of spatial navigation, a different perceptual horizon for movement through a landscape. Hosono Haruomi once noted one of the unique things about the contemporary Tokyo landscape is that due to the absence of a grid system and the way the preponderance of tall buildings tends to block out what might otherwise have served as orientating landmarks (such as Mt. Fuji, Tokyo Tower, or Sky Tree), there is little sense of a stable background against which urban life transpires. Instead, people have the sense of being immersed in a fluid and malleable environment with constantly shifting horizons.[32] This orientational instability is close to that found in a densely tangled jungle environment—one of the reasons jungle crows love Tokyo so much. When the visual field becomes this complex, sound serves as an important alternate channel for humans to locate themselves in space.

Kurokawa describes *rheo* as an attempt to render the dynamic sonic energy of these uncertain horizons into a more sensible mediated form. The work provides an immersion in the complex and sliding rhythms of five shifting landscapes and uses digital techniques to synesthetically blur the boundaries between sight and hearing, the inner rhythms of the body and the outer rhythms of the mediated world.

It might seem strange to think of video as an atmosphere, since the moving image has traditionally served as a medium demanding more focused attention. As ambient video exemplifies, however, part of what happens to the image in the postindustrial period is a general reversal of the dominance of vision over sound, with sound now often taking priority as the organizational driver of audiovisual experience.[33] One reason for the increasing importance of sound, I propose, is the more flexible modes of attention and focus it allows. To return to the original meaning of *ambi-* discussed in the introduction, it is easier for a sound to "surround on both sides" than it is for a visual image. Yet ambient media is never simply a privileging of hearing over vision: the new emphasis on sonic atmospheres is paired with new styles of visual display as well, emphasizing modes that can register on the body even in peripheral vision. Consider, for example, the short video advertisements playing on the video screens now commonly installed above each set of sliding doors inside Japanese trains: silent so as not to be too intrusive; short and rapidly edited so as to support and sustain varied levels of attention; and streaming on an endless loop just above eye level in the most conspicuous place in the train. In cases like this, a rhythmic visual style serves as way to allow audiences more freedom to determine their own modes of attunement and allows moving-image media to blend more seamlessly into existing environments. By modulating the shifting body rather than engaging the focused mind, both BGV and ambient video adapt to the competing attentional demands of the city. But while BGV most often seeks to sell products or provide utilitarian moods, ambient video responds to this situation by seeking out more expansive forms of urban attunement.

As DeNora writes, understanding the varied ways physical embodiment meshes with environmental materials provides a different way of understanding sociality, one helping to dissolve the seeming opposition between self and environment or, in this case, care for the self and engagement with a broader world: "The body—its limits, processes, capacities, thresholds—is reconceived as an emergent and flexible entity, as reflexively linked to the material–cultural environment and what that environment may afford. . . . The body/environment divide can be replaced by a concern with how 'bodies' are configured."[34] Seeing embodiment as emerging with and through environmental forms of attunement provides a much better sense of what is at stake with ambient subjectivation. While turning away from the discursive, ambient video engages the social at the level of atmospheric affordances and environmental agency. By approaching the city through the eurythmic potentials of rhythm, ambient video functions as a technology for tinkering with how the self might dance with and through the complex cadences of contemporary life.

/4/

SOFT FASCINATIONS
IN SHALLOW DEPTH

Imagine stepping off the streets of Tokyo into a dark and quiet gallery space. In the far corner is a five-meter-wide panoramic image, glowing in high-definition, four times wider than it is tall. The upper and lower edges of the frame are blurred, softening the border between the projected light of the image and the darkness hugging it from above and below.

Fade from black to a series of lush floral compositions in soft tones. The white petals of a lotus flower fill the entire frame as everything in the image slides slowly to the right. This partially dissolves into two more views of the same bloom, now drifting slowly downward, revealing a large grouping of mint-green stamen rising from the center of the blossom. As the different images slide across each other, their diagonally radiating petals mesh, casting shifting shadows across the surface of the screen.

The framing hugs the petals tightly. The flower never appears in its entirety, pulling viewers in toward the gentle curves and soft textures. Some parts of the image are semitransparent, giving a partial glimpse of the layers underneath. The petals appear supple and porous as felt. But there is something unnatural about their pristine high-definition surfaces. They glow in an uncanny space between photo-realism and a vacuum of digital purity.

A minute in, dark reflections appear across the surface of the image. These sliding patches of shadow eventually coalesce into the outline of a face. More shadows appear, slowly drifting horizontally across the screen. A title appears superimposed across the bundle of stamen as the music swells for the first time: "Swimming in Qualia." The flower image fades to black, and then, slowly, the title follows it into the darkness (Figure 13).

These are the opening moments of *Swimming in Qualia,* an ambient video installation presented as part of the *STILL/ALIVE* group show

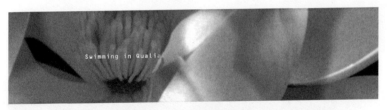

FIGURE 13. Title with lotus flower. Still from Ise Shōko, *Swimming in Qualia.*

at the Tokyo Metropolitan Museum of Photography (December 22, 2007, to February 20, 2008). The visuals are by Ise Shōko. The music is by Steve Jansen (1959–), electronic music composer and former drummer for Japan (the English rock band).[1] Through close attention to the role of image compositing in this and related works, in this chapter I focus on how ambient techniques of self-care are translated into a digital audiovisual register.

My emphasis is on the compositing of what I call *shallow depth,* a space of relationality both literal and metaphorical seeking to situate a narrow space of autonomy within a complex assembly of external controls. As this chapter examines, the shallow depths of ambient video present viewers with a degree of freedom, allowing attention to drift in and out while providing a sustained mood of indeterminate calm. The depth of the visual compositions provides a hint of the unknown, but not enough to overwhelm the relaxed and freely drifting awareness cultivated by the shifting surface layers. Yet these tightly controlled digital images, built through the airtight vacuum of software compositing, form a potential challenge to the presumed autonomy of the contemporary viewer. The ambient videos I examine avoid this threat by seeking out contingent freedoms in the footage imported into the compositing space, using these to determine the shape of the final video. This, too, allows a shallow space of autonomous movement to drift in through an otherwise overdetermined digital landscape. In both ways, the shallow depths of ambient video provide coordinates for the postindustrial self, freely floating through and among accumulated layers of data.

COMPOSITING IN SHALLOW DEPTH

In installation form, *Swimming in Qualia* has two video channels: the first, "Ascent," consists of a slow-paced loop of around twenty-four minutes in length. A second projector displays a much shorter loop,

"Glimpse," six minutes long and organized around a faster but still in-determinate cycling. Both channels are mixed from the same set of imagery: rippling waters, shifting silhouettes, foggy forests, railroad tracks slipping by, and a lush landscape of lotus blossoms and leaves. The two parts are projected on adjacent perpendicular walls, so the two images meet flush in the corner of the room. The longer section, "Ascent," was later projected as a single-channel work during a live concert by Steve Jansen at the Meguro Persimmon Hall in Tokyo (February 29, 2008). Live musicians arranged in front of the screen performed an improvisatory version of Jansen's score.[2]

From the felt-like flower petals to the gently rippling water appearing later in the piece, most of the material in *Swimming in Qualia* registers to vision as soft to the touch. What is not soft in itself is wrapped in a substance that is: trees in the forest are bathed in fog; railroad tracks are blurred with movement. Colors are saturated and smoothed through shading and added grain, and a soft twilight wraps the environments in warm tones. The visuals glow gently in the darkness of the projection space. Soft focus blurs hard lines, particularly around the edges of the image itself (Figure 14). Ise avoids hard cuts in favor of gradual dissolves. Rhythm, particularly in the "Ascent" portion of the work, manifests as a slow ebb and flow as the dynamic pulse of sounds and images gradually accelerates and decelerates over time. The video appears to breathe softly with this undulating pulse as the images drift across the screen.

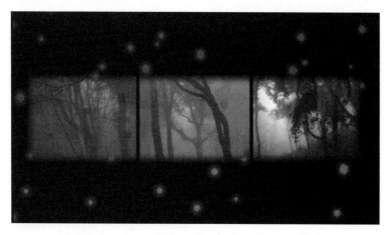

FIGURE 14. Soft fascinations and blurred borders. Still from Ise Shōko, *Swimming in Qualia.*

To share a dark space with these audiovisuals is to be pulled out of the task-oriented, identity-based self of everyday life and toward an impersonal immersion in pure sensation, as promised by the title of the work. *Qualia* is a philosophical term referring to the subjective contents of sense perception, the various qualities perceptible in objects only through the medium of the human senses. The soft porousness of *Swimming in Qualia*'s stimuli produces a blurring effect on the subjective level. The feelings produced are highly sensual, but the objects of these feelings shift and slide as the piece progresses, never stabilizing around a single focus. These ambiguous sensory impressions provide an experience of "swimming" with the qualia themselves, rather than a more direct encounter with the objects giving rise to them. In so doing, the video avoids reference to any more stable form of reflective human identity, allowing audience attentions to disperse and a more impersonal, phenomenological mode of awareness to emerge.

Unlike the more closely integrated rhythms of the works discussed in the previous chapter, *Swimming in Qualia* sits at a further remove from the pressures of everyday life. Audiences leave the noise of the Tokyo streets to slip into the cool darkness of the exhibition space and drift among these indeterminate sensations. The lush yet muted textures and the deliberately slow pacing of the video guide these dissolving bodies and pull them toward a more relaxed, meditative, and yet mobile state. People in the audience are together in their shared orientation to the screens but dissolved as people, blending with the larger atmosphere. And yet, at the same time, this escape from self-concern produces a form of subjectivation eminently suited to the neoliberal focus on self-care.

The spatial logic of *Swimming in Qualia* has similarities with older traditions of image composition that render depth not through orientation to a distant horizon but through a layered accumulation of surface textures. Complicating this push toward flatness, however, is the presence of photo-realistic three-dimensional space. This brings us to the central aesthetic problem in ambient video compositing: how to blend flat, two-dimensional graphic surfaces with three-dimensional photographic images.

The seeming opposition between "surface" and "depth" has long structured discourse on modern Japanese aesthetics. The contrast is often narrated as a choice between a native and/or "postmodern" mode of composition, "in which depth comprises layers of planes without regard to graduated perspective," and the geometric mapping of three-dimensional space arranged around a vanishing point, the singular essence of the Cartesian self.[3] In this reading, perspectival depth is associated with centralized power, control, and hierarchy (famously materialized in Jeremy Bentham's panopticon), whereas (as early postmodern critics liked to argue) the play of surface layers is inherently more free, unsystematic, and outside hierarchy.[4] As Thomas Lamarre notes in his work on the animation table, however, there is nothing inherently less rational about organizing depth not through gradated perspective but through distributed planes. In fact, most science and engineering has long since moved on from the fixed perspective of Cartesianism to explore more layered and flexible ways of mapping the world. Envisioning a three-dimensional space as a series of two-dimensional layers provides a much more precise (and machine-friendly) mapping of relations between points in space. Lamarre gives the example of assembly diagrams produced in orthogonal perspective, where a three-dimensional object is mapped in two dimensions by tilting it forty-five degrees from the page and envisioning it as a series of parallel two-dimensional layers—as in the "exploded view" showing how the components of a machine fit together.[5] But there is more to this than simply a greater compatibility with machine vision. Visual perception researchers have argued human vision may be fundamentally oriented toward distinguishing between layers, with the sensation of depth only a later, higher-order addition inferred through the shifting of surface planes. As James Jerome Gibson argues, "What we see is not depth as such but one thing behind another."[6]

If this is the case, why were postmodern theorists able to see a world of distributed planes as something beyond hierarchy and less susceptible to control? Lamarre argues this seemingly "flat" space could be understood as more unsystematic and free only through contrast with the Cartesian model and the totalizing gaze it implied. In Japan this cofiguration was especially overdetermined, with the latter identified with "Western" colonial modernity and the former with a pre- and/or postmodern Japan simultaneously more authentic and more futuristic. Postmodern Japanese thinkers sought to position the distributed-plane model outside modern systems of control and surveillance when, in fact, this could not be further from the truth.[7]

While insightful, Lamarre's explanation does not fully account for the broader postindustrial turn to imagining space as a series of distributed planes, with or without the need to reject the Cartesian or invest in facile assertions of Japanese particularity. I suggest one significant reason layered space came to appear more "free" starting in the late 1970s was it served as a useful spatial model for the emerging neoliberal self and its own desire to be distributed, flexible, and in-determinate. As Rose describes, the rise of neoliberalism marked a shift from a psychological model of "hidden depths" at the core of the person to an understanding of the self as a "flattened field of open cir-cuits."[8] In other words, neoliberalism no longer seeks to ground iden-tity deep within but rather conceives of the self as a series of distributed nodes—a composite of data layers. This transformation comes with a biopolitical twist: distributed and dispersed, people are liberated from the all-seeing gaze of centralized power—providing an actual, verifiable sense of freedom—while their bodies are opened up to new forms of data manipulation and surveillance far below the threshold of a unified perceiving subject. The "flat" rhetoric of postmodern self-determination and autonomy obscures this rise in environmental con-trols, emphasizing only the gains in personal freedom and mobility. But the two cannot be separated. To return to Foucault's comments from *The Birth of Biopolitics* lectures discussed in the introduction, this is a society "in which the field is left open to fluctuating processes, in which minority individuals and practices are tolerated, in which action is brought to bear on the rules of the game rather than on the players, and finally in which there is *an environmental type of intervention in-stead of the internal subjugation of individuals.*"[9] While Lamarre finds possibilities for divergence within this "distributive field," the intervals between layers also allow for a more precise fixing of bodies in space.

Nowhere is this relationship between environmental control and personal flexibility more vivid than in the realm of motion graphics compositing software. Lev Manovich's *Software Takes Command* de-scribes how a layered form of spatial organization gradually became dominant as software engineers sought to incorporate practices of graphic design, animation, filmmaking, motion graphics, and photog-raphy into the unified space of moving-image compositing programs. By the late 1990s, previously incompatible media genres became inte-grated into a hybrid and mutually intelligible computer workflow. This was thanks to the emergence of a range of different image-compositing programs, including Photoshop, Illustrator, Flash, Final Cut, After Ef-fects, and Maya. The techniques and traditions of previously distinct fields—for example, graphic design and digital video—were now avail-able in a single unified interface. The consolidation of these varied media into a small number of compatible software platforms effectively blurred the professional boundaries between different fields as well, allowing even small firms and freelance designers to operate in several fields simultaneously.[10] As noted in the previous chapter, this was the dawn of the Japanese *eizō sakka,* multimodal image creators working in a number of different media at once—and layering them together within a single software space.

For much of the twentieth century, bringing different media types within a single work (for example, hand-drawn animation, live-action imagery, and typography) meant editing them sequentially (moving from one form to another) or combining them within a single, static image. Compositing moving images of different kinds simultaneously was both labor intensive and technically complex. With the advent of motion graphics software, however, artists gained the ability to mix numerous moving-image layers within the same software space, precisely adjusting their position, opacity, and movement across a work's running time and between its image layers. As Manovich notes, with the advent of moving-image compositing, visual media were catching up with the studio revolution in recorded music, where multichannel recording had generated a new spatial musical aesthetics from the 1970s onward.[11]

The creative process shifted from a resolutely time-synced mode of moving-image construction, with the frame as the indissoluble unit of a linear montage sequence, to a nonlinear software canvas composed of groups of objects arranged across a layered spatial field, each of which may be discreetly modified in size, shape, and movement. The hard cut became less important in this new aesthetic, in exchange for visual forms organized around the "continuous transformation of image layers" and rhythms of "rewriting, erasing, and gradual superimposition."[12] As with the rise of multitrack nonlinear music production, the shift in focus to a nonlinear model of distributed layers in motion graphics brought the practice closer to the world of "flat" two-dimensional media. Painting, animation, photography, and 2D design became increasingly prominent reference points for the emerging aesthetics of digitally composited motion.[13] With digital compositing software, all forms of audiovisual media were brought under the guiding framework of the distributed multiplanar image.

Even with this new hybridity, however, a larger aesthetic problem remained: how to integrate the animation and graphic-compositing techniques of the past with the flexibility and portability of the video camera and its lens-based perspective on existing three-dimensional environments. By the early 2000s, compositing software had begun to incorporate 3D computer graphics and architectural modeling as well, enabling software users to directly manipulate 3D shapes. As Manovich argues, this was a qualitatively different approach from the essentially 2D space of 1990s compositing. Whereas 2D compositing software treats everything as a flat 2D layer, 3D compositing treats even 2D layers as objects to be positioned in 3D space, not unlike the arrangement of screens in a gallery. These two modes of compositing each foreground different aesthetic concerns: as noted, the former draws heavily on the history of 2D media, although with increased degrees of control. The latter draws more from architecture.

In both cases, however, the software remains object oriented, or what Manovich calls "modular." Each element in a composition, whether placed on a 2D layer or in a 3D space, is defined as an *object* with particular values such as size, orientation, transparency, and an array of other textures and effects. This includes image data imported from outside the software, such as video clips and photographs. Every object imported into the software space is immediately situated in virtual depth in relation to other objects. Instead of the black box of the frame (or the cel, in cel animation), the malleable software *object* becomes the irreducible compositional nucleus within compositing software. From the perspective of the software, "a media composition is understood as a set of independent objects that can change over time."[14]

Manovich does not emphasize this point, but I want to draw attention to the persistence of the *object* here as the one element resisting dissolution within this new regime of spatial organization and control. The properties of the object may be radically transformed, and the object can be duplicated, split, or deleted at will. But within the logic of the compositing software, the frame of the object remains absolute. For compositing software, the object is an indissoluble building block, there to be manipulated but never compromised in itself.

While the underlying code might remain hidden, the software object itself is fixed in place, transformed into a set of data points. When humans encounter an object in lived 3D space (outside software), it comes conditioned by what Gibson calls the "ambient optic array," the visual cues helping us situate an object within a wider environment like light, shadows, and the edge between one object and another behind it. With nonlinear software compositing, these atmospheric components of visual perception threaten to dissolve into a world of seemingly discreet and isolated data objects with no inherent relation to one another. As Gibson emphasizes, with human perception the world only ever reveals itself partially: as a person moves through space, some perspectives are revealed, others are concealed.[15] In contrast, in the nonlinear, distributed field of motion graphics software, the ambient array has been eliminated in favor of a distributed field of complete visibility. Objects become data sets that are fully present, all of the time.

If graduated perspective can be understood as the core visual strategy for the Cartesian quest to be all-seeing, the software object layer—composed, mapped, moved, and manipulated over space and time through an ever-expanding range of variable data points—makes a good candidate for envisioning how visibility functions within contemporary societies of control. Rather than fix it in relation to a single point, an object is covered over with metrics until little space is left to imagine anything outside the frame.

Ambient videos like *Swimming in Qualia* respond to this situation by developing specific multiplanar strategies to open out a shallow space for the unknown within these overcoded contexts. I focus on two strategies here. First, *soft fascinations* give viewers the freedom to determine what degree of attention they will give to a work while implying much more lies beyond. Second, *contingencies* are introduced into the vacuum of software space via footage of found movement in lived space.

SOFT FASCINATIONS

Building on the work of William James as well as contemporary neurobiology, environmental psychologists Stephen and Rachel Kaplan describe two forms of human attention used in everyday life: voluntary and involuntary. A person calls on voluntary, or directed, attention when attempting to focus on something by inhibiting awareness of other parts of the environment of equal or greater interest. This inhibitory mechanism is susceptible to fatigue from overuse. Attentional fatigue is common in urban environments, which often present exhaustive demands on directed attention. Crossing a busy street safely, for example, demands attending to many different objects moving in many different directions while inhibiting attention to many others.

In contrast, involuntary attention does not fatigue. It occurs when attending to objects of inherent fascination in the absence of competing stimuli. The Kaplans describe two varieties of involuntary attention: *hard fascination,* which arrests a person's entire concentration, and *soft fascination,* which supports attention but does not demand it. The Kaplans' "attention restoration theory" proposes soft fascinations serve to relieve attentional fatigue by resting the inhibitory function as well as providing a reflective space for attention to wander freely.[16]

The Kaplans identify several specific aesthetic qualities inherent to environments of soft fascination, including *being away* (the feeling of being outside everyday space and time), *extent* (the feeling the environment extends beyond the horizon of perception), and *mystery* (the promise of further intrigue). The Kaplans' clinical research demonstrates how exposure to this combination of environmental qualities effectively contributes to the restoration of directed attention, with benefits in both convalescent settings and the everyday attentional demands of urban life.[17]

The Kaplans' theory provides important clues for understanding how ambient media are able to support various levels of attention while generating restorative moods. First, they argue familiar aesthetic criteria like otherworldliness and mystery are integral to the experience of soft fascination. This implies when standard forms of BGM and BGV "strip away all sense of doubt and uncertainty" (to paraphrase Eno), they not only eliminate their interest as works of art but also undermine their ability to provide restorative moods as "ignorable as they are interesting." In other words, the presence of uncertainty in an ambient work is not incidental to its ability to provide attention restoration but integral to it. Feelings of being away, intimations of a world beyond the perceptible, and a sense of mystery are all inherent properties of ambient "healing." When a work of BGM or BGV fails to maintain this mystery, it *also* fails as an effective source of attention restoration.

Second, the Kaplans' emphasize the contingent and unpredictable aesthetic details of the nonhuman world are often the best providers of soft fascination, leading to their emphasis on "nearby nature" (parks, trees, and other green spaces) as a solution to urban attentional fatigue.[18] This helps explain why phenomena still not fully subject to human control so often feature in ambient works: the movement of clouds, the rippling of water, the patterning of plants, the voices and gestures of nonhuman animals. What makes these materials effective tools of ambient subjectivation is not the fantasy of "nature" as a pristine place outside human civilization (a clichéd image found in many more-generic works of BGV) but how these objects draw viewers away from their human identities and hint at a less familiar world of indeterminate borders. By cultivating perceptual uncertainty, soft fascinations point to a world of effects and influences beyond what is immediately apparent to human viewers. This confluence between attention restoration and aesthetic interest is key to understanding how ambient media reconfigures earlier aesthetic styles as practical resources for self-care.

Swimming in Qualia cultivates soft fascinations through the permeability of each of its constituent parts. Transparency, softness, drifting fog, rippling reflections, and gentle lighting make permeable the boundaries between the different objects sliding around the screen. Ise draws on software-based image compositing only to push against its object/layer ontology, rendering a world of porous surfaces and blurred borders. The bodies of the viewers can then mirror this amorphousness as they attune to the surfaces of the work.

In the "Ascent" portion's second sequence, overlapping black silhouettes of humans' upper torsos appear as if gathered to watch something deeper in the image, gently lit by a turquoise background. This assembly of still and slowly moving bodies is arranged in superimposed layers of differing sizes with varying degrees of transparency. Some bodies are semipermeated by the turquoise light. The figures shrink in size with each receding layer, providing a perspectival illusion of shallow depth against a background color field while retaining a sense of flatness (Figure 15).

The figures' sliding is situated in an uncanny valley between human and computer-generated movement, convincing in general contour but in its particulars always a little too smooth.[19] This also holds for the dolphin swimming through the blue-green background late in the sequence, with its slightly unrealistic tail thrust. Just as Ise suffuses these semitransparent humans with an impossibly pure light, she mixes photo-realistic and computer-generated movement beyond the point of visible discernment, compositing a shallow space of indiscernible volume and substance.

In both museum and concert versions of the piece, the screen architecture of the work further undermines any clean distinction between its constituent parts. In the museum identical source material is recast in continuously varying combinations on the two adjacent screens. The two loops' disparate lengths result in a continuous shifting of the relationship between the two screens, scrambling attempts to discern an overarching narrative or a firm beginning and end. The perpendicular angle between the two projections forces museumgoers to either approach both walls from an oblique perspective or favor one in a frontal approach and relegate the other to peripheral vision. In either case, as curator Ishida Tetsurō points out in the *STILL/ALIVE* exhibition catalog, it is impossible to focus fully on both screens at once.[20] By eliminating the possibility for complete frontal attention, the screen architecture of *Swimming in Qualia* blurs the border between foreground and background forms of awareness.

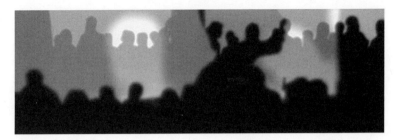

FIGURE 15. Semitransparent layers of uncertain depth. Still from Ise Shōko, *Swimming in Qualia.*

The concert version cultivates a different form of perceptual ambiguity. A *mise en abyme* emerges in the visual echo between the live space of the concert hall (with its audience seated in rows facing musicians arranged in front of a large screen) and the layered silhouettes visible within the screen during the second section of "Ascent," assembled in rows of their own. With the sudden appearance of the dolphin in the deepest layer of the image, the glowing turquoise backdrop is reframed as a tank filled with water, and the silhouettes become legible as an audience in the darkened space of an aquarium. The tank's light wraps the dark frames of the silhouettes in front of it, much as the live theatrical audience watching this scene see those seated in the rows before them bathed in the light of the video's own projected glow.

Steve Jansen's ambient score provides further resources for ambient subjectivation via soft fascination. Reverberant sliding synthesizer motifs slow in speed as they trickle like birdcalls from the speakers across the length of the piece. Through these slowing gestures, the music provides a sensation of continual deceleration even as it flows steadily onward. As with Hosono's "Fossil of Flame" (described in chapter 2), these slowing cadences provide a sonic framework for the audiences' own gradual physical relaxation.

In the theatrical version of *Swimming in Qualia,* this drift toward stillness culminates in an extended section near the middle where the musicians put down their instruments and the screen fades to an indiscernible darkness. Slowly eased into deeper immobilities, the audience sinks into a collective rest feeling more like a fall back into sleep than a break in the flow of the piece.

When the musicians resume playing and the screen begins to glow again, the audience returns from this interstitial slumber with attention refreshed and even less able to discern where the piece ends and their own reflective drift begins. *Swimming in Qualia* aims for this blurred space between dissolution and drift, implying an unknown beyond while remaining unthreatening enough for attention to relax and recover. Characteristic of ambient video, the work emphasizes the uncertainties of the image but ensures this uncertainty never threatens to overwhelm. By providing immersive spaces of contained and "safe" complexity—another form of shallow depth—ambient video serves as a soft refuge for sensory reintegration.

This provision of a sensory refuge is enhanced when an ambient video is ensconced within an art gallery, museum, or theatrical space. Often located in densely populated urban environments, these contained spaces are nonetheless protected from outside noise and immediate demands for focused attention. The mostly bare walls serve as a way not only to better absorb the media on display but also to block out the more cluttered and demanding environment waiting outside. In the case of projected video, lowered lighting and covered windows further deepen the gallery's role as an intermediary space between the private and the public, the inward and the outward. But unlike the darkness of a movie theater, the gallery most often calls upon visitors to remain engaged in organizing their moment-to-moment movement, deciding where to position their bodies in relation to the screen and to other visitors. As noted, audiences can try out different angles of perception, deciding how close and how long to linger. In this, the gallery serves as an ideal space for a more autonomous encounter with soft fascinations, allowing visitors to approach them as they see fit (literalizing the sculptural quality of Satie's *Gymnopedies,* discussed in chapter 1).

As presented at the Tokyo Metropolitan Museum of Photography, *Swimming in Qualia* is structured through nested pools of shallow depth. The perpendicular screens draw audiences closer to the image than is typical for such a large format projection, luring the mobile viewers into an unresolved search for a stable perspective. At the same time, the visible spaces within the projected images are, with few exceptions, focused on layered surface textures continually slipping between two- and three-dimensional space. Petals fold on top of one another; silhouettes slide in front of other silhouettes; trees emerge here and there in the middle distance. One seeming exception is the sequence focusing on the railroad tracks, in which an overhead shot shows two parallel rails zipping by horizontally at high speeds, with no overlays. Here, however, the image is presented in triplicate, with slightly different tracks side by side, pulling the spatial familiarity of the original three-dimensional shot back into the two-dimensional arrangement of a triptych.[21] Ambiguous shadows occasionally pass across one of the inset windows, and rain falls on the "surface" of a transparent foreground layer, further flattening the overall texture. A similar two-dimensional splitting of the three-dimensional image occurs in a later lotus flower sequence. Here, the flowers and leaves break up into a series of vertical bands that slip and congeal as they slide laterally across the surface of the screen (Figure 16).

Swimming in Qualia constantly plays with this tension between two-dimensional graphic surfaces and a shallow three-dimensional depth of field. This latter space is itself established not through linear perspective (lines moving from near to far, from viewer into a gradually shrinking distance) but through accumulated surfaces occluding the deeper layers of the image.

Movement in *Swimming in Qualia* is mainly movement across rather than between these two-dimensional layers. The few dives into the image consist of software zooms rather than three-dimensional camera movement. In a zoom into a forest scene, for example, the size of the trees grow larger, giving the impression of moving forward in space, yet the perspectival relations between the different parts of the image do not change. What resembles movement in depth at the same time registers to perception as simply the enlargement of a flat, two-dimensional surface.

Feelings of drift in *Swimming in Qualia* are largely the result of this software-based interplay between perceptual depth and the surface of the projected image. The movements of objects within the frame have no clear beginning nor end and lack a visible instigator within the image. The different layers appear to be moved by an unknown hand, an absent creator, an invisible software instruction lurking unseen in the background of the image. Individual scenes fade out before the moving parts can settle into any static formation. The sheer number of moving surfaces and their variable speed and direction make it difficult to see everything as a gestalt. Just as the perpendicular angle of the two projections resists a singular focus, so does the indeterminate relation of the nested frames within each screen. Repeatedly displaced from any stable perspective, attention is left to drift among the qualia.

SWIMMING IN CONTINGENCY

But even with all of these manipulations of transparency and depth, compositing software still presents a challenge to soft fascination: how can qualities like mystery and extent (the feeling of something beyond

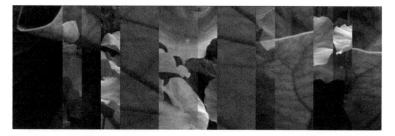

FIGURE 16. Laterally shifting vertical bands flatten the image. Still from Ise Shōko, *Swimming in Qualia*.

the horizon of perception) be achieved within the airtight vacuum of overcoded object layers? Visual effects notwithstanding, contingency has been evacuated in exchange for the precise mapping of each object's properties and movements at every moment of the video's running time.

Ambient video's answer is to undermine the modular logic of the compositing software by seeking out ways to sneak in the material uncertainties of soft fascination from the outside world. Rather than take the software-coded object as a discreet and isolated set of parameters, ambient video artists leverage environmentally inflected objects discovered in existing environments as a means to introduce soft fascinations back into the vacuum of composited space. In this way, these objects can maintain a sense of mystery and depth, pointing viewers beyond the space of the software itself and back into the perceptual uncertainties of their original ambient optic array.

Before giving a few examples of how this functions in *Swimming in Qualia* and other recent works of ambient video, it is worth noting this incorporation of external contingencies into controlled environments has an extensive history. The *Sakuteiki* (Records of garden making) is the world's oldest known text on the aesthetics of gardening. Written by Tachibana no Toshitsuna (1028–94) sometime in mid- to late eleventh-century Japan, the work focuses on the selecting and placing of stones as the primary act of garden formation. The author advises the would-be gardener to "follow the request of the stone" (*ishi no kowan ni shitagahite*) in choosing where to place it. In Toshitsuna's time a stone's shape was thought to express its own intention and dictate its proper use and position in the garden. For example, taking an upright stone from a mountain and placing it upside down in a garden was considered taboo and thought to lead to the death of the garden's

owner. If a stone had landed upside down after tumbling off a mountain and enough time had passed for it to weather and settle in its new
position, however, the stone could be used in this new orientation
without the threat of evil spirits: "This weathering is not the work of
man. Because the stones have weathered naturally, they can be set or
laid in the garden as they are found in nature without impediment."
Over nine hundred years later, worries over evil spirits may have faded,
but the visual fascination of this contingent "weathering" has not. Ambient video works toward a similar incorporation of the contingent
texture of found objects into the highly controlled space of the digital
"garden."[22]

The interplay between the contingency of found objects and their
subsequent framing is also a well-established theme in more recent
camera-based arts. Ise is also a photographer, and despite her reliance
on compositing, her video work in many ways shares more with the
techniques of street photography than it does with feature filmmaking
and other forms of prescripted moving-image media.[23]

Whereas a still photographer might be searching for found compositions frozen in time, video calls for a search not only for compelling
images but interesting movement patterns as well. There is an abiding
interest in Ise's work in found movement, in unscripted physical events
encountered in a public landscape and surreptitiously recorded as they
occur in front of the camera. As noted in chapter 3, Ise's pieces often
begin with her wandering around local environments looking for interesting visual rhythms. Her videos are then built around this found
material, whether from the city streets, the zoo, the park, the forest, or
the sky. By letting these found movements guide her later compositing
choices, Ise uses the software to reach back toward the contingencies
of the space before her camera.

The use of found 3D movement to guide composited 2D effects
was also popularized by video artist and composer Takagi Masakatsu
(1979–), who began developing these techniques after disbanding his
initial live video project with Aoki Takamasa, Silicom. Takagi's *Journal for People* series of video works (2001–2) uses an array of heavily ef-
fected imagery of figures sliding smoothly through space: ice skating,
swimming, jumping, and running, among other forms of movement.[24]
The most provocative combination of 2D and 3D in the collection does
not feature human movement, however, but the circular rotation of a
carnival ride. *Light Park #2* begins with medium and close-up shots
of a rotating swing ride, the kind where individual swings hang by
chains from a large carousel shaped like a spinning top. As the carousel

picks up speed and lifts off the ground, the swings (and the riders they carry) are pulled centrifugally outward. The video presents images of the rotating swings in high contrast, with the seats, chains, and riders presented in glowing and slightly ghosted white silhouettes against a background of solid black (Figure 17). The removal of nearly all visual texture from the image, save for the uniform gray blurring at the border between the two colors, simultaneously flattens the composition and reveals the fundamentals of the 3D rotational movement with all the more clarity.

Video artist Kawamura Yuki (1979–) explores similar overlaid rotations in a series of video works from 2005.[25] *Slide* and *Port* both draw upon footage of objects rotating on an axis tilted away from the vertical surface of the image. *Slide* eliminates most visible details from the original video, a medium shot of a revolving door. The only remaining elements are the gray outlines of light reflected off the spinning glass, rotating at various speeds through empty white space. Near the middle of the piece, the pace shifts to introduce a strobe effect, with individual figures walking toward and away from the camera. The figures themselves are turned into washed-out fields of color, overlaid one on the

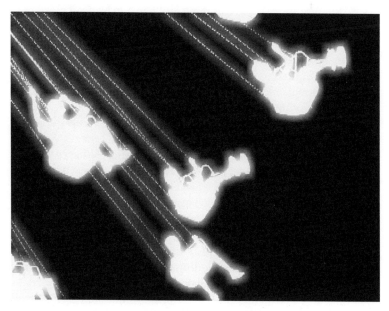

FIGURE 17. Between two and three dimensions. Still from Takagi Masakatsu, *Light Park #2.*

next with various layers of transparency, while over each figure various fragments of refracted light (akin to lens flares) float around like particles in the air. *Port* begins with a similar shot of a revolving door, but here the framing focuses on one section of the threshold, with the spinning axis off to the right. The figures and the outlines of the door itself are again drained of detail, the passersby visible only as shadows reflected within the spinning glass. Depth is obscured to the degree it is difficult to discern which direction the door is spinning. The edge of the door itself appears to be sliding left and right in 2D space, despite the visual cues signaling rotation. As with Takagi's work, orbital 3D movements captured by a camera guide the postproduction 2D effects, but in ways that leave much of the original scene ambiguous. *Jour de reve* brings in a similar carnival theme, this time focusing on a spinning carousel heavily overlaid with layers of color and translucent water droplets (Figure 18). Again, the original footage is heavily obscured, allowing the rotation of the carousel to determine the vectors of the swirling colors and shapes overlaid upon it.

While opening up greater degrees of porousness between 2D and 3D space, these four works simply replace the mechanics of the software with the geometrical mechanics of an object in front of the camera. A different approach to this same problem is to bring in movement less predictable than the rotation of an object on a stable axis. Takagi's work often focuses on the undisciplined and lively physicality of young children. Works such as *Rama* (2002) and *Aura* (2003) organize a complex series of 2D color and pattern layers around footage of running, playing, skipping, and tumbling kids as they move toward, away from, and around his camera.[26]

Animal movement, particularly bird movement, emerges as another prominent source of spontaneous motion. Takagi's *Birdland* (2001-2) plays with the partial revealing and erasing of images of crows on electrical wires and in trees. As in *Light Park #2*, image detail is reduced to solid color fields—this time, black silhouettes against a white background. The compositing intervention in this piece centers on the active drawing and erasing of the original image (lines emerging and branching off from each other, growing rhizomatically into new shapes and connections, only to disappear again). Amid this 2D mutability, attention falls to the occasional glimpse of the 3D movement of the crows themselves—a turning head or a leap into flight.

Ise also has a range of pieces organized around the contingencies of animal behavior. In *Number of Blinks* (*Mabataki no kazu,* 2003), the eyelid movements of a primate shot in close-up and presented in

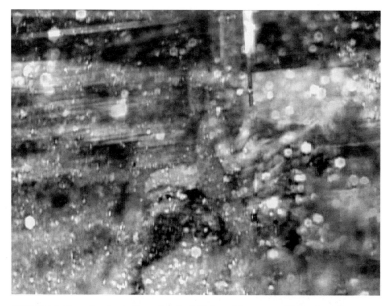

FIGURE 18. Rotation in shallow depth. Still from Kawamura Yuki, *Jour de reve.*

heavily saturated pinks determine the editing of the piece itself.[27] As noted in the previous chapter, a central section of *+Intersection* (2002) features overlaid images of semitransparent flamingos wading around a shallow pond. In these videos, as with the aforementioned examples, the blurring of color and the shifting of semitransparent layers mesh the animals' movements through 3D space with the sliding of their silhouettes across the surface of the image.

Over time ambient video artists began developing more subtle approaches to 2D/3D porousness not dependent on such dramatic manipulations across the entire canvas of the image. This shift to exploring more localized transformations within the visual frame was aided by technological changes in image delivery. In *The Language of New Media* (2002) Manovich predicted larger screens and higher resolutions would generate an aesthetic of "spatial montage," where only parts of an image move at any given time, allowing attention to slowly shift to different parts of the frame. As Jim Bizzocchi points out, this is exactly what has happened with the proliferation of large high-definition televisions in the past decade.[28] The flatter screens blend more easily into their surroundings, while the higher resolution has allowed video to begin to rival painting or still photography in visual detail, reducing the need for constant movement and variety to hold viewers' attention. Rather than relying on editing and narrative to maintain interest, high-definition video could focus on a more gradual shifting of image layers.

Along with *Swimming in Qualia,* Ise explores this new approach in a series of four looped pieces entitled *Passage* (2008).[29] The final loop, *Noema,* consists of a single image of the upper part of a nearly leafless tree shot against a dull, gray background. Large and small branches fork out to fill up the entirety of the frame, with dozens of black birds perched upon them. In stark contrast with the other works I have described, Ise's software-based manipulations of this image are simple and restrained. Every time a bird flies off from the tree or returns from out of the frame to alight on a branch, a thin, red line appears in the bird's wake, tracing a path through space on the surface of the image (Figure 19). These lines persist even after the birds have landed or departed, so the screen gradually begins to fill up with a tangle of red-threaded flight patterns.

Noema makes for a stark contrast to Takagi's *Birdland,* in which bird movement emerges only in brief glimpses while the image layer undergoes continual and forceful manipulation by the virtual brush of the software. In *Noema,* compositing choices are led entirely by the unscripted movement of the birds. After determining the basic structure, Ise allows the contingencies of the found movement to determine the ultimate form of the graphic 2D surface.

While the distributed field of compositing software can be understood to embody the larger biopolitical drive for environmental surveillance and control, ambient video seeks to mobilize the attentive freedom of soft fascination and the contingencies of found movement to carve out shallow spaces of autonomy within this coded world. This ambiguous fusion of analog contingency and digital control can be understood as the visual equivalent of the return to acoustic instrumentation in Hatakeyama's *Minima Moralia* and other recent ambient music discussed in chapter 2. Instead of bringing objects fully into the malleable world of digital data, ambient media seek ways to open the enclosed virtual space of the computer to the contingencies of the wider (as yet uncoded) environments outside.

Time spent swimming in these shallow depths has real effects on viewers, slowing the breath, allowing for attention restoration, and opening up more flexible ways of relating to moving-image media. At the same time, this emphasis on soft fascinations and spatial contin-

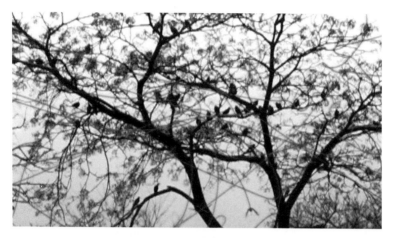

FIGURE 19. Composited contingency. Still from Ise Shōko, *Noema*.

gency serves to compensate for just how shallow this constricted space of subjective autonomy really is. Ambient video can imagine a self free to float with the water and drift with the wind, yet the atmospheres on offer are as tightly controlled as any have ever been.

What does it mean, ultimately, to be subject to such carefully designed atmospheres? In order to pursue this question further, the final two chapters return to the social and historical context of ambient subjectivation, focusing on how ambient media force us to rethink the ethics of emotion regulation (chapter 5) and confront the cultural politics of "therapy culture" more broadly (chapter 6). In the process we will look at how ambience functions within the more narrative contexts of the feature film and the novel.

/5/
SUBTRACTIVISM

While both music and video provide powerful aesthetic affordances for ambient subjectivation on the somatic level, they also come up against the more intractable domains of intersubjective life: personal attachments, familial ties, and the realm of stronger emotions not so easily swayed. The final two chapters expand this book's focus to consider not only how media can serve as technologies of ambient self-care but also what this means for the ethics of care, interpersonal relationships, and social life more broadly. To accomplish this, I look at how ambience functions in feature films and novels, media able to both cultivate powerful ambient moods of their own and narratively reflect back on the social implications of ambient media use.

Unlike ambient music and video, narrative film and fiction do not slip so easily into the background. Effectively attuning to them demands fairly continuous focused attention. For this reason, in narrative media ambience tends to be situated not just in the background of the audience's everyday life but also in the background to the environments within the story, surrounding audiences indirectly by surrounding the characters set before them. In practice this distinction between the moods a narrative work attributes to its characters and setting and the moods it produces in its audience is often blurred. As Sianne Ngai writes, the "tone" of a fictional work is "reducible neither to the emotional response a text solicits from its reader nor to representations of feelings within the world of a story."[1] When audiences attune to characters, they also get into their moods.

Of course, this back-and-forth between mood and story can be found within almost any narrative work. Background music in narrative film is perhaps the most familiar example of the importance of mood in even the most plot-driven stories. Or consider the descriptive passages in many novels that set the tone but do little to advance the mechanics of the story. For example, as Hans Gumbrecht notes, references to weather in novels are almost always there in the service of atmosphere.[2]

In some narrative styles, however, tone plays a more pronounced role, and the aesthetic emphasis skews decisively toward mood and away from plot and characterization. In film, atmospheric styles have gone by various names, from *contemplative cinema* to the *mood film* to the *cinema of slowness*.[3] Internationally, critics have often associated Japanese cinema with this kind of moodiness, particularly in the wake of influential Mizoguchi Kenji films like *Ugetsu* (1953). In their seminal 1959 study of Japanese cinema, Joseph L. Anderson and Donald Richie repeatedly make the claim that "to the Japanese director, atmosphere is often more important than plot."[4] But this was hardly unique to Japan: a similar assertion could be made for the works of postwar European auteurs like Theodoros Angelopoulos, Michelangelo Antonioni, Alain Resnais, and Andrei Tarkovsky. Beginning in the 1980s, atmosphere again became associated with Asian art cinema, with directors like Hou Hsiao-hsien, Tsai Ming-Liang, and, later, Jia Zhangke and Apichatpong Weerasethakul often noted for their emphasis on tone. In Japan a younger wave of post-1970s directors including Sōmai Shinji, Ichikawa Jun, Kurosawa Kiyoshi, Aoyama Shinji, Kitano Takeshi, Koreeda Hirokazu, Kawase Naomi, Oshii Mamoru, and Oguri Kōhei have explored atmospheric styles, often leavening them with tropes from other genres.[5]

What I refer to here as *ambient cinema* is part of this larger tradition of mood films, but with one more specific criterion. Ambient films not only serve audiences as a resource for ambient subjectivation via atmospheric affordances, but also use narrative to reflect on the role of mood-regulating media in the lives of their characters. In this way, ambient cinema works both sides of the atmosphere/story divide, providing not just a mood that dominates a narrative but also a narrative about mood.

The key example of ambient cinema I turn to here is the 2004 film *Tony Takitani*, directed by Ichikawa Jun (1948–2008). The film cultivates a somber and reflective mood through its sets, cinematography, costumes, sound design, and, above all, soundtrack, by composer and former Yellow Magic Orchestra member Sakamoto Ryūichi (1952–). The narrative, based on a Murakami Haruki short story set in the 1980s, depicts an attempt by three solitary souls to cover their inner pain and loneliness with the ambient resources of music, illustration, and designer fashion. The atmospheric affordances of these aesthetic materials help obscure the more troubling and intransigent parts of the characters' emotional lives. At the same time, the atmosphere of the film as a whole mimics its characters' approach to personal mood regulation, providing soothing surface consolations for audiences as they quietly witness the tragedies and healing depicted on-screen. As this chapter explores, this cinematic approach to ambient subjectivation operates on a principle of *subtractivism,* a smoothing of the self by designing out the need for strong emotional attachments, whether to other people or to the past itself.

SOLITARY STYLE

Tony Takitani was highly anticipated as the first feature-length adaptation of a story by Murakami Haruki (1949–), who at the time was near the height of his international popularity.[6] Aware of these heightened expectations, Ichikawa went out of his way to capture Murakami's atmospheric brand of introspective solitude, even as he made some significant changes to the original story.[7]

The most immediately striking aspect of the film's ambience is its deliberately restrained aesthetic palette. Nearly every sequence was shot on a small, specially fabricated outdoor set built on an empty lot in Yokohama, with the minimal interior furnishings of Tony's office and apartment shifted around for each scene.[8] The concrete of the city, the gray sky, and the local power lines provide the urban backdrop for the film's small and contained world (Figure 20). Nearly every object in the film is gray, black, white, indigo, or some shade in between. The cinematography returns over and over to a slow low-angle left-to-right tracking shot as a way to transition between scenes. As the view shifts from one space to the next, out-of-focus walls slide by close to the camera, bracketing each scene while avoiding hard cuts in favor of a steady forward progression of time. Nishijima Hidetoshi's narration—with lines often taken directly from Murakami's story—is delivered in muted monotones, with characters on-screen sometimes finishing his lines for him. The sound design features a number of repeated motifs echoing through the film: ticking clocks, construction whistles, wind in the trees. The casting is also minimal, with the two lead actors, Issey Ogata and Miyazawa Rie, each playing double roles.

This repetition of a small number of images, sounds, objects, and actors allows the film to develop a strong and cohesive mood, and this repetition of mood cues itself becomes the central affective logic of the film, above and beyond the story or its characters. These slow and quiet repetitions continually bring the film back to an impersonal stillness, a solitary rhythm allowing the stronger emotions pulled up by the narrative (grief, loneliness, desire) to evaporate into a low-affect

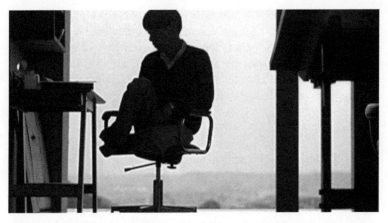

FIGURE 20. Tony (Issey Ogata) alone in his studio, set against the gray horizon of the city. Still from *Tony Takitani*.

mood before the film once again begins sliding forward at a slow pace. As encapsulated in the steady left-to-right tracking shot, time and space in the film is governed by an aesthetic impartial to narrative events or dramatic propulsion. The film's slide forward feels as inevitable as the secondhand moving around a clock, pushing the human drama to the periphery and allowing viewers to let go and submit to the ongoing flow.

At the same time, the film's narrative provides a succinct distillation of painful histories covered over in the turn toward impersonal drift in the late 1970s and 1980s. The opening montage sequence begins by introducing Tony's father, Takitani Shōzaburō, a simple man who spends World War II playing trombone in Shanghai and sleeping with lots of women. After pure luck keeps him from being assassinated as a POW, he returns to Japan to discover his immediate family was killed in the Tokyo air raids. He marries a distant cousin, but she dies soon after giving birth to a baby boy. On the advice of a U.S. Army jazz friend and expecting American culture to be popular for some time to come, Shōzaburō decides to name the boy Tony. Ostracized as a result of his unusual name, Tony learns to keep to himself while quietly developing his skills as a technical illustrator. His eye for mechanical detail makes him a popular commercial artist amid the emerging materialism of the 1970s and 1980s, and his career flourishes even as his solitude intensifies.

Tony's quiet but secure life is isolated but peaceful until one day a

younger woman arrives at his office wearing her clothes with a lightness he has never seen before. At age thirty-seven Tony is suddenly
in love and, for the first time in his life, finds he cannot live without
someone else. He persuades this woman, Eiko, to marry him, and for
a time they live a life of what appears on the surface to be domestic
bliss. Tony suddenly becomes aware of how lonely he was before and,
as the narrator notes, for a brief period becomes deathly afraid of being
alone again. This feeling soon fades, however, as he settles into his new
life with Eiko.

Tony's main attraction to his wife is her taste in clothes—the way
she seems to almost meld with them into a lighter-than-air vision of
physical transcendence. It gradually becomes apparent that for Eiko,
however, purchasing high-end fashion is a compulsion she is powerless
to resist. She buys far more outfits than she can ever hope to wear,
eventually filling up an entire room of their Setagaya, Tokyo, apartment. She claims the clothes cover an emptiness inside. Eventually,
Tony confronts her about her habit, and she promises to try to cut back,
only to quickly become despondent (Figure 21). A short time later, her
mind drifting while driving home after returning a recent purchase at
an Aoyama boutique, Eiko dies in an off-screen car crash.

As Tony begins to cope with the sudden loss of his wife, the most
difficult question is what to do with her enormous wardrobe. The luxury clothes soon begin to haunt him, shadows of the woman who left
them behind. Tony eventually asks a dealer to take the clothes away.

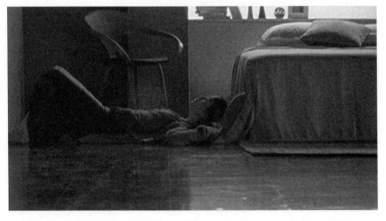

FIGURE 21. Eiko (Miyazawa Rie) struggling not to buy more clothes. Still from
Tony Takitani.

Soon after, his father dies of liver cancer, leaving behind a large collection of jazz LPs. Tony places this pile of records in the now-empty wardrobe and once again confronts the mute shadows left by a person who once lived through them (Figure 22). While these emotionally charged objects remain in his apartment, Tony has difficulty mourning the loss of his wife and his father. Only after selling the records and emptying the wardrobe one last time does he begin to find peace in solitude once more. As the narrator states near the end of the film, only then is Tony, at last, "completely alone."

EMOTIONAL CAPITALISM AND LOW-AFFECT LIFESTYLES

At first glance, this seems to be a tale of misfortune and tragedy: Tony has a difficult childhood, finds happiness briefly as an adult, and then must work through grief when this happiness comes to a sudden end. But the ambience of the film tells a different story, orienting audiences toward the calm of Tony's baseline solitude more than his ill-fated brush with intimacy. Tony is as alone at the end of the film as he is at the beginning. But the film's mood presents this not as the result of accumulated tragedy or the whims of fate but as simply the way things have to be. Time passes; emotions come and go; and the people and objects provoking them fade away. Tuning in to this wistful passage of time ultimately serves as the film's strategic response to the drama and trauma of postwar Japan: keep calm and carry on. This might at first seem like a Buddhist image of impermanence (*mujō*), as famously put forth in classic Japanese texts like the *Hōjōki* (An account of my hut, 1212) and *Heike monogatari* (The tale of the Heike, circa 1371). I want to suggest, however, it has a lot more to do with the contemporary strategy of subtractivism: a kind of strategic impermanence streamlining the self in order to stay mobile and unattached.

Before I look more closely at what *Tony Takitani* reveals about subtractivism, it will be useful to provide some historical context for this low-affect approach to the self. The emphasis on keeping calm as a practical means of self-care has roots in modern regimes of emotion management and in many ways parallels the history of background music outlined in chapter 1. With the emergence of psychoanalysis and psychological consulting in the late nineteenth century, capitalist societies first became cognizant of the value of mood regulation as a means to increase efficiency and productivity. This happened earliest in the United States and the United Kingdom. Eva Illouz has traced the importation of Freudian ideas into American business practices early

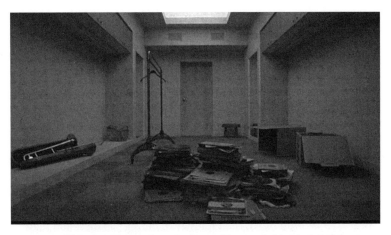

FIGURE 22. Shōzaburō's records as shadows of the man left behind. Still from *Tony Takitani.*

in the twentieth century. This is the origin of what she calls *emotional capitalism,* or the business of "harnessing the emotional self more closely to instrumental action."[9] Under the influence of new efficiency studies pioneered by Frederick Taylor and others around the time of World War I, career success began to be understood less as the result of a person's capacity for hard work and more as the product of a complex assembly of traits and skills any given person might possess or make their own. It no longer mattered if these habits were innate or acquired, and in most cases, the management literature argued, they could be taught.[10] The criterion for success was no longer personal determination but the careful fine-tuning of individual and group psychology.

While earlier disciplinary principles favored blunt demonstrations of authority to keep underlings in their place, these new practices of "management psychology" equated power and influence with self-mastery and emotional control. A new "expert" squadron of psychological consultants advised against the expression of strong or divisive emotions in the workplace, with the aim of ensuring the smooth and efficient flow of interpersonal communication. A positive morale was to be preserved at all costs. To achieve this, therapeutic techniques of emotional control were increasingly called upon to try and guarantee everyday equanimity. As Illouz writes, while the new therapeutic worker "dwells excessively on his or her emotions, he or she is simultaneously required not to be moved by them."[11]

Unlike the United States, in Japan emotional capitalism as a managerial style made little headway until after the end of the Pacific War in 1945. It could build, however, on a longer tradition of self-help aimed at personal advancement. This tradition had its origins in the shifting employment patterns and various self-improvement programs appearing in Japan around the turn of the twentieth century. The 1870 Japanese translation of *Self-Help* by Scottish author Samuel Smiles during the rapid industrialization of the Meiji period (1868–1912) became the era's best-selling book, and with the help of the rapidly expanding mass media, this set off a popular boom in personal advancement (*risshin shusse*) literature. Smiles's success was replicated in 1911 with the Nitobe Inazō best seller *Shūyō* (Self-cultivation).[12] These books promised limitless advancement for the persevering and enterprising (male) worker. Until 1900 or so, the rapidly expanding Japanese job market and an upwardly mobile class of newly educated laborers made such aspirations plausible. Around the turn of the century, however, the number of educated young men entering the workforce began to outpace the production of new jobs. Advancement was no longer secured, and an atmosphere of conformity took hold as the only way to slowly work one's way up the corporate ladder.[13] Nevertheless, the discourse of self-improvement persisted even as the career benefits it promised became increasingly hard to attain. Literary critic Maeda Ai has argued that in response to the shrinking economic possibilities for rapid upward mobility, the self-improvement disciplines promoted by self-help transformed into "valid personal goals in themselves," exceeding their original aim of success in the workplace.[14]

Yet it was not until over a half century later, during the postwar reconstruction and the gradual transition to a service-oriented economy in the 1970s and 1980s, that Japanese corporate discourse shifted to prioritize employee moods along the lines of American management psychology. Rose notes that what UK management psychologists of the time found laudable about this new Japanese management style was companies' "consideration for the self-esteem of employees" and a corporate culture where "all employees can identify with the aims and objectives of the company and which encourages and recognizes the individual contribution of all." In Japan as elsewhere, a new neoliberal approach to personel management was emerging, stressing autonomy and self-regulation rather than top-down control. This new approach imagined workers as invested in both their own well-being and the "collective entrepreneurialism" of the corporation as a whole. Work no longer was just about doing the job or advancement in a particular career but was a technique for the overall production of the self.[15] Just as in the Meiji period, however, it was easy to promise self-actualization at work but much harder to deliver, particularly after the bursting of Japan's economic bubble. A new therapy culture quickly bloomed in other areas to take up the slack, offering to help "develop" the self outside the context of work.[16]

Tony can be understood as an early exemplar of this new approach to work and self, organized around emotional control and low-affect living. In college in the late 1960s, he witnesses the ideological debates and political passions driving the work of his fellow art students but responds with the cool judgment of one who simply cannot understand the need for such emotional turbulence. As the narrator states, "Tony couldn't fathom the value of the kinds of paintings his classmates argued over—paintings imbued with artistry or ideology. To him, such paintings were just immature, and ugly, and inaccurate." In the context of the new push for self-regulated affective autonomy, the messy emotionality of the 1960s student movements could be recast as simply juvenile.[17] The emerging emphasis on personal mood regulation promoted a more rational and efficient self that didn't let unruly emotions get in the way.

COSUBJECTIVITY

This emphasis on low-affect living also served as a pragmatic response to the subjective challenges of urban life. As Robert Fink argues, the insistent repetitions of popular media might be understood to refer not just to a particular psychological state but to a wider *culture of repetition* invested in finding pleasure in the highly organized patterns of consumer society. Fink focuses on the role of television advertising in developing an audience sensitive to the aesthetics of repetition in everyday life.[18] The fashion industry and the omnipresent rhythms of the city (as described in chapter 3) also no doubt played a role in developing a taste for pattern recognition as a way to lend a flexible structure to the emotional ups and downs of everyday life. This act of giving oneself over to repetition and drift is a familiar strategy for those, like Tony, seeking to blend in with the anonymous city. Georg Simmel, in his seminal 1903 essay "The Metropolis and Mental Life," points out that unlike less densely populated communities, where only a small number of familiar faces are encountered over the course of any given day, life in a metropolis is characterized by countless daily interactions with strangers, most of which are brief and based on the exchange of goods and services. There is little time or incentive for getting to know all but a few selected people beyond the level demanded by utilitarian exchange. What this means, among other things, is that the more textured emotional engagements characterizing human interaction in more intimate settings are in large part replaced by an ongoing series of brief and trivial interactions. In the metropolis other people are often simply fellow travelers in peripheral vision.[19]

By the end of the century, this urban demand for a shallower sociality had developed into new forms of being together in shared space, often relying on atmospheric subjectivation to provide an implicit set of guidelines for communal behavior. In her sociological study of music use in everyday life, Tia DeNora introduces a distinction between *cosubjectivity* and *intersubjectivity*. Cosubjectivity is a form of social relation

> where two or more individuals may come to exhibit similar modes of feeling and acting, constituted in relation to extra-personal parameters, such as those provided by musical materials. Such co-subjectivity differs in important ways from the . . . notion of "inter-subjectivity," which presumes interpersonal dialogue and the collaborative production of meaning and cognition. Inter-subjectivity . . . involves a collaborative version of reflexivity. . . . By contrast, co-subjectivity is the result of isolated individually reflexive alignments to an environment and its materials.[20]

Cosubjective modes are most prevalent in crowded urban spaces designed around flexibility and mobility—in other words, the neoliberal city. In these contexts the strategic use of media allows other people to contribute to a shared energy and collective orientation without ever demanding foreground attention themselves.

Cosubjectivity allows for a semblance of individuality without getting in anyone else's way. In a highly differentiated consumer society, high-density diversification paradoxically creates the need for a highly regulated public anonymity in order to keep all these "individuals" from imposing on one another. In the metropolis it is easier for people to coexist with others who share their ideal of comfortable invisibility and low-affect sociality. The urban self comes to be defined less through interpersonal relationships and more, to return to DeNora, through "isolated individually reflexive alignments to an environment and its materials."

The Tokyo metropolitan area might be understood as one of the world's great experiments in cosubjectivity, bringing tens of millions of people right next to one another while for the most part relieving them of any need to actually speak to one another.[21] Cosubjective environments like cafés and public transportation networks are remarkable for being able to accommodate many and alienate few. Of course, these places too have their own particular rules and regulations, and it is certainly possible to feel unwelcome and out of place. Every overcrowded rush-hour train is a reminder of how fraught and fragile the orchestration of cosubjectivity actually is. There are reminders in the film, too, like the scene where a pile of oranges for sale in a grocery store suddenly rolls to the floor and the woman closest to the display immediately declares (ostensibly to Tony, who is standing nearby), "It wasn't my fault, right?" When operating smoothly, cosubjectivity allows for personal differences to be maintained while living, working, and traveling peacefully in close proximity to one another. As easy as it is to be skeptical about what this means for social life, there is also something immensely practical going on here. For effective navigation through the city, cosubjectivity may be just as important, if not more important, than the molding of a more distinctly bounded and reflective interpersonal self.[22]

As with emotional capitalism, cosubjective environments favor a mobile, dispersed, and anonymous self. To assert a more specific, bounded identity would serve only to restrict personal mobility. Cosubjective sensory dispersal offers the tantalizing promise of being able to render the self invisible, avoiding the potential discomforts of a more solid and stable identity. Over time this approach to shared urban space became internalized, combining with workplace mood regulation to serve as an effective way of dealing not only with other people but also with the emotional ups and downs of the self.

Starting in the 1970s, Japanese social critics have often portrayed this desire for impersonality as a form of social apathy, describing it as the result of a loss of the "grand narratives" and cohesive ideologies to which prior generations supposedly subscribed. Popular 1970s terms like *sanmushugi* (triple nothingism) described a sense the generation coming of age at the time did not care about much of anything, with no spirit (*mukiryoku*), no interest (*mukanshin*), and no responsibility (*musekinin*).[23] This supposedly apathetic generation was followed by the *shinjinrui* (new-type human), a name the media invented for a 1980s generation who could (it was hoped) more effectively tap into the libidinal logic and impersonal effervescence of the new "postmodern" age.[24] After Japan's entry into a full-blown economic recession in the 1990s, the short-lived enthusiasm for the *shinjinrui* gave way to worries over yet another apathetic generation, this one coming of age around the turn of the century. Saitō Tamaki, the Lacanian psychoanalyst and social critic famous for his work describing the social recluse (*hikiko-mori*) phenomenon, goes so far as to diagnose the impersonal styles prominent in the art of these younger Japanese as a form of "deper-sonalization disorder," referring to someone unable to express strong opinions and more comfortable floating in indeterminate space.[25]

Generational narratives are a perennial favorite of the Japanese media, and it is important to question whether these descriptions are actually representative of the majority of Japanese coming of age during these periods. In any case, rather than explaining the desire for anonymity as a symptom of generational apathy, I suggest this seem-ing depersonalization has a lot more to do with the practical utility of cosubjectivity for contemporary Japanese life, particularly in a neo-liberal context intent on preserving personal liberties while ensuring the smooth and efficient movement of people.

THE AGE OF SUBTRACTION

A more affirmative take on the low-affect lifestyle comes from Arai Man, the Dentsū ambient video producer introduced in chapter 3. Arai cheerfully tags the new era starting in the late 1970s as "the Age of Subtraction" (*hikizan no jidai*). He proposes a general fatigue in Japan from too much stuff and too many people, leading to a desire for emptied-out environments with no one around. In the turn to subtrac-tivism, Arai sees the younger generations of Japanese rejecting both the hubristic self-assertion of earlier ideologies and the "greediness and materialism" of the high-growth years. He sees younger Japanese embracing impotency (*funō*), showing little interest in either physical or cultural reproduction. Their only desire is to empty out their lives in the hopes of achieving some kind of "balance."[26]

As evidence Arai notes the popularity of Erik Satie's music; the focus on the minor and inconsequential in novelists like Murakami Haruki, Ikezawa Natsuki, and Yoshimoto Banana; and the "subtrac-tive merchandise" made popular by brands like Mujirushi ryōhin (lit-erally "no-label quality goods," commonly abbreviated as Muji). Arai proposes the rejection of attention-grabbing aesthetics, and the shift to more diminutive styles in many fields was the result of a shared cul-tural "overripeness." With too many people and too much to focus on, having less to attend to became appealing in itself.[27]

As with his own ambient video practice, what Arai calls the "subtractive arts" (*hikizan geijutsu*) are based on a minimalist strategy of stripping away everything extra until only the most basic and essential components remain. Arai argues this subtractive impulse seeks to balance decades of overproduction, hyperstimulation, consumer overindulgence, and overblown egos. Subtraction becomes a form of "ventilation," emptying the surrounding environment and letting in some fresh air.[28]

As noted in the previous chapter, the urban sensorium in itself places increased strain on the human capacity for directed attention, a faculty that can fatigue through overuse. As proponents of "attentional economics" argue, within the information-dense environments of contemporary cities, attention itself has become an object of scarcity.[29] Aesthetics has responded to this situation in a number of ways. Two of the most prominent strategies for commanding attention are novelty and scale: make your object something nobody has ever experienced before, or at least make it bigger and louder.[30] In stark contrast with these pushes for new kinds of "hard fascination," a subtractive aesthetics places no additional demands on human attention. Purposefully diminutive, subtractivism provides something nearly as scarce as attention itself: ignorability. Rather than competing for the increasingly scarce commodity of focused attention, the aesthetics of subtraction responds by staying out of the way.

In the world of computers, for example, Lev Manovich notes how with the emergence of the graphical user interface (such as the first commercially available Macintosh operating system in 1984) the self-contained image lost its privileged position at the center of attention: "No longer completely filling the screen, it is now just one window among many." With this proliferation of windows, a new aesthetic imperative arose: "the peaceful coexistence of multiple information objects on the computer screen, exemplified by a number of simultaneously opened windows."[31] Too many competing windows gave rise to the need for a style that didn't focus on one at the expense of the others but strove instead to blend in and remain in the background of attention.

In a prescient aside in *The Language of New Media,* Manovich describes a "no-style style" popular with global new media artists in the 1990s: "no labels, no distinct design, no bright colors or extravagant shapes." Manovich points to designer fashion labels like Hugo Boss and Prada as forerunners of this style, later taken up by designers in other fields. He could have just as easily pointed to prominent Japanese fashion designers of the 1980s like Kawakubo Rei (of Comme des Garçons) and Yamamoto Yohji or, on a more everyday level, subtractivist life-style brands like Muji. Like Arai, Manovich describes the no-style style as a response to an overabundance of choice and a subsequent reluctance to side too much with any one choice among others:

> In a society saturated with brands and labels, people respond by adopting a minimalist aesthetic and a hard-to-identify clothing style. Writing about an empty loft as an expression of a minimalist ideal, architecture critic Herbert Muschamp points out that people "reject exposing the subjectivity when one piece of stuff is preferred to another." The opposition between an individualized inner world and an objective, shared, neutral world outside becomes reversed.[32]

Following Muschamp, Manovich reads the no-style style as a refusal to choose one identity over another, an internalization of aesthetic and affective neutrality as a way to always be ready to engage with whatever and whomever comes along next. Subtractivism attempts a return to the zero point of style as a practical way to "fit in" to a complex world of proliferating choices. By the 1980s subtractivism would fully emerge as a lifestyle of its own, an atmospheric camouflage for a newly anonymous urban subject. With its sleek lines, muted colors, and refusal to make any deliberate statements, subtractivism provided a style embodying the neoliberal ideals of flexibility, mobility, lightness, and efficiency.[33]

I suggest understanding subtractivism as one of the basic aesthetic strategies underlying the soft fascinations of ambient media, as well as a much broader range of contemporary fashion, architecture, and lifestyle design. If cosubjectivity is about the blending of diverse people in a shared space of anonymous moods, subtractivism aims for something similar in the design of aesthetic objects—a stylistic orientation toward what we might call *coobjectivity,* or the ability of objects to blend seamlessly and anonymously into their surrounding environment.

DRESSING FOR A BURNT-OUT FUTURE

Subtractivist styles are evident in Japanese consumer trends starting in the early 1980s—right around the time Tony begins finding a ready market for his "emotionless" illustrations in the film. Yoshimi Shunya reads the transformation from the consumer fantasies of the 1970s to the no-style style of the 1980s through two of the premier retailers of the period, Parco and Muji—at the time both owned by the larger Seibu conglomerate. In the 1970s the Shibuya, Tokyo, branch of the Parco department store was the epicenter of consumer culture for young women. As Yoshimi notes, Parco sought to transform the central area west of Shibuya station into an "integrated advertising environment," a set of staged fantasy spaces based on the premise of allowing consumers to escape the mundane pressures of their everyday lives.[34] In the 1970s the premier retail atmospheres on offer were largely of the exotic variety, with an emphasis on stepping outside everyday life (not unlike Hosono's "sightseeing music" described in chapter 2). In this early stage of the emerging Japanese consumer culture, Parco's advertising campaigns pushed women to assert their freedom and break away from traditional domestic spaces, if only to shop. In contrast, Yoshimi describes Muji's strategy in the 1980s as

> the absolute opposite of Parco's distancing from the everyday.... It was based on comprehensively supplying the materials that would allow customers to live with a reasonable degree of aesthetic satisfaction. These materials were things that could be found anywhere, that were absolutely ordinary, and made no attempt to lecture to the customers.... What we find here is a burnt-out future that affirms only what is private and commonplace.[35]

Yoshimi associates Muji's designs with the increasing mediatization and fluidity of urban Japanese environments in the 1980s, part of a global transformation toward what at the time was coming to be called the "information society."[36] While the 1980s are often imagined as the height of consumerism in bubble-era Japan, in actuality consumption was already in decline following its heyday in the 1970s (well before the larger bursting of the economic bubble and Japan's entry into a full recession in the early 1990s). By the early 1980s personal consumption had entered a steep decline, and marketers publicly worried young people were "no longer buying things." While private investment was still on the increase, the role of personal consumption in Japan's GNP was actually shrinking.[37] As Arai notes, increasingly what consumers wanted to buy was not more but *less*. The subtractivist style became a way to sell it to them.

While Yoshimi describes this as the arrival of a "burnt-out" future, his analysis misses the subtractivist principles governing the soft tones and anonymous ambitions of Muji products. Muji began in December 1980 as a product line of Seibu supermarket chain Seiyū and opened its first dedicated Muji store in Aoyama (Tokyo) in 1983. In 1989 it left Seibu to become independent and, as of February 2015, has almost three hundred stores across Japan and over three hundred overseas on four continents, including 128 in China. The company's stripped-down, muted designs are emblematic of the emphasis on coobjectivity in Japanese consumer design from the 1980s onward. One of the original developers of the Muji style, designer Tanaka Ikko, describes the idea behind the brand's emphasis on "everyday" and "basic" products as follows:

> You may feel embarrassed if the person sitting next to you on the train is wearing the same clothes as you. If they are jeans, however, you wouldn't be worried, because jeans are what we could describe as "basic" clothing. All Muji products are such "basic" products.[38]

Putting modernist principles to minimalist ends and echoing the purposeful ignorability of BGM, Muji goods are styled through the "careful elimination and subtraction of gratuitous features." Geared toward the anonymous city, Muji fashions allow their wearers to blend in and, perhaps, to dissapear. As Julian Holloway and Sheila Hones point out in an essay on the brand's "mundane geographies":

> Muji objects are designed to blend into non-Muji surroundings. This aspect to the Muji design aesthetic is emphasized in the company's catalogues with repeated assurances that the objects are anonymous, adaptable, and useful . . . "guaranteed to blend and never dominate." Thus, throughout its catalogues, Muji commodities are presented as "discreet," "muted," "never visibly branded," "transparent," "understated," "unobtrusive," and "unostentatious."[39]

With Muji, subtractivist style went mainstream. Just as Satie's furniture music was designed to blend with the sound of knives and forks, Muji's knives and forks were designed to blend with everything else you might have lying around. These subtractivist goods were designed to fade into the background, allowing the person who uses them to blend in, too.

In the film Eiko favors more upscale designer clothing (mainly Parisian boutique brands), but the apartment she shares with Tony looks like it could have been ordered straight out of a Muji catalog. In rendering Tony and Eiko's low-affect lifestyle, the film explores the impact of a subtractivist approach to interpersonal life, exploring how cosubjectivity and coobjectivity might function in the context of close personal relationships. Ichikawa cuts away the interpersonal and dialectical aspects of classical film style (over-the-shoulder dialogue shots, hard cuts, montage in the service of storytelling) in favor of soft surfaces, delicate melodies, and drifting camerawork. With its emphasis on impersonal atmospheres, muted tones, and smooth, understated objects, the film embraces subtractivism as an aesthetic approach. At the same time, it hints at the ethical and intersubjective problems possibly following from such an attempt at self-erasure.

Tony Takitani is full of characters using material objects and the soothing influence of others to maintain calm and cover over more painful emotions. Tony's father keeps to his jazz trombone as a way to avoid confronting the larger implications of the war, his brush with death as a prisoner of war, the loss of his family, and the death of his wife. Similarly, Tony uses his technical illustration practice to cordon himself off from his own feelings of loneliness. Rather than dwell on the loss of his mother, the meaning of his unusual name, his social isolation, and the emotional pain of those around him (including his new wife), Tony seeks to make peace with solitude, keeping his life and surroundings purposefully plain and simple as if to design out more volatile feelings.

This is paralleled by Eiko's admission the reason she spends most of her salary on expensive clothing is to "cover over the emptiness inside" (Figure 23). The comforting surfaces of her clothing become a way to smooth over her own moods, and in turn this helps comfort Tony as well. When Shōzaburō asks Tony what it is he likes about Eiko, he simply states, "It's like she was born to wear clothes." Reflecting a gender dynamic common to emotional labor more broadly, the ability of Tony's wife to be a soothing presence for him forms the basis of his attraction and their subsequent partnership.[40] While Tony and Eiko never appear to discuss it explicitly, they make an implicit pact to avoid confronting their respective sadnesses and stay together in the shallows and soft surfaces of their quiet domestic life. The one exception to this is when Tony dares confront Eiko about her clothes-buying compulsion, a breach of protocol leading immediately to tragedy.

THE SOUNDTRACK TO *TONY TAKITANI*

The film's soundtrack allows audiences, too, to indulge in the delicate atmospheres of Tony and Eiko's subtractivist solitudes. The composer,

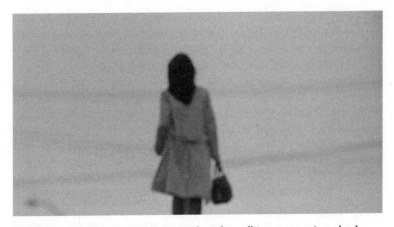

FIGURE 23. Clothing the emptiness inside: Eiko walking away against a backdrop of power lines. Still from *Tony Takitani.*

Sakamoto Ryūichi, has long fashioned himself as a Satie-esque ambient celebrity for the new century, a master of soothing melancholy. A former member of Yellow Magic Orchestra along with Hosono Haruomi and Takahashi Yukihiro, he went on to write pop songs and operas, appear in whisky advertisements, win a Grammy and an Academy Award for his film scores, curate art exhibitions, act in films, lead a publishing house, pursue environmental and antinuclear causes, and even interview the Dalai Llama—each activity now folded into his persona as the elder statesman of highbrow Japanese pop. In press photos he is usually seen wearing minimalist black and gray Yamamoto Yohji–style designer clothing, not too far from the upscale monochrome fashions worn by the characters in the film. Sakamoto composed a minimalist piano soundtrack for one of Yamamoto Yohji's fashion shows in 1995, and he brings a similar aesthetic to his work for the *Tony Takitani* score. [41]

Sakamoto's music has played an important role in lending mainstream respectability to the ambient style. A case in point is his surprise 1999 hit "Energy Flow," the first instrumental ever to reach the number-one spot on the Oricon charts (the Japanese equivalent of the Billboard rankings). The music was produced for a TV spot for the vitamin energy drink Regain EB. The commercial shows Sakamoto playing his grand piano in the center of a busy intersection, soothing the tired office workers hurrying around him. Industry media at the time attributed the single's unexpected success to how the ad had "apparently struck a chord with middle-aged people coping with Japan's lingering recession and the end of the country's work-obsessed, high-growth era."[42] What was being sold in the case of "Energy Flow" was primarily an atmosphere of affective solace rather than a drink or a CD single. There is more than a little Satie in the melody and in the way the track can offer both the detached refinement of the classical piano and the rational utility of the energy drink, without either seeming to compromise the integrity of the other.

Sakamoto's piano score plays through the first twelve minutes of *Tony Takitani,* setting the mood for everything to follow. After wrapping up the location shoot, Ichikawa sent a rough cut of the film to Sakamoto in New York and asked him to create music that "might as well not have been there" (*nakutemo yokatta yō na*).[43] Sakamoto responded with three quiet themes for solo piano, each presented in several versions. The somber and sparsely textured "DNA" matches the film's methodical and unhurried journey through Tony's family background at the start of the film. "Solitude," the quietly propulsive main theme, is carried by minor-chord arpeggios and features a wistful melody shifting between different octaves as the film progresses. Last is "Fotografia," an Antonio Carlos Jobim–style piece matching Tony's brief period of marital bliss with a playful melody in a somewhat brighter key.

Almost 60 percent of the film's seventy-seven minutes is underscored with piano music, and the first half hour of the film features almost constant piano—only two and a half minutes are without the backing of Sakamoto's score. Along with the horizontal camera movement and the sparse but repetitive sound design, the steady minimalist pulse of these cues gives a strong sensation of the slow but inevitable passage of time. At the same time, the music infuses the whole film with a nostalgic and sentimental light, as if everything happening on-screen was already drifting off into the past. Operating much like Eiko's designer clothing, the music blankets the pain inside the story with a shimmering coat of beautiful solitude. The soundtrack functions as an ambient medium coming between audiences and the world of the story, allowing for a more detached appreciation of Tony's minimalist life as a fashionable object in its own right.

The exceptions that prove the rule are the few moments when the music stops, momentarily interrupting the sentimental drift. In the first two-thirds of the film, this happens only briefly and always during moments of heightened emotional tension: after Tony is first visited by Eiko and finds himself in love, while he is nervously waiting for her response to his marriage proposal, and when he finally confronts his wife about her uncontrollable spending. When after each of these pauses the piano returns and the camera begins to track right again, it brings with it a palpable sense of relief. Structured this way, the film's soundtrack encourages audiences to join Tony in taking refuge in the soft surfaces and ambient moods.

MELANCHOLY AND MOURNING

It is difficult to avoid getting wrapped up in the mood while spending time with the film. But step back, and it becomes clear this kind of subjective drift is exactly what is allowing Tony and Eiko to avoid confronting their own pain and the pain of others. Tony dwells neither on his absent mother and nearly absent father nor on how his father might be haunted by a war about which he himself has largely avoided thinking. He lives with his American name without ever reflecting on what exactly it means and why it causes others to treat him differently. Meanwhile, Eiko—who left another man to marry Tony, possibly as a way to fund her shopping compulsion—relies on clothing to cover over her own emotional struggle.[44]

As with many Murakami stories, it is tempting to try and understand the characters' motivations in psychoanalytical terms, even as missing details continually frustrate the attempt. This is true of minimalist music as well. Musicologists attempting to understand the pleasures of minimalist repetition have often turned back to Freud's analysis of melancholia and its strong association with the compulsion to repeat.[45] In contrast to mourning, which acknowledges the reality of loss, Freud saw in melancholia an attempt to repeat an imaginary past in order to avoid confronting the reality of the present. In this context, taking refuge in wistful moods and soft surfaces seems to mark a preference for aestheticizing a melancholic past rather than confronting a mournful present. This easily blends with the wider "culture of repetition" Fink notes as characteristic of consumer societies.

The culture of repetition and its techniques of emotional self-care are everywhere in the film, from Eiko's insatiable need to purchase new clothes to the repetitive structure of the cinematography and music. Japanese psychologists began to recognize compulsive shopping for high-end brands (*burando izonshō*) as a social problem beginning in the late 1990s, part of the fallout of the shift from the consumerism of the early 1980s to the recessionary years that followed. But the film never presents Eiko's attempt to cover her pain with aesthetic objects as a psychological strategy unique to her alone. Rather, by drawing parallels between Eiko's wardrobe and Shōzaburō's record collection, *Tony Takitani* begins tracing a more widespread practice of care for the self through consumer goods, even implicating the film itself in the process. The records reflect back directly on the role of the soundtrack, and the focus on fashion points to the many ways soft designer surfaces work to cover over more painful social realities. In the same way as the records and the clothing soothe Shōzaburō and Eiko, the ambient moods of *Tony Takitani* lend a comforting emotional sheen to the potentially disturbing histories the film evokes, feeding the repetition compulsion by allowing audiences to enjoy Tony's loneliness through a wistful backward gaze.

Yet even as the film flirts with the enticing repetition of consumerism, it never completely allows audiences to sink into a complacent drift. Following Eiko's death, Tony gradually begins to shift from melancholy to mourning, pulling himself out of the minimalist haze and learning to see others not as mere affective mood resources but as independent people with needs of their own. The mood of the film shifts too, as Sakamoto's score completely disappears from the soundtrack. Eiko's car accident is followed by what, in the context of what we have heard so far, is an extraordinarily long time without music: a full seventeen minutes. It is in this time Tony finally begins to confront the realities he so far has kept covered by the minor repetitions of his daily routine.

At first Tony is in shock after his wife's sudden death. He posts an ad in the newspaper for a woman of Eiko's measurements to come to his office wearing the outfits his wife left behind. But the substitute breaks down sobbing on coming into contact with Eiko's clothes. The only explanation she can offer—in a line straight out of Murakami favorite *The Great Gatsby*—is she has "never seen so many beautiful clothes all at once." Echoing Fitzgerald, here Murakami marks the affective power of objects above and beyond human comprehension.

Tony's *Vertigo*-style attempt to replace his wife with a look-alike at first seems absurd, but as Yamane Yumie notes, by seeing another woman in Eiko's clothing, Tony is finally able to begin distinguishing his wife from her many outfits, perhaps for the first time.[46] In doing so, he comes to understand her as a unique, irreplaceable human, beyond the surface of her clothing and its soothing affordances. Only then can he begin coming to terms with his wife's death. With this recognition of otherness—of Eiko as more than just a comforting surface—both Tony and *Tony Takitani* begin to shift from the repetition compulsion of melancholia to a process of mourning and gradual recovery.

The relative lack of music in the last half of the film marks this transition, dropping the ambient overlay of Sakamoto's score to present the lighter air of a life lived with less mediation. Music returns briefly at the one-hour mark, with the "DNA" theme again marking Tony's relationship with his past (this time as it is being reconfigured). The final six minutes of the film are again without music. Unlike the awkward silences of the first half of the film, however, these final unscored minutes are rich with the bustle of the outside world, textured with the sounds of the lives of others. Tony is still quiet and alone, but his melancholic mood begins to give way to an improvisational curiosity more willing to engage his surroundings.

This is a different type of quiet than what we experienced earlier. As the final voiceover implies, Tony becomes truly alone not when the people in his life disappear but when he finally empties his house of Eiko's and Shōzaburō's belongings. By letting go of his wife's clothing and his father's records, Tony distances himself from the use of mood-regulating objects as melancholy technologies of self. This in turn triggers a reconfiguration of the film's own approach to atmosphere. Sakamoto's score drops away once Tony lets go of the clothing and records, and the film begins tuning in to a more open form of ambience.

Seo Inwoo argues Tony's rejection of melancholic loneliness marks possibly the first moment in Murakami's writing where he begins to critique his generation's tendencies toward historical apathy and social isolation, qualities often embodied by his early narrators. This newfound respect for the social self would spur on Murakami to a series of more historically informed works later in the 1990s.[47]

In the case of Ichikawa's adaptation, however, it is difficult to know if the turn away from melancholic repetition really registers with audiences during the final seventeen minutes of the film, particularly when Sakamoto's wistful "Solitude" theme returns to accompany the ending credits. Sakamoto's score is almost overpowering in its articulation of Tony's wistful solitude, dominating the mood of the film as a whole and making it difficult for audiences to follow Tony's break with melancholy in the final minutes of the film.[48] Structurally, the film simply doesn't give enough time for a new mood to form.

However, the lighter mood at the film's end might also be understood as the culmination rather than the rejection of Tony's approach to low-affect living. Tony's move to eliminate all material connections with the past and be reborn afresh—as he lies in a fetal position in the now-empty wardrobe—is in itself a characteristically subtractivist response to the problem of historical memory (Figure 24). As Ahmed describes in her analysis of the 2002 British film *Bend It Like Beckham,* the melancholic is often figured as one who cannot "let go" of painful memories in order to move toward a happier future. But what if this past is something worth remembering? In the case of an assimilationist film like *Bend It Like Beckham,* Ahmed argues, the painful history of racism is precisely what the immigrant family learns to "let go" of in order to join the dominant white culture and its promise of happiness. The film visualizes this past through shots of the immigrant home's "dark and cramped" domestic interiors, contrasting this with the promise of freedom and mobility the main character finds when she leaves it behind to join a "multicultural" Britain on the outdoor soccer field.[49] In a similar way, the fashion and records cluttering Tony's apartment and weighing down his mood can be understood as more than consumer mood aids: they also serve the film as displaced markers of historical pain, from Shōzaburō's colonial exploits in Shanghai to Eiko's attempts to mask her own unspoken grief. From this perspective, when Tony sells these painful memories and finds peace in his now-empty home, he is letting go of not just melancholy but the past as well.

As Renu Bora has argued, the smooth, pristine surfaces often featured in "postmodern" design are not simply neutral and transparent:

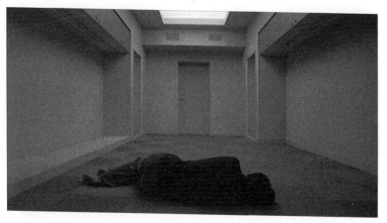

FIGURE 24. Tony lying in the now-empty wardrobe. Still from *Tony Takitani.*

by refusing to register any trace of prior tactile contact, they come to signify the "willed erasure" of their own history.[50] What makes an ambient film like *Tony Takitani* so resonant, I suggest, is how it positions viewers *both* to feel the immediate pleasure of this practice of self-erasure, of rubbing subjectivity smooth, and to feel the melancholic absence this subtractivism leaves behind. In this sense, it is important the film doesn't let viewers completely follow Tony into his blissful state of forgetfulness at the film's close but turns back to the wistfulness of Sakamoto's "Solitude" theme. As noted with the turn to isolationism in chapter 2, ambient media both aestheticize the peaceful dissolution of identity and mark the loss of what had to be subtracted to get there.

By implicating viewers' own desire for the beautiful solitudes it presents, the film makes Tony's attempts to break free from this lifestyle all the more emotionally resonant. It is this double-sidedness that makes *Tony Takitani,* in Manohla Dargis's succinct formulation, "a delicate wisp of a film with a surprisingly sharp sting."[51] In other words, the film expertly attunes audiences to the lush atmospheres of the subtractivist style but leaves an uneasy feeling that despite the calm drift of the film all is not quite right with the relationships it describes. While amply demonstrating the power of atmospheric design, the film pushes viewers to reflect on their own relationships with personal mood regulation, the way they too might use beautiful surfaces to cover over the emptiness inside.

As Washida Kiyokazu remarks at the beginning of his classic study of the phenomenology of clothing, when it comes to fashion it is often surprisingly difficult to distinguish pleasure from numbness.[52] Everyone and everything in Tony's life disappears over time, literally fading from the screen. This might at first sound traumatic, but within the ambient logic of the film, this exercise of subtraction comes across as a relief more than anything else, even as it remains tinged with a wistful melancholy. In a crowded and complex world, subjective ventilation becomes desirable in and of itself, even as it problematically renders other people mere obstacles (or tools) to getting there, and ultimately leaves Tony isolated and alone (Figure 25).

As the narrator describes in the final minutes of the film, Tony is eventually able to forget almost everything about his past, including his father and wife, but the one image he cannot shake is the memory of Eiko's substitute crying in the face of "so many beautiful clothes." Rather than match Eiko's despondency over the "emptiness inside," the film, like subtractivism more generally, follows her lead in covering the self with smooth, clean, and beautiful contours, avoiding pain as

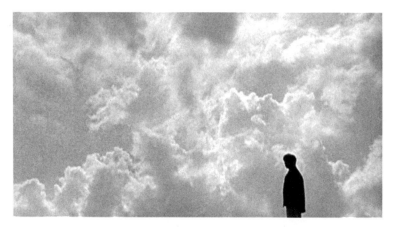

FIGURE 25. Subjective ventilation: Tony set against the open sky. Still from *Tony Takitani.*

much as possible by designing out stronger emotions, hurtful memories, and stubborn attachments. In this world personal autonomy is everything and can be found only through letting go. But as the ambient design of Ichikawa's film insistently reminds us, this world of soft surfaces and low-affect living will always arrive tinted by the sadness of all that was left behind.

/6/
HEALING STYLE

AMBIENT LITERATURE AND THE AESTHETICS OF CALM

Near the middle of Kurita Yuki's (1972–) novella *Hamizabesu* (Hamisabeth, 2002), a young woman becomes annoyed when a former coworker calls and pesters her for a date:

> I hung up the phone.
>> I pulled out the plug.
>>> Angry, I went to take a shower. While wandering around the room naked, my whole body started to tingle. It seems that because I was upset my circulation had improved. (66)

In Kurita's later novel *Oteru moru* (Hôtel Mole, 2005), a woman asks her boss why she was picked for the job of hotel receptionist. The boss replies:

> Your features. I knew when I saw your resume photograph, and I knew for sure when you came for the interview and I saw you sitting at the front desk. Your face is a face that invites sleep, or what in the industry we call a "sleep-inducing appearance." When customers see that face, they feel they are going to sleep well that night. (52)

These two scenes reveal two aspects of ambient mood regulation in postindustrial Japan. In the first example, the woman does not dwell on why the phone call was annoying. Instead, she shifts her mood by shifting her sensory environment: "Angry, I went to take a shower." She deals with ill feelings not with thinking but through water on the body and air on the skin. She displaces irritation on the level of affective sensory cues not dependent on cognition for their efficacy.

In the second example, the boss employs this same strategy of sensory displacement for commercial purposes. The receptionist's face generates a calming mood for customers, helping them to forget their worries. In both cases, the affective cues employed are not situationally specific. Characters use the shower, the air on naked skin, and the calming face for their ability to afford calming moods irrespective of context.

Such forms of transposable calm emerged in Japan in the mid-1990s as marketable commodities, both in therapeutic guises (relief from anxiety) and more generally in contexts of relaxation and stress relief. Around this time a new persona emerged in the media, the "healing style" (*iyashi-kei*) individual: a person (often but not always female) who puts those around them at ease.[1] This use of the term first emerged in reference to female television talk-show personalities and later expanded to include actresses, fashion models, comedians, politicians, and even academics. In more casual contexts, to dub someone healing style became shorthand for a personality type particularly adept at making others feel comfortable. Before long, self-help books emerged, usually for woman, on how to embody the healing style persona for advancement both professionally and personally. For example, Hanebayashi Yuzu's 2005 *Iyashi-kei josei ni naru hinto* (Hints on becoming a healing style woman) gathers one hundred relationship counselors to advise readers on how to "make him feel relieved and fall in love."

As a supplement to this kind of emotional labor, other healing style objects went on the market promising to help their purchasers attune to a more relaxed self, including products for a wide variety of therapeutic modalities (aromatherapy, pet therapy, color therapy, plant therapy, sound therapy, art therapy, massage therapy, sex therapy, etc.), television shows, pornography, and robots. Desperate for an expanded demographic to make up for the declining birthrate in Japan, toy companies like Bandai began marketing relaxation toys directly to adults. One example is the million-seller Primo Puel series of talking dolls, introduced in 2000. The toy was initially marketed to twentysomething working women but soon found popularity among the middle aged and elderly as well. One version produces four hundred phrases, such as "kiss me" or "I'm lonely," and recognizes spoken phrases like "I'm home" and "let's play."[2] Ambient media was incorporated into this larger boom in healing products, alongside a wider range of relaxation-oriented art, music, photography, and video. Healing style goods emerged not to "heal" any particular illness but to serve as technologies to help the bedraggled subjects of recessionary Japan tune in to the low-affect urban ideal. All of these products shared the promise of producing calm for (and in) the consumer. Market watchers began to speak of a "healing boom."

Ironically, these "healing goods" (*iyashi guzzu*) could promise relaxation in part because they offered a break from all of the other affective appeals encountered daily in contemporary Japanese media. In contrast to commercially motivated affective appeals, *iyashi* goods offered their users the chance to construct a personal affective space free of outside intervention. At the same time, the marketing of these goods gave rise to an advertising discourse of "stress relief" and "healing" aimed at the creation of new consumer desires and demands for self-care.

As journalists and cultural critics never failed to point out, the "healing boom" emerged directly in the aftermath of the two largest traumas of late twentieth-century Japan: the Kobe earthquake and the Aum Shinrikyō sarin gas attacks, both in early 1995. These episodes of national trauma—along with the more widespread effects of the economic recession and subsequent restructuring—were often said to have provided the emotional context for the emergence of calm as a lucrative and marketable feeling.[3]

While the widespread anxiety triggered by these events may have played some role, the explosion of healing goods in the late 1990s was but the most pronounced stage of a much longer-term shift toward technologies of mood regulation. As historian Tanaka Satoshi describes, the *iyashi* trend is the most recent in a long string of healing booms in modern Japan. Early twentieth-century trends included practices such as the all-vegetable-soup diet, the drinking of one's own urine in the morning, and the practice of attaching coins to the body with cellophane tape, to name only a few examples.[4] Another boom occurred in the 1960s and 1970s with the emergence of "natural" healing products promising to provide restoration and relaxation and guard against the stresses of "modern life." The emerging therapy industry introduced a remarkable string of supplements and exercise trends around this time, particularly once the mass media recognized self-care as a perennially popular (and low-cost) focus for television and print media. Early commercial successes included the comfrey boom in the year following the Tokyo Olympics (1965) and the best-selling book on "garlic healing methods" by Watanabe Tadashi (1973).[5] This was followed by a parade of new health trends from 1975 to 1980, most of them still on the market today: goji berries, *umeboshi,* shiitake, kombucha, maifan stones, bamboo foot massage, rice vinegar, Manchurian wild rice, hydrangea soup, pollen, deep-sea shark liver oil, chlorella, pickled chicken eggs, aloe, reishi mushrooms, geranium, digestive enzymes, magnetic necklaces, treadmills, and exercise equipment for hanging upside down (*burasagari kenkōki*). Candy maker Kotobuki opened Natural House, Japan's first natural food supermarket, in Jiyūgaoka, Tokyo, in 1978.[6]

The stated goal of these new health trends was often less gaining a competitive edge and more simply "coping" with the perceived stresses of contemporary society. One of the principles Tanaka notes at the heart of the high-growth-era healing trends is a tendency to equate human civilization (*bunmei*) with illness and nature (*shizen*) with health—a core tenet of romanticism updated for the age of therapy culture. This emphasis on the "natural" was a significant shift in focus from health fads earlier in the century, which often touted their origins in cutting-edge science to prove their futuristic powers to overcome sickness.[7] In part, this backlash against scientific progress reflected the growing public awareness of human-generated environmental problems. The hard sciences lost much of their futuristic allure, and attention turned toward the creation of environments felt to be more "organically" suitable for nurturing human health. By the 1970s advertisements for healing goods shifted to promote therapies based on supposedly more natural, ecological, and holistic principles.

Yet what was on offer in most cases here was rarely what was explicitly claimed: a return to a more "natural" way of living or a return to a state of health before the onset of stress or illness. Rather, what the new goods implicitly promised was the ability to manage one's personal comfort and energy levels. Once "illness" became generalized into a failure to adapt to the demands of city living, "healing" could transform into a euphemism for this ongoing pursuit of increased emotional control and a comfortable, mood-regulated lifestyle.[8] Such forms of self-care no longer were only a temporary need in an otherwise productive life but turned instead into core techniques of ongoing subjective maintenance. The emphasis was on somatic technologies as "techniques of the self" (to again use Foucault's term), to be used by a person to manipulate his or her own daily emotional and energetic rhythms. This more personal approach to mood regulation—beginning in the late 1970s and peaking in the late 1990s—was the first to emphasize transposable calm as a personal means of coping with the contemporary.

Japanese fiction has reconfigured its affective appeals in order to compete with and reflect upon this mood-regulating culture through what I call "ambient literature." Like the other ambient media described in this book, ambient literature is an aesthetic response to the demand for transposable calm. Ambient literature rethinks the novel as a mood-regulating device. Like the ambient cinema discussed in the previous chapter, ambient literature has two major aims: to generate calming moods and to provide a space to reflect back on therapy culture as a whole.

Kurita Yuki's work can be situated in a growing body of ambient literature that, like other ambient media, embraces the affordance of calming moods as a primary objective. Japanese fiction began to reflect the new culture of mood regulation as early as the late 1970s with Murakami Haruki's debut novel, *Kaze no uta o kike* (Hear the wind sing, 1979). In a 2002 book on "post-Murakami" literature, literary critic Nakamata Akio cites this work as the first major example of what would become a dominant trend in Japanese literature of the 1980s and 1990s: the "healing style novel" (*iyashi-kei shōsetsu*). Murakami's narrator states at the outset of the book his reason for writing is a "small attempt at healing himself." Nakamata elaborates:

> Murakami Haruki starts writing as a "small attempt to heal himself," but at the same time he also heals [*iyasu*] many of his readers. It is well known Murakami managed a jazz bar during his student years. It might be too much to imagine Murakami as a barkeep, soothing the souls of his customers by listening to their worries. But in fact, Murakami's writing can be read as one kind of "healing style" fiction.[9]

While the term *healing style* dates to more than a decade after Murakami's debut novel, Nakamata's anachronistic use of the term is apt. Murakami's early work charts much of the affective terrain of what came to characterize later ambient literature, including, as Nakamata points out, an avoidance of psychological interiority and a preference for light, transparent diction.[10]

Yoshimoto Banana (1964–) is also well known for the calming effect of her writing, beginning with her debut novel, *Kitchen* (1988). Ann Sherif describes how Yoshimoto's narratives concern "the process of grieving and healing and exhibit a steadfast belief in the possibility of reintegration into society, even after extreme alienation or trauma." She quotes Tokyo psychiatrist Machizawa Shizuo, who describes how even his suicidal patients are able to find in Yoshimoto's novels "an optimism and brightness absent in their own lives."[11]

In the wake of the popular success of Murakami and Yoshimoto, a number of younger novelists developed styles engaging mood regulation and healing themes more directly. These include Kurita Yuki (1972–), Seo Maiko (1974–), and Ōshima Masumi (1962–).[12] These novelists began their careers at a time when literature was competing for affective space with the more directly mood-oriented practices of the therapy culture industry. This chapter focuses on the ambient literary style they devised in response and the way it negotiates between narrative tension and the atmospheric affordance of calm.

THE HÔTEL DE MOLE DORMONS BIEN

Kurita's works are particularly compelling in their exploration of an ambient literary aesthetics.[13] This chapter focuses on her 2005 novel *Hôtel Mole,* a work deftly deploying the calming resources of ambient literary style at the same time as it casts a critical (and sometimes satirical) gaze on therapy culture itself. The novel tells the story of twenty-three-year-old Honda Kiri, a young woman beginning her first real job: a night-shift attendant running the front desk of the Hôtel de Mole Dormons Bien. She soon learns the Hôtel de Mole is no ordinary Japanese business hotel. Everything about the hotel is geared toward providing the highest-quality sleep possible. Interviews are conducted with potential guests concerning personal sleep history. Check-in occurs immediately after sunset, and checkout, at sunrise. The guest rooms are entirely underground—up to thirteen floors down—and have regulated light timers to ensure ideal levels of darkness. The lobby, which Kurita describes in great detail, is designed to generate relaxing, soporific moods as guests make their way to their rooms. As the human face of the hotel's relaxing promise, Kiri is trained to impart a warm and soothing welcome to hotel guests. The narrative follows Kiri from her job interview, through her training, and on to her first weeks alone on the job. Along the way she begins to unravel the mystery of how the hotel generates such deep sleep. Interspersed with these episodes are scenes set at Kiri's home focused on her complicated relationship with her sickly identical twin sister.

The popular reception of Kurita's fiction has been marked by an emphasis on the soothing quality of her writing. In a review of *Hôtel Mole* in the literary journal *Bungakukai,* Higashi Naoko reports on the powerful physiological effect the novel had on her: "Several times while reading this mysterious story, I was overcome with sleepiness. This certainly was not because I was bored. . . . In the same way a delicious description of food triggers hunger, the qualities of sleep were so powerfully portrayed here that I became quite sleepy."[14] Higashi ends the review by noting she plans to keep the novel near her pillow at night to function as a sort of talisman to prevent insomnia and promote restful sleep. In a review of an earlier Kurita work, *Onuiko Terumii* (The seamstress Terumii, 2004), critic Yoshida Nobuko writes in a similar vein, reporting that just after reading she felt full of warmth. Novelist

Kakuta Mitsuyo likewise feels her spirit is lifted after reading Kurita's novels.[15]

Hôtel Mole affords its readers therapeutic forms of calm not just through its sleepy setting but through the strategic deployment of an ambient literary style. While the act of reading demands at least a minimum degree of attention, ambient literature deploys a range of techniques to develop emotionally calming and environmentally immersive atmospheres. As I describe in the next section, Kurita's work draws upon all levels of textual form to generate these moods, beginning with the most minute elements—individual words—and building outward to the level of narrative flow and the emotional dynamics of the story as a whole.

AMBIENT LITERARY AESTHETICS

The words in *Hôtel Mole* are mostly common, familiar terms. The vocabulary is not the sort to give readers pause or confusion. This does not mean the words express simple meanings, simply that they are simply put. For example, to describe mystery, Kurita sticks to the most familiar adjective available, *fushigi* (mysterious). The novel does not engage in the refinement of emotional tone through descriptive variety. Instead, *fushigi* remains *fushigi*—a familiar term for the unfamiliar. Common words like *fushigi* cue a mysterious atmosphere but do so in a nonspecific way. While every reader of Japanese has a familiarity with this word, the word is at the same time general enough to be unlikely to cue any specific details or images. This allows it to invoke a general atmosphere of mystery while maintaining a dispersed, amorphous state of attention. *Fushigi* is an ambience.

This same aesthetic of ambiguity through transparency is replicated on the level of the sentence. The text on the back cover of *Hôtel Mole*, likely the first description readers will encounter upon picking up the book, summarizes the novel in three straightforward lines:

> Maiban, Oteru Moru ni wa nemuri o motomete hito ga
>   atsumaru.
> Shiawase na nemuri o teikyō suru fushigi na hoteru.
> Nichijō kara hon no sukoshi kairi shita sekai de
>   motarasareru monogatari.

> Every night, people in search of sleep gather at the Hôtel
>   Mole.

> A mysterious hotel offering happy sleep.
> A story taking place in a world just a little separated from everyday life.

The words employed here—with the minor exception perhaps of *kairi shita* (estranged or separated)—could hardly be more everyday. This is a mysterious story about people who gather at a hotel to find blissful sleep. This curious premise is stated as matter-of-factly as possible. As the final line signals, this is a mystery departing just a tiny bit (*hon no sukoshi*) from the familiar (a "world on the other side of daily life," to borrow Ise's phrase from chapter 3). This is not the gaping anxiety of a mystery threatening to topple the known world. Instead, just a touch of mystery surfaces, contained and vaguely familiar, not unlike a daydream.

Notice the last two sentences in the summary are fragments. The copula is implied, but its absence emphasizes the final nouns in both lines. A mysterious hotel. A story detached from everyday life. The nouns are invoked in parallel as if the hotel and the tale (*monogatari*) were one and the same. The idea of gathering for a pleasant sleep provides an assurance of calm while the little bit of mystery—the curiosity of a hotel designed entirely for sleeping—promises comfortable uncertainties and soft fascinations to let the imagination wander.

This basic equation of familiar simplicity plus comfortable mystery governs the emotional architecture of ambient literature. Sentence structure, like diction, tends toward the straightforward and evocative. The phrasing is short, light, and succinct. Kurita's readers often comment on the sense of ease afforded by the lightness and precision of her language. Ishii Shinji, in the afterword to Kurita's 2002 novella *Hamisabeth,* describes her diction as exact (*seikaku*), avoiding vague nuance and "using the ordinary meanings shared by everyone."[16] He notes surplus exposition is studiously avoided, as is any belabored explanation of characters' emotional states. The story flows by smooth and easy.

But Ishii senses something more than simplicity of language has contributed to the smooth (*surusuru*) experience of reading Kurita. Here, he turns to the mystery part of the equation and in the process uncovers precisely what is "healing" about Kurita's style:

> Kurita doesn't write about unknowns as if they were knowns. The unknown is enshrined in the depths of the novel as it is [*sonomama*] and expressed with exquisite precision, as if affixed with a pair of tweezers, in a language

everyone can understand. For the reader, the meanings
of the various words are easily understood. But at the
same time, just beyond this surface covering of language,
the structure and meaning of the "unknown"—as an
"unknown"—becomes thoroughly absorbed.[17]

What Ishii describes here is the way ambient literature paradoxically
reaches at mystery through a language that does not reach at all. Unlike
the Kantian sublime, which seeks a direct confrontation with the enor-
mity of the unknown in a moment of shock and terror, the ambient
approach to mystery is simply to leave mystery as mystery, transmuting
the unknown not by attempting to arrest it in language but through
a careful evocation of the familiar qualities leading in its (unspoken)
direction. Instead of attempting to plumb the depths directly, ambient literature's placid language evokes the depths through the translu-
cency of its shallow surfaces.

SENSORY INVOCATION

Kurita achieves perceptual clarity while maintaining semantic uncertainty by emphasizing sensory detail. As Elaine Scarry describes in
Dreaming by the Book, writers can achieve a high degree of perceptual vivacity by instructing readers to imagine the material conditions
necessary to produce a given sense perception. When reading literature, "what in perception comes to be imitated is not only the sensory
outcome (the way something looks or sounds or feels beneath the
hands), but the actual structure of production that gave rise to the perception."[18] Ambient literature makes extensive use of this technique,
with detailed mimetic depictions of characters encountering soft fascinations in their sensory surroundings—the soothingness of sound,
texture, color, light, temperature, and so on. Many of these encounters focus especially on the tactile qualities of objects. The characters'
hands here operate not as levers to move things around but as media to
feel and explore the textures of the atmospheric spaces inside the story.
As Deleuze writes, "It is the tactile which can constitute a pure sensory image, on condition that the hand relinquishes its prehensile and
motor functions to content itself with pure touching."[19] In this way the
characters' perceiving hands become extensions of the hands of the
reader, which are themselves occupied with holding the book.
     During Kiri's first visit to the hotel, her attention is drawn to the
chair behind the front desk as she waits to be interviewed:

> The chair was nice. Tall enough to support the back of the head, with armrests as well. The surface felt like velvet, making me want to keep stroking it. I reached out my hand to touch the back of the chair. My fingers felt something hard. Taking a closer look, I saw a plastic plate about the size of my little finger. It said "Cowhide." Was this to explain what the chair was made of? I tried sitting down. Even through my clothes, I could feel the suppleness of the leather on my skin. I closed my eyes and soon felt my body yielding to the softness. A moan of comfort began to bubble up from deep within my throat. (13)

While this paragraph does not move the plot forward in any significant way, Kiri's hands here play the crucial function of invoking a receptive sensory awareness of the surrounding environment and in turn reinforcing the overall ambient mood. This type of tactile encounter reappears throughout the novel.

As Ishii points out, Kurita's descriptions of such seemingly mundane objects as a desk chair are characteristically careful and precise. This textual precision is thematized in the narrative by the small plastic plates Kiri finds affixed to objects throughout the hotel, each revealing the material used in the object's construction. At first, Kiri is puzzled by such attention to detail, but when she later asks her boss about the plates, she receives the rather oblique answer that they are there "so the employees do not become confused" (36). As Kiri eventually comes to recognize, part of generating a relaxing atmosphere in the hotel involves paying attention not only to visual appearances but also to the more immediate tactile qualities of the hotel's surfaces.

There is, however, more to this passage than the introduction of precise material details. The vivacity of this description comes through how Kiri does not so much tell readers how the chair feels but rather guides them through the perceptual experience of her body coming into contact with the material. Readers sense the chair not as an isolated visual object but through the caress of a hand against its surface, the feeling of support along the head and arms, the cool yielding of the leather under the weight of the body. Scarry notes such passages are made vivid by how "the people on the inside of the fiction report to us on the sensory qualities in there that we ourselves cannot reach or test."[20] Kiri's sensory contact evokes readers' own haptic responses. Notice how differently the passage reads with Kiri's presence removed: "The back of the chair was tall, with armrests. The surface was velvety. On the back was a hard plastic plate reading 'Cowhide.' This may have been to explain what the chair was made of. The leather was soft." This more objective description gives just as much technical information about the chair but has almost none of the sensory and emotional resonance of the original. As Scarry emphasizes, moments of imagined contact give described objects their sense of solidity and weight: the hand on the leather, the body on the chair, the head on the headrest. Such moments bring a sensory immediacy to the chair it otherwise lacks.

But what makes this encounter with the chair so soothing? This paragraph in microcosm contains all the criteria for a calm encounter: a sense of suppleness and ease combined with a stable base of embodied security and support. The headrest and armrests are crucial here. What enables Kiri to sink into the chair, even closing her eyes, is not only the velvety softness of the leather but also the sense of safety, of ontological security, of being held. Scarry describes John Locke's notion of the vital emotional role played by the perception of solidity. By promising to stop "our further sinking downwards," solidity "establishes the floor beneath us that, even as we are unmindful of it, makes us cavalier about venturing out."[21] This supportive background is crucial for creating an ambient space. In ambient literature tactile feelings of ontological security provide the absolute background against which the imagination can venture out and explore the unknown. Securely held by these literary furnishings, a reader can confidently explore ideas and experiences that might otherwise be too unfamiliar or threatening.

After adjusting to the soft surfaces of the hotel, Kiri realizes the tension she was feeling in anticipation of her job interview has dissipated, and she feels so relaxed she almost starts to yawn. In the novel itself, however, no causal relation is ever asserted between the hotel's design and Kiri's relaxed state. Despite Kiri's detailed description of the objects around her, she never offers any explicit reflection on how these ambient aspects of the hotel are working to make her sleepy. Instead, she leads readers with her through a number of sensory encounters and then simply describes how she is feeling. These descriptions serve as direct physiological cues for readers, much in the way reading about yawning is often enough to make a person begin to yawn.

The high redundancy of emotional cues in *Hôtel Mole* pointing toward a relaxing mood helps ensure that even if every reader does not respond to every affective cue and even if individual cues are of varying impact based on the different sensory proclivities of each reader, the cumulative effect will still be to firmly establish an ambient mood. This additive process is especially crucial in the early pages of the book. Establishing this strong emotional framework early on serves to orient readers' expectations for the remainder of the novel. Later, even if comparatively discomforting emotional cues appear, the strength of these earlier sensory experiences helps to weight the novel's affective focus toward a dominant mood of calm. Moods have a great deal of inertia. Already in a relaxed mood, readers are apt to focus on elements reinforcing this atmosphere of calm and to deemphasize those elements working against it.[22]

This is not to say a shift in emotional tone later in the text would have no consequences. To maintain a mood, emotional cues must be reintroduced periodically. This is precisely what happens throughout *Hôtel Mole*. Over the course of the book, Kiri makes her way deeper into the hotel (from the lobby to the elevator, the bedrooms, and finally the lowest floor in the building), each time describing in detail her sensory surroundings. Each scene reinforces a mood of calm uncertainty while venturing deeper into the unknown.

ESTABLISHING AN INCUBATORY SPACE

Like other forms of ambient entrainment, ambient literature builds an enveloping space around readers as they read. The "healing" aspect of the healing style refers not to the alleviation of a particular ailment but to the restorative atmosphere within which healing can occur. This safe enclosure provides a heightened level of protection from exterior threats, allowing a person to redirect energies usually devoted to coping with the outside world to the interior task of physical and emotional healing. This incubatory structure is found (at least ideally) in in-patient hospital care, in the protected emotional space of the therapy session, and, perhaps in its oldest guise, in the practice of the spiritual retreat.[23]

The design of the Hôtel de Mole focuses on nurturing this sense of envelopment, of being held within a warm, safe, womb-like space. To reach the front door of the hotel, Kiri first passes through an inconspicuous alleyway hidden between two buildings. The alley is so narrow it seems impossible to pass to the other side, but by turning sideways, Kiri is able to slide through. She announces her name over the intercom, and the doors slide smoothly open. She enters and feels the doors quietly slide closed behind her. Before her is a long hallway. The walls are beige; the ceiling, a deep wine red. As Kiri walks forward, every step sinks softly and inaudibly into the carpet. Everything is quiet. The lighting is faint, and she cannot see her wristwatch through the darkness. As she looks up, she realizes the ceiling is unusually low.

After some time, Kiri reaches the end of the hall and emerges into a large reception area. The walls are concave, giving the room a spherical shape. Long curtains made of a thick and heavy material hang from the ceiling. They are also a dark and rich shade of wine. To one side sits the front desk and the leather chair previously described. On the other side hangs a large painting, about the size, Kiri notes, of a double bed. The painted image is abstract and composed entirely of dark colors. Nearby, a small source of light flickers near one of the walls. It wavers now and then, like a candle. Kiri smells a faint hint of wax in the air. Below the painting sits a sofa. Or rather, something like the seating area of a sofa curves directly out of the wall, part of the building itself.

These descriptions, each related through Kiri's perceptual experience, vividly instruct readers to conjure the sensory experience of entering the enclosed space of the hotel. Everything is designed to be womb-like, a place of perceptual softening and incubated security. The initial obstacles to entering position the space "a little bit apart" from everyday life. The low lighting, hushed acoustics, and faint aromas allow the senses to relax and open, while the soft fabrics, warm colors, round walls, and low ceiling provide a feeling of being enveloped and held.

The novel evokes this setting within its first twenty pages, establishing a vivid sensory space where the more fleeting, almost ghostly presence of the characters can drift. The hotel mixes familiar comforts with an edge of the uncanny—an unknown safe enough to drift through calmly. Immediately after these initial encounters, Kiri relates her experience entering the hotel in just this manner:

> My impression of the entrance hall is rather different from other hotels I have visited. It isn't like a resort hotel, a city hotel, or a love hotel. But it isn't strange enough to feel unfamiliar. I feel like I have been somewhere like this before. But then it isn't like any of my friends' homes, or the room of a lover—of course, this isn't a house at all. Why does it feel so familiar, I wonder? (15)

Kiri is intrigued that despite the lack of windows and plants, the space does not feel lonely. The entrance hall is strangely comforting. At the same time as being incubatory, however, the space is open and porous. The Hôtel de Mole is a space of social circulation, with a new population every night. Like airports, train stations, and waiting rooms, hotels are public spaces to the degree they welcome any person who can afford access and agree to follow the rules. While the hotel establishes a space set off from the street, it still maintains a conduit to the outside. The space is designed to be welcoming yet anonymous, a familiar path into the unknown.

This is also true for books, if we understand them as portable worlds that can accompany movement through urban space. The small format of many Japanese novels—especially paperbacks—makes them ideal companions during the long train commutes of many urban Japanese readers.[24] The paperback, no less than the portable audio player, can be thought of as a mobile technology of mood regulation. On reading *Hôtel Mole,* these transitory commuter spaces resonate with the transient spaces within the novel, allowing the hotel's restorative mood to seep into the space surrounding the book. In this way, readers of ambient literature are made comfortable about venturing out while in the act of venturing out—affording, perhaps, a new way of relating to public space.

AMBIENT SUBJECTIVATION IN LITERATURE

In carving out a space of mystery within familiar everyday rhythms, readers find new ways of relating to routine. As we have seen with ambient music, video, and film, one way ambient media move through the familiar to the unknown is by tapping into the estranging and vitalizing qualities of repetition. The time of ambient literature follows the tempo and repetition of a regulated modern life. The pace of *Hôtel Mole* is organized around the workday. Kiri applies for a job, has her interview, commutes back and forth to work, and slowly becomes adjusted to working at the hotel. She wakes, goes to work, comes home, dreams, wakes, and goes to work again. Adhering to the temporality of the workday evacuates narrative momentum from the novel and replaces it with a sense of expansive, nondirectional time. Ambient literature avoids spectacle and drama, producing a sensation of perpetual drift rather than movement through a sequence of events.

The free-floating repetition of the everyday merges with the atmospheric quality of the self in ambient literature, where identities are shadowy and rarely asserted with force. While Kiri's physiological state is described and the subplot concerning her troubled twin sister serves as the emotional trauma upon which the healing qualities of the hotel work their powers, the characters in *Hôtel Mole* mostly remain lightly sketched, only barely outlined, never fully coming into view. As Nakamata points out, this type of "empty" characterization is common in contemporary Japanese literature from Murakami Haruki onward. Nakamata proposes this downplaying of psychological interiority has something cinematic about it, as if the narrator was a free-floating camera-eye, unreflective but carefully recording every sensory detail.[25] Such ambiguity allows a character to become a medium through which readers can wander and feel these unfamiliar spaces. Whereas plot-oriented narratives structure themselves around identification with characters, in the aesthetics of ambience "identification is actually inverted: the character has become a kind of viewer."[26] As noted, Kiri acts less as a self-conscious subject than as a sensing body, lending her perceptual organs to the reader.

As noted earlier, the emergence of such forms of decentered self has often been explained by referring to the collapse of larger narrative orientations, which in Japan is often linked back to the traumas of modernization, World War II, "postmodern" culture, or the recent recessionary decades. As I have argued throughout this book, however, this mode of dispersed subjectivity might be described not as a symptom of social collapse but as a creative and highly adaptive form of engagement with the designed environments of postindustrial life. The technologies of personalized mood control have spurred a recognition that affective environments play a fundamental role in humans' sense of being in and amid the world. These sensory modes of being run parallel and in some ways prior to more narrative, interiorized forms of identity. Like other forms of ambient media, ambient literature enables readers to dissolve discrete identities into moods of open-ended affective exploration, free from the usual demands of their social and discursive selves.

Compared with more plot-oriented styles, where sensory spaces are mapped onto a relatively rigid architecture of plot and character, ambient literature prefers the internal flexibility of the incubatory space, allowing readers to enter in, feel around, and let their own emotional and affective responses seep into the work. Echoing Roland Barthes's distinction between writerly and readerly texts, Kurita, in dialogue with novelist Kakuta Mitsuyo, discusses the difference between novels more geared toward a writer expressing himself or herself and texts asking the reader to step into the novel's space and collaborate in the production of meaning. Kakuta observes how, compared with other writers, Kurita expressly writes for her readers, consciously opening a line of communication with them. Kurita responds by emphasizing the need to leave a space open for the reader to become involved in the text: "I like novels where I can think while I am reading. The novel is there, and I am there. I like things that create this space [*ma*] for me. Novels where, in this space, we can begin to influence each other."[27] Kurita here identifies a key function of her writing: like Eno wrote of ambient music, ambient literature provides "a space to think." The combination of the incubatory envelope and the blurring of self allows readers to engage with the novel not as discrete and bounded people but as malleable bodies that can roam a space and be transformed by its atmosphere. Deleuze describes how in such amorphous spaces "we no longer know what is imaginary or real, physical or mental, . . . not because they are confused, but because we do not have to know and there is no longer even a place from which to ask."[28] Ambient subjectivation relaxes the usual borders of self and not self, allowing for a more porous and improvisatory engagement with the senses. As Hans Gumbrecht notes, "The literary elaboration of atmospheres and moods, whose structure one need not recognize, makes it possible to be transported, via imagination, into situations in which physical sensation and psychic constitution become inseparable."[29] Ambient literature provides a means for the usual specificities of self to relax into the more indeterminate contours of imagined space.

ATMOSPHERE–NARRATIVE COUNTERPOINT

Crucially, however, ambient narrative forms never abandon the structural dynamics of storytelling—the buildup of tensions and their eventual release. Instead, they draw upon the larger rhythms of narrative description in order to fold these moments back into an overarching ambient mood. *Hôtel Mole* oscillates between more explicitly ambient scenes of calming evocation set in the hotel and more narrative character-driven scenes set in Kiri's home. As with ambient cinema, this allows ambient literature some space for the novel to critically reflect on therapy culture at the same time as it pursues its own relaxing strategies.

The home scenes in *Hôtel Mole* serve two main functions. First, they reveal just enough about Kiri's character for readers to begin to empathize with her. We learn Kiri is selflessly raising her twin sister's child, after this sickly sibling again entered the hospital for a long-term stay. We learn working at the Hôtel de Mole is Kiri's first real job after graduating from school and that her career has so far been postponed in order to care for her sister and her sister's child. Without delving into complex psychological motivations, this home context helps develop a stronger resonance between Kiri's feelings and the reader's own.

The second function of this subplot is to set into motion a gradual narrative trajectory from illness to wellness. "Healing" itself, after all, implies a narrative arc from sickness to health. Over the course of the book, Kiri comes to terms with her twin's continued ill health and gradually achieves competence in her position as front desk manager. The novel ends as the tension of both these challenges is finally and fully dissolved. The emotional contour of the narrative is something like a steadily smoothing sine wave. The novel begins by oscillating between scenes of calm sensory evocation in the hotel and less ambient scenes of Kiri and her family at home. While these latter scenes allow us to get to know and empathize with Kiri outside work, they also offer emotional interludes; comparatively familiar and normative spaces serve as a counterpoint to the strange ambience of the hotel. Over the course of the book, these two realms gradually merge, first through Kiri's dreams (she has a particularly vivid dream of childhood while testing out one of the hotel beds) and finally by introducing the ill sister into the healing space of the hotel itself. The peaks and troughs of this quiet/disquiet oscillation slowly level out and eventually synthesize in the harmonious sense of integration that ends the book. Kiri's troubled relationship with her sister begins to improve precisely as she gains competence in running the hotel. In this unraveling pendular structure, characteristic of the ambient novel, we experience—and we *feel* in the slowing pace of the text—how ambient spaces can unravel all narrative tensions. Everything merges with the night.

AFFECTIVE CONTRACTS

Kiri's emotional journey might have turned out differently. The candle in the lobby might have tipped over and burned the hotel down, shifting the emotional trajectory of the story and displacing the ambient mood. But this would take it out of the genre of ambient literature, breaking the affective contract implicit to the form. Genre functions as a mood-orienting frame. Film theorist Noël Carroll notes how "some genres seem to traffic in certain specifiable emotions essentially. That is, certain genres appear to have as their abiding point the elicitation of specifiable emotional states in audiences."[30] Different genres also promise a different spectrum of emotional diversity. Epics, for example, often mix in feelings associated with romance, action, tragedy, suspense, and comedy within the same narrative. Other genres are more focused on delving deep into a single emotional register. Ambient media belong to the latter category, and audiences often come to the works primed for a calming affective experience.

As Kurita notes, these emotional expectations are present not only in the way readers approach particular genres but also in readers' expectations for specific authors.[31] A regular reader of an author's works knows from experience the limits on the type of episodes (and the associated emotions) a writer will invoke. Readers can trust the author will see them through to the end of the story without breaching these boundaries. They are then safe to open themselves emotionally to the novel, reading with a sense of ease and security and knowing their emotional investment will not be suddenly betrayed as the story progresses. As in ambient music, video, and film, atmosphere in ambient literature depends on the gradual building up of trust between audience and text, through the continual reinforcement of calming affect in a variety of registers, allowing readers to relax into the atmosphere of the work.

Paradoxically, the overarching stability of the ambient atmosphere allows for some freedom in the moment-to-moment texture of the story. As Kurita points out, as long as this trust is maintained, the author can include some rather disturbing episodes, and readers will still be able to entrust themselves to the author's care (*mi o makaserareru*).[32] There are some fairly traumatic episodes even in *Hôtel Mole*. In one of the few flashbacks to Kiri's past within the novel, we learn she returned home one day to find her boyfriend having sex with her twin sister, leading to the sister's pregnancy and the birth of her niece. Meanwhile, at the hotel Kiri at times becomes nervous about her new responsibilities managing the front desk. All of this is narrated within a general context of ambient calm, however, ensuring these obstacles do not derail the overall mood of the novel. The atmospheric stability provides an opportunity to reflect back on traumatic experience from a more equanimous perspective.

In sum, ambient literature generates calm uncertainty through the accumulated effects of the techniques described here: transparent diction and sensory invocation, the generation of incubatory spaces around which ambient subjects can roam, and the gradual development of embodied security within the safety of the affective contract. All of these small- and large-scale affordances additively form the enveloping mood of an ambient work.

The approach to literature outlined here treats mood regulation as the primary work done by a text—literature creates mood spaces through which identity can become more malleable, affording relaxation and repose. Needless to say, adapting literature to be a tool of ambient subjectivation marks a shift away from earlier models of literary and aesthetic production. The final section considers the arguments of those who pushed against the turn toward the healing style in Japanese literature and situates ambience within larger debates over the role of therapy culture in contemporary Japan.

HEALING DEBATES

As noted earlier, ambient literature's ability to engage in a free play of subjectivation always comes with a trade-off: in order to develop an incubatory calm, the ambient novel must distance itself from the outside world and the more upsetting or exciting forms of emotion that might be triggered there. "Healing" incubation demands the emotional aperture opening onto the outside world be narrowed down. So while ambient literature may provide a space to think, it does not necessarily provide a space to think anything particularly distressing. Eno's assertion ambient music "must be as ignorable as it is interesting" also marks the limitations of ambience as a method of direct social critique.

Criticism of ambient literature often expresses concern over this prioritization of personal affect in contemporary Japanese culture. In a well-known complaint about Murakami Haruki, novelist Ōe Kenzaburō directly laments the "Muzak" elements in Murakami's writing:

> Murakami doesn't take an active attitude toward society, or even toward the immediate environments of daily life. He works by passively absorbing influences from various genres, as if he were listening to background music. He just goes on spinning within his interior fantasy world.[33]

As Ōe's comments indicate, the aspects of ambient literature most troubling to its critics are its apparent "passivity" with regard to social and political issues and its tendency to retreat into imagined interiors.

Literary critic Kuroko Kazuo, in an article critiquing both Yoshimoto Banana and the larger "healing" trend, worries over Yoshimoto's steadfast belief in the power of mood regulation. Kuroko cites Yoshimoto's description of how sometimes, when she is feeling bad, simply eating a piece of cake is all that is necessary for her to turn her feelings around and be happy for the rest of the day. Kuroko points to this therapeutic use of food as an example of Yoshimoto's apathy toward wider social struggles.[34] Similarly, Ann Sherif ends her own essay on Yoshimoto with a broad denunciation of the author's optimism: "While her works entertain us and give us a temporary sense of hope for the world, the nuclear threat that Yoshimoto Banana so blissfully ignores remains steadfastly by our sides, for other authors to recall."[35] These critics regard healing style media as a solipsistic practice, a way of using close-at-hand positive affect to block out and ignore the more threatening and intractable aspects of social and political life.

Understandably, the postindustrial emphasis on comfort as an end in itself has triggered a great deal of concern among politically engaged critics. When I have asked various academics inside and outside Japan how they feel about this comforting culture, more than one has replied along the lines of, "Well, *I* think people should be more uncomfortable." This perspective sees the focus on material amenities during and after the high-growth years as a way for people to avoid more serious matters: dealing with the legacy of war, assuming political responsibility both locally and globally, and actively participating in the democratic process, to name just a few.

These arguments come in many sizes and shapes. Philosopher Morioka Masahiro describes contemporary Japan as a "painless civilization" carefully screening out the struggle and suffering he sees as essential for developing personal meaning and identity. As noted in the introduction, Asada Akira has sardonically described postindustrial Japan as a culture of "infantile capitalism," where ordinary people are content to not question those in power as long as their comfortable environments and personal pleasures continue to be provided. Tomiko Yoda elaborates on Asada's description of Japanese society as a "passive maternal medium," a "noncoercive force that controls individuals by 'wrapping' and 'embracing' them in its fold."[36]

A similar discourse emerged simultaneously in the United States, where critics saw therapy culture as abandoning self-discipline and the ethical imperative to care for others in favor of a single-minded pursuit of personal sensory gratification. Christopher Lasch's *The Minimal Self* (1984) sounded an early caution about the emergence, in art and literature, of "a self uncertain of its own outlines, longing either to remake the world in its own image or to merge into its environment in blissful union."[37] Lasch describes a post-1960s American retreat from an increasingly threatening, complicated, and fractured world, followed by a subsequent flight into self-care:

> Confronted with an apparently implacable and unmanageable environment, people have turned to self-management. With the help of an elaborate network of therapeutic professions, which themselves have largely abandoned approaches stressing introspective insight in favor of "coping" and

behavior modification, men and women today are trying to piece together a technology of the self, the only apparent alternative to personal collapse.[38]

Later critiques of postmodernism sound similar notes, most famously Frederick Jameson's warning of the "waning of affect." Jameson positions the aesthetic collapse of interior/exterior distinctions and modernist notions of "depth" as harbingers of a new era of superficiality in which people are unable to draw on historical contexts to organize a coherent narrative of self. Experience becomes fragmentary, and political investments start to atrophy.[39]

The most trenchant critiques of the comfort orientation have surfaced in debates surrounding the influence of therapy culture on education. Oguma Eiji and Ueno Yōko have highlighted the use of "healing" rhetoric in 1990s campaigns by right-wing groups to have depictions of Japan's wartime atrocities removed from school textbooks. The campaigns argued students would be better off without the added stress and trauma of confronting Japan's past—allowing therapeutic concerns to trump historical understanding.

Similarly, Yagi Kōsuke describes in his book on "'healing' as discrimination" how an overemphasis on avoiding uncomfortable feelings can lead to avoidance rather than tolerance of others different from oneself. Yagi points to how, in a society prioritizing comfort and positive feelings, minorities who in their appearance remind "normal" Japanese of uncomfortable histories they would rather ignore are in turn accused of failing to "blend in," as if sticking out from the crowd were a willful action on their part.[40] Such examples raise troubling questions about the impact of a society oriented toward therapy and self-care above all else.

I will not attempt here to sort out the significant differences between each of these arguments, only to point out how each tends—at its most rhetorical, at least—to imply an ethical choice must be made between a strong, active, socially and historically aware subjectivity and a passive, therapeutic, mood-regulating one. In more casual contexts, it has become common to hear complaints of the "peace-drunk" (*heiwa-boke*) stupor of younger Japanese, implying peace and comfort is to blame for the nation's cultural, economic, and political stagnation.

While such arguments against comfort can be compelling in the abstract, there is a danger here of reducing complex social and emotional contexts to a simple divide between "active" and "passive" social positions, denouncing comfort and presenting discomfort as a corrective in and of itself. As Ahmed notes, this overlooks the varied access people have to "active" and critical social roles:

> Maintaining an active position of "transgression" not only takes time, but may not be psychically, socially, or materially possible for some individuals and groups given their ongoing and unfinished commitments and histories. . . . Assimilation and transgression are not choices that are available to individuals, but are effects of how subjects can and cannot inhabit social norms and ideals.[41]

Conversely, needs for comfort and healing often correlate directly to how "out-of-place" a person may be within the normative social landscape, whether as a result of illness, disability, gender, sexuality, physical appearance, or ethnicity—not to mention the more general precariousness produced by the neoliberal withdrawal of social supports.[42]

By portraying comfort as inherently regressive and irresponsible, anti–therapy culture critiques can easily situate themselves in a heroically transgressive position that plays into readers' desire for critical transcendence—and discounts the real healing needs of many participating in the larger "healing boom." These critiques also risk falling into a vapid nostalgia for a less "emotionally sensitive" time, whether for the more explicit political commitments of the 1960s (on the left) or for a time prior to the war-renouncing Article 9 of the Japanese constitution (on the right).[43] Ironically, this perspective on history parallels therapy culture's own equation of contemporary society with illness and some prior era as more human and true.

I follow Eva Illouz here in offering not a defense of therapy culture but a call to take affect regulation seriously as an increasingly important dimension of subjectivation—one that over the past half century has proved robust and resilient if necessarily limited as a tool of social critique. Illouz writes (from the perspective of sociology):

> By insisting that the therapeutic lexicon "depoliticizes" problems that are social and collective, many sociologists have made it difficult for themselves to understand why the new middle classes and women have enthusiastically endorsed the therapeutic discourse—other than by presuming, somewhat implausibly, that theirs is a "false" consciousness or by presuming that modern societies are governed by

a seamless process of surveillance equally embodied in com-
puterized control of citizens and in the therapist's office.[44]

Illouz does not necessarily argue against those who emphasize the
ideological dangers of therapy culture but rather insists we be willing
to set aside this critique long enough to understand how and why such
a culture developed in the first place. Illouz describes this as a model of
"immanent critique" that "must emerge from a 'thick' understanding
of people's desires and goals and cannot bracket the actual understand-
ings and strategies of lay actors."[45]

Studies focusing on these "lay actors" have tended to produce a more
balanced perspective on contemporary forms of mood regulation. John
Clammer, for example, affirms the role of desire and emotion in late
twentieth-century Japanese consumer culture, emphasizing the consumption of material goods is as much about inventing new forms of self
as it is about complacency and conformity. Clammer describes the advent of consumerism in Japan as "an entire reorientation to life, to what
is possible and to the realization of the idea of the making of the self as an
at least partly autonomous project rather than as simply the plaything of
history or of social forces beyond the control of the individual."[46]

An understanding of the structural transformations underlying
neoliberalism also helps illuminate what drives the therapeutic emphasis on self-care. Micki McGee's work on the American self-help industry points out how self-help became popular in the United States at the
same time as employers were systematically cutting back on benefits
and services geared at employee development and well-being. With
fewer social supports in place, employees were left to their own devices
when it came to psychological health, workplace struggles, retraining,
and forced career change. The ideology of self-help, McGee argues,
helped naturalize this reduction in social supports. Through personal
effort, positive thinking, self-knowledge, and private study, the self-
help literature argued, nothing was beyond reach. Should a person fall
short of his or her wildest dreams, it was to be seen as a personal failure, not something to do with the system as a whole.[47]

The healing boom in Japan was born in a similar moment of neoliberal industrial reforms. After the economic downturn in the early
1990s, many Japanese businesses moved to restructure along the lines
of this streamlined American model. The lifetime-employment ideal
of the postwar decades began to be replaced by more flexible, temporary, and cheaper forms of labor. On-the-job training—a mainstay of
the previous model—declined, and workers were often on their own

in the struggle to remain competitive. Worker vulnerability has only increased since with the spread of companies relying on exploitative labor practices (*burakku kigyō*) and other precarious employment structures.[48] These shifts in employment practices provide a larger impetus for self-care as part of the struggle to remain competitive (or at least physically and emotionally sound) while working in such environments.

Ambient literature has largely avoided addressing these structural changes head on, preferring to focus instead on affording particular affective moods giving audiences the space to think for themselves. Authors tend to understand their role as providing an atmospheric space for reflection and recovery rather than directives on what exactly needs to change. In a 2005 interview, Kurita describes her attempt to provide some feeling of positive affect toward the future, particularly at moments when the present has become a struggle:

> When I read a novel or see a film, and it displays tragic events just as they are, I think "but I already knew that . . . ." I want to say "but still there are people who are trying to move forward." . . . Even amidst all this sadness, it is a positive action to find a way to lift your spirits by enjoying novels or films or music. When you are really feeling bad, you don't have those kinds of good feelings. Because of this, though I don't want to affirm reality just as it is, I feel like it is natural for me to somehow calm down and write stories with a hope for the future.[49]

Hope, in this case, comes through a partial withdrawal from the pressure of worldly events, affording the space, perhaps, for thinking and feeling something new.

What is at stake here is the role of media in relation to society: is it to be a reflective critique or an emotional tool? Older critics such as Ōe and Kuroko insist on a critical literature and warn against the solipsistic dangers of an excessive therapeutic focus. The (mostly younger, mostly female) authors of healing style literature, meanwhile, emphasize the therapeutic benefits of calm for those in need of healing and are more comfortable situating literature alongside other therapeutic objects.

I suggest the tension between self-care and social critique itself is what deserves our attention; ambient media demonstrate the two approaches are not as incompatible as they may first appear. Just as

Brian Eno asserts ambient music's critical distance from the commercial banality of Muzak, what I am calling ambient literature contains the seeds of a critique of the therapy industry as a whole. In *Hôtel Mole* Kurita explores how a hotel geared entirely toward generating relaxation for its guests can still be stressful for its employees. Kiri's main struggle during her first week of work is simply staying awake in such a sleep-inducing space. At one point during an early morning shift, she simply cannot keep herself from dozing off and replaces the relaxation music playing in the lobby with a punk album, dancing wildly to the music to keep herself awake. Her boss later complains about this, worrying the music's energy will seep into the building and disturb the guests sleeping below. But even the hotel membership structure guards against sleep becoming an end in itself. Initial interviews ensure guests have real sleep disorders they need to address, and whenever they become well enough to sleep soundly, even outside the hotel, they are asked to cancel their membership. Higashi Naoko picks up on this in her review of the novel: "What must be understood is the novel is not saying humans live in order to sleep. The hotel also acknowledges this. After all, in order to make waking life as rich as possible, the body and brain need to be well rested."[50]

Kurita, whose own experience working as an overnight hotel receptionist helped inspire the novel, also documents the more discomforting aspects of emotional labor.[51] Kiri's boss is strict and demanding and anything but healing style toward hotel employees. Kiri's position—up all night working and allowed little restful sleep herself—serves as a reminder of all the tiring effort necessary to create a restful space for others. This type of labor has ambient dimensions, too, in the way it often operates at the periphery of hotel guests' attention, largely out of view (and this is precisely what makes it effective). Alongside the novel's own calming affordances, *Hôtel Mole*'s focus on emotional labor helps bring this less comfortable side of therapy culture to the foreground. As Kurita's novel demonstrates, ambient literature can still engage with the more critical modes emphasized in earlier forms of literary practice, depicting the complexities and contradictions of therapy culture while fully participating in it as a mood-regulating medium. Of course, this is not an easy balancing act, and perhaps no full-throttle social critique can be waged in an atmosphere that has carefully pacified all strong forms of negative feeling.

Such a contradiction is present in Eno's original demand for ambience to produce both "calm" and "a space to think": the only way to ensure both is to make sure not to think of anything that would upset the calming mood. The shallow depth of this space to think, while as amorphous and creative as I have described it in this book, nonetheless has therapeutic contours limiting where such thoughts may travel. Recognizing these limitations, however, can lead to a better understanding of what role calm and comfort might play as part of a socially responsive literature. By providing spaces of ambivalent calm, access to an impersonal self, and reflections on the work involved in building a healing mood, ambient literature asserts the value of not just healing as an end in itself but the labor involved in these acts of care.

CONCLUSION

This book has sought to map out "both sides" of ambient subjectivation, attending to both the real mobility and healing on offer and the potentially dubious aspects of mediated mood regulation and therapy culture. Nikolas Rose notes this doubled-edged quality as something inherent to neoliberal techniques of self:

> On the one hand, in freeing many questions concerning the proper conduct of life from the authoritative prescriptions and proscriptions of political, religious, and social authorities, [neoliberalism] pluralizes the answers that can be provided, opening up a field of diversity within which each subject is obliged to locate themselves. On the other hand, in relocating these questions of the conduct of life within the field of expertise, in tying it to norms of truth and health, it binds subjects to a subjection that is the more profound because it appears to emanate from our autonomous quest for ourselves—it appears as a matter of our freedom.[1]

In closing the book, I want to similarly emphasize how ambient subjectivation results in both actual gains in personal freedom (a partial reprieve from the totalizing demands of an isorhythmic identity) *and* more insidious forms of social control (operating in ways more environmental and atmospheric and thus more difficult to consciously register and perhaps resist). As Rose notes, this places an immense amount of responsibility on people seeking to steer their own subjective well-being, asking them not only to monitor and design their own subjectivations but to remain vigilant against social environments increasingly mobilized to tune them in ways often well below conscious awareness.

Over the course of the book I have touched on some troubling aspects of the turn to therapeutic media, and it is worth continuing to question the type of mood-regulating self ambient media produce. There is always far more to life than how you feel about it. At the same time, however, ambient approaches to subjectivation hold out the possibility for attunement to something besides the status quo. I will end on a hopeful note by considering some of these alternative trajectories.

Ambient media may remain limited as tools of critique, but by providing "calm, and a space to think" they are never simply operating as a social anesthetic. While neoliberalism pretends the foreground can operate independently of the background, the rise of ambient subjectivation might also provoke a shift away from this modern conception of the strong self and its posture of independence from the surrounding environment. Ambient media might emphasize everyone's entwinement with the affective attunements of shared space and call on audiences to become reflective and participatory agents in the design of these collective moods. An ambient understanding of self necessarily situates the person in an intimate relationship with larger ecologies, affirming our interdependency not only with other people but with the affordances of the objects and environments we live with and through.

Tellingly, experiences of physical weakness and vulnerability have often served as instigators for a turn to this type of ambient awareness. Consider Brian Eno's well-known story of "discovering" ambient music while immobilized in his apartment, in bed convalescing after being run down by a taxi. A friend comes by and puts an album of harp music on the record changer on low volume and leaves while it is still playing. Eno feels compelled to adjust the volume but with his broken bones cannot get up to do so. Forced to keep listening, he discovers how the low-level music blends with the sounds of the street outside, mixing together into a restful soundscape and leading Eno to imagine an "ambient music" designed for this more environmental form of audition.[2]

Hosono Haruomi's turn to ambience grew from a similar encounter with his own physical limits. In interviews from just before his ambient period, he is forthcoming about his own difficulties dealing with stress, particularly after achieving celebrity as a member of Yellow Magic Orchestra. In a 1984 interview with Yoshinari Mayumi, he describes using music as a technology of personal stress relief:

> Lately, I tend to get neurotic. There are difficult times
> when I feel emotionally oppressed. At the same time as I
> feel it mentally, it also tends to manifest physically, and my
> stomach starts to hurt. I feel how the body and mind are
> connected. . . . The only thing that helps me for stress relief
> is making music. I don't have any other way. It's like music
> is a place to deposit stress [*laughs*]. During YMO, I used
> to joke that music was my "fatigue deposit box," but lately
> this has become even more true. It feels like it's reaching a
> critical stage. I really want to find some way to help use up
> all this tension [*laughs*].[3]

This growing fatigue eventually resulted in a painful but fortuitous experience not unlike Eno's. Hosono discusses this in a casual 2000 conversation with former YMO bandmate Sakamoto Ryūichi:

> **Sakamoto:** Speaking of YMO, I am wondering why you were so uptight in those days...
>
> **Hosono:** I don't know. We were young.
>
> **S:** [*laughing*] That's it?
>
> **H:** Hmm, looking back now I think that was what "youth" meant.
>
> **S:** You were in your thirties then, Hosono. You were pretty high strung.
>
> **H:** I wonder why I was so tense. Now I'm easy going. I think I mellowed out after I broke my leg fifteen years ago. Until then I maintained that tense state from YMO. The environment around me was like that too ... including the record label staff and the fans. I felt like I had to respond to that pressure all the time. But when I broke my leg, they gave up. If it had just been a fever or broken arm, they wouldn't have.
>
> **S:** You couldn't walk...
>
> **H:** I had just started thinking I had no other choice but to get sick to get out of there, when I slipped and broke my leg in heavy snow. I had to take more than half a year off, and the people surrounding me just vanished. That's when I felt relief, you know. One month after I broke my leg, I took a "real" rest for the first time in my life. I just stayed home, playing Nintendo and being goofy. One day I found whitish spots on my eyelids. My doctor told me I had been under excessive stress and the spots were a kind of sign. Intracranial cholesterol is discharged from the eyelids via the hypothalamus. If it is not discharged, you retain it in your body, which is dangerous.[4]

Fifteen years before this interview works out to 1984 or 1985—not long after Hosono's conversation with Yoshinari. As with Eno, broken bones forced Hosono to slow down and rethink what it means to be vulnerable to environmental influence, just as he was getting into ambient music as a style.

Arai Man tells a similar tale, recalling how he first developed an interest in ambient aesthetics after falling seriously ill while a college student at Sophia University in Tokyo. Losing half his body weight before recovering, he realized his life had been too much about "adding" and not enough about "subtracting."[5]

For Kurita Yuki an ambient emphasis on recovery came about in the context of care for someone else. While writing her first novella, *Hamisabeth,* a close friend was hospitalized. As Kurita imagined her work being read by this sick friend, themes of illness and healing began to seep into her writing.[6]

Each of these ambient origin stories point to a growing awareness of personal vulnerability and a growing understanding of how media can serve as atmospheric tools for healing self and others. After coming face to face with physical weakness, these people found ways of transforming environmental susceptibility into an opportunity for healing. Riffing on Giovanni Vattimo's concept of "weak thought" (*pensiero debole*), Hosokawa Shūhei describes the emergence of what he calls "weak listening" (*yowai chōshu*): an approach to recorded music that doesn't call for or even allow the kind of concentrated focus of the modern concert hall setting.[7] Weak listening blurs the dichotomy between audience and recording, allowing for a sense of self emerging with and through the influence of the surrounding world, rather than asserting the mastery of a unified subject over and above it. In weak listening, the listener (or hearer, since the listening/hearing distinction is largely meaningless here) submits to the recording and through this finds a kind of freedom based in and through its atmosphere. It is precisely this "weak" aspect of the sensing body ambient media embraces, carving out forms of environmental agency from within this seemingly passive position.

There need not be anything passive about this embrace. As Washida Kiyokazu notes in <*Yowasa*> *no chikara* (The power of "weakness"), looking at the world with an awareness of vulnerability and understanding the responsibility involved in looking after the weakness of others leads to a different set of principles for organizing human life.[8] The pursuit of personal power gives way to the humility of collective care. At their most ethical, ambient media are rooted in both an affirmation of this weak self and an awareness of the environmental responsibilities accompanying it. As I hope this book has shown, Japanese ambient producers have already provided us with many compelling models of how this might work.

Alongside this affirmation of weakness, the foregrounding of ambience helps make clear how much atmospheres can serve to either *reinforce* or *reconfigure* normative social behaviors. While environmental media often seek to offer ready-made aesthetic solutions to the management of cosubjective feeling, they can also cultivate an increased awareness of the way designed atmospheres directly modulate the behaviors and attitudes of self and others. This leads to a number of important questions about the cultural politics of atmospheric design within shared space. Who determines the ambient mediation of everyday life, and how is this control established and maintained? What modes of social engagement and subjectivation do particular moods afford, and what forms do they inhibit? What principles should determine the selection and design of mediated atmospheres in public space? How can an atmosphere allow for a more inclusive range of beings to feel at ease and at home, without at the same time designing out the possibility for intersubjective encounters with difference?

Locations where these questions make themselves felt most acutely in Japan include the spaces in and around train and subway stations, the quasi-public parks surrounding new urban office towers, and the enormous retail/office complexes increasingly dominating the urban Japanese landscape, such as the Mori Group's Roppongi Hills (2003) and Omotesando Hills (2005), the Mitsui Group's Tokyo Midtown (2007), and Tōkyū's Hikarie complex next to Shibuya station (2012). On the surface these are each open and inviting environments, and often welcoming and comfortable to wander through. At the same time, these spaces are implicitly oriented toward a particular demographic: those with the economic and cultural capital to blend in smoothly and behave as expected, without lingering too long.

For those who don't "fit" this mobile and transparent neoliberal ideal, these ostensibly open and comfortable spaces can produce feelings of being alien and out of place. Any failure or refusal to "read the air" properly—loitering, making too much noise, partaking in what is often a long list of prohibited behaviors—will soon summon the security guards. Ahmed's description of comfort gives a good phenomenological sense of what is at stake: "To be comfortable is to be so at ease with one's environment that it is hard to distinguish where one's body ends and the world begins. One fits, and by fitting, the surfaces of bodies disappear from view. The disappearance of the surface is instructive: in feelings of comfort, bodies extend into spaces, and spaces extend into bodies." In contrast, "pain or discomfort return one's attention to the surfaces of the body *as body*."[9] In this context atmosphere—built through the shape and texture of building materials, lighting, acoustics, background media, etc.—is a way to draw lines of inclusion and exclusion without making them obvious or explicit. Those for whom the spaces have been shaped can easily extend themselves through them, whereas others might find themselves on the defensive for being unwilling or unable to go with the flow.

As with neoliberal forms of governmentality more generally, this reliance on atmosphere as a mechanism of indirect social control often allows for increased freedom and self-determination at the local level. These are still, on the whole, fairly inclusive spaces, and as I have argued, cosubjective attunement remains an important method for allowing eurythmic diversity in tight quarters. At the same time, the lines the atmosphere draws become, in their transparency and ubiquity, all the more difficult to contest. With an atmosphere the rules lie hidden in plain sight, largely invisible until someone accidentally or willfully "misreads" the air.

As a successor to the environmental arts of the 1960s, one of ambient media's most important roles might be to draw attention back to the subjective coordinates laid out by an atmosphere and imagine what else atmosphere might accomplish as a medium of collective life. As Eno envisioned in the late 1970s, whereas "canned" moods often attempt to eliminate all conflict and uncertainty from the affective landscape, ambient media might seek other ways to calmly confront the more contentious spaces of the contemporary world. In this sense, one of the main challenges taken up by ambient media is how to develop more inclusive and possibly even critical atmospheres, modes of subjectivation capable of maintaining a clear-eyed calm while moving through environments of uncertainty and difference. These atmospheres might even register the need to sometimes set aside a surface calm in the name of deeper and more unsettling truths.

At their best, ambient media help us to "remember the air," to paraphrase Luce Irigaray. Echoing Newton's description of air as an ambient medium, Irigaray notes how the air has qualitative dimensions—temperature, pressure, humidity—that inevitably shape the other energies passing through it, albeit in ways often so subtle these qualitative changes become attributed to the solid objects we see before us rather than the air that serves to filter our impressions. The air is often forgotten, and the space it fills comes to be regarded as nothing but an empty container across which "direct" perception can take place. To remember the air radically undermines this illusion of perceptual mastery at a distance.[10]

Ambient media might teach us to read the air itself as a site of subjectivation, providing a resource for recognizing how the atmosphere is tuning our affective lives. To learn to read the air in this way is to embrace the weak, partial, and embedded agency of the environmental self. On recognizing the atmosphere as an aesthetic force, people can begin developing personal and public strategies for the creation of moods more true to where they are and where they want to be. The strong self's denial of environmental influence only contributes to a continued forgetting of the air and the power it helps render invisible. In contrast, the only way to not be led astray by ambience is to begin to understand how it works and how it might work better.

ACKNOWLEDGMENTS

This book grew from a long-term fascination with the molding of sub-jectivity through media. For this I credit growing up in California, with its stubborn belief in the power of self-reinvention through lifestyle en-gineering, and time spent getting lost in Tokyo, with its endless maze of carefully curated spaces. I admire the pragmatism of both places' willingness to experiment with new forms of living, at the same time as I remain haunted by so much of what these surface designs strive to cover over. I first thank my parents, Deborah and Gregory Roquet, not only for their steady support but also for modeling an open-minded skepticism that has continued to help guide me across these uneven landscapes.

The aesthetic ideas here emerged from a long time spent immersed in mediated moods of many kinds. KSPC radio at Pomona College gave me a chance to explore new ambient and experimental music on the air. Kyoko Kurita helped me explore the interface between sound and Japanese literature early on. A year of postgraduate "acoustic ecol-ogy" research traveling through the South Pacific and Southeast Asia on a Thomas J. Watson Fellowship provided an extended opportunity to study the relationship between soundscapes and urbanization. I am grateful to the late Katherine Hagedorn for her enthusiastic support for this project.

At the University of California, Berkeley, this book would never have grown as it did without Alan Tansman's encouragement, sincer-ity, and intellectual generosity. Miryam Sas provided crucial feedback on early versions of the manuscript, and the first inklings of some cen-tral ideas here came together in her Japanese Aesthetic Theory semi-nars. Dan O'Neill's close reading of urban space in modern Japanese literature proved an early impetus as well. Lalitha Gopalan strength-ened my dedication to experimental film and video, while Andrew Jones demonstrated why sound studies and Asian studies resonate better together. UC Berkeley's Townsend Center and Arts Research Center provided opportunities to work across disciplines and engage with a lively community of lateral thinkers. The Center for Japanese Studies provided further support for research trips to Japan early in the project.

A Fulbright IIE Doctoral Dissertation Research Fellowship made possible the first of what became three years of research activities in Tokyo, ably administered by Toyama Keiko at the Akasaka-mitsuke office. Uno Kuniichi graciously hosted me at Rikkyō University and helped push my thinking in unexpected and always rewarding directions. Hasegawa Hitomi of the Moving Image Archive of Contemporary Art generously ushered me into the Japanese video art community.

Subsequent years at Stanford University as an Andrew W. Mellon postdoctoral fellow in the humanities provided an ideal environment to complete the book while pondering both the future of the aesthetic disciplines and the strangeness of Silicon Valley. Thanks go to J. P. Daughton, R. Lanier Anderson, James Reichert, and the other Mellons for their support and guidance.

The final state of the book owes a great deal to the incisive feedback of two anonymous readers for the University of Minnesota Press, Danielle Kasprzak's editorial guidance, and anonymous reviews from the *Journal of Popular Music Studies* and the *Journal of Japanese Studies* on earlier versions of chapters 2 and 6. A wide range of artists and musicians contributed to this research through interviews, providing study copies of works or helping point me toward materials I was unaware of. I am grateful to Ise Shōko, Hatakeyama Chihei, Tetsu Inoue, Kano Shiho, Goshima Kazuhiro, Satō Minoru, Kurokawa Ryōichi, Idemitsu Mako, and Taki Kentarō. Thanks also go to Ochiai Nozomi of Mainichi Video-Audio Systems and Nakaue Atsushi of Dentsū Music and Entertainment for their research assistance.

The ideas here developed on a more day-to-day level through conversation and coffee with fellow travelers, including Marië Abe, Sean Callaghan, Michael Craig, David Humphrey, Kim Icreverzi, Miki Kaneda, Nick Kaufman, Yumi Kim, Namiko Kunimoto, Andrew Leong, Diane Lewis, Daryl Maude, Xiao Liu, Patrick Luhan, Patrick Noonan, Mark Roberts, Maria Römer, Jordan Smith, Joanna Sturiano, Robert Szeliga, Max Ward, Jeremy Yellen, Ken Yoshida, and Alex Zahlten. Special thanks go to Momoko Shimizu for refusing to tolerate academic blather and *kijō no kūron* (armchair theorizing).

Finally, I am grateful to all those taking the initiative to create more thoughtful, enlivening, and inclusive atmospheres, whatever the context. Often, all it takes is a willingness to experiment a bit with the BGM.

NOTES

INTRODUCTION

1 The creators of the disc are video artists Kikkawa Hiroshi and Kodama Yūichi, musicians Furuya Kenji and Cube Juice, and photographer Suzuki Tokiko. The jellyfish are from the Enoshima Aquarium, a popular tourist spot on the Shōnan coast two hours south of Tokyo.

2 Tia DeNora writes of the use of aesthetic materials (rhythms, textures, musical structures) to provide forms of mediated physical *entrainment,* the "alignment or integration of bodily features with some recurrent features in the environment"—often in ways not entirely conscious. Greg M. Smith provides a useful model of how this kind of entrainment can produce sustained moods. Repetition plays a key role. Emotional responses to affective stimuli tend to be over in a matter of seconds and may differ depending on personal history and mode of attention. Smith notes films often work to get around this variability by presenting a wide spectrum of similar mood cues across the running time of a work. Aesthetic elements including lighting, music, sound effects, dialogue, editing, and camera work combine to present a unified emotional tone, ensuring that even if a viewer doesn't respond equally or predictably to each and every "mood cue," attunement with the overall atmosphere will eventually occur. As this book explores, this strategy of affective overdetermination to produce sustained moods functions similarly in other media like music, video art, and literature. DeNora, *Music in Everyday Life,* 79; Smith, *Film Structure and the Emotion System,* 149–51.

3 Cited in Spitzer, "Milieu and Ambience," 39. For a fascinating approach to human perception building from this Newtonian understanding of air as an ambient medium, see Gibson, *The Ecological Approach to Visual Perception,* 17.

4 Water can also be an ambient medium, should this body jump in the river to swim with the jellyfish.

5 *Funiki* was first coined as a translation of the Dutch term *lucht* in the mid-nineteenth century. As with *atmosphere,* the original meaning referred simply to the layer of air surrounding the earth. Near the beginning of the Meiji period (1868–1912) and the rush for modernization, the valence of *funiki* expanded to keep pace with the European notion of the feeling or mood of a place. "Funiki," *Seisenban Nihonkokugo daijiten.*

6 Pinkus, "Ambiguity, Ambience, Ambivalence, and the Environment," 91.

7 Spitzer, "Milieu and Ambience," 39; Morton, *Ecology Without Nature,* 34. Rickert provides additional perspectives on the word's origins in *Ambient Rhetoric,* 5–8.

8 I follow Thomas Lemke's definition of neoliberalism as "a political rationality that tries to render the social domain economic and to link a reduction in (welfare) state services and security systems to the increasing
call for 'personal responsibility' and 'self-care.'" See Lemke, "The Birth of
Biopolitics," 203. On the social effects of neoliberalism in Japan, see Borovoy, "Japan as Mirror"; Hayashi, "From Exploitation to Playful Exploits";
and Allison, *Precarious Japan*. Though she doesn't discuss neoliberalism
specifically, Tessa Morris-Suzuki's *Beyond Computopia* highlights related
aspects of the Japanese government's push for an "information society"
starting in the late 1960s. To be clear, neoliberalism as an approach to national governance was established in Japan only gradually, with key neoliberal reforms enacted only in the late 1990s and early 2000s during the
Hashimoto and Koizumi administrations. It is clear, however, the more
cultural side of Japanese neoliberalism I focus on here has a much longer
trajectory, growing through the 1970s and 1980s and intensifying in tandem with the government's later neoliberal turn.

9 See McLuhan, *Understanding Media*; on ubiquitous computing and what
it means for media aesthetics, see Ekman, ed., *Throughout,* and Kassabian,
Ubiquitous Listening, 1–19.

10 Foucault, *Ethics,* 225. Foucault's *les techniques de soi* is often translated
as "technologies of the self," and his use of the term encompasses both
"techniques" and "technologies" in their common English definitions. As
I will be addressing a wide range of more specific technologies later in the
book, I have chosen to use "techniques" to translate Foucault's term and
save "technologies of the self" to refer more specifically to the use of media
technologies as tools of personal subjectivation.

11 Foucault, *The Hermeneutics of the Subject,* 1–19.

12 "Being affected by sound or weather, while among the easiest and least obtrusive forms of experience, is, physically, a concrete encounter (in the literal sense of *en-countering:* meeting up) with our physical environment."
Gumbrecht, *Atmosphere, Mood, Stimmung,* 4.

13 Heidegger, *Being and Time,* 132–33. Emphasis in original.

14 Gumbrecht, *Atmosphere, Mood, Stimmung,* 7–8.

15 German philosophy was considered state of the art in Japan at the time,
and Watsuji had traveled to Germany to learn as much as he could.

16 Watsuji, *Watsuji Tetsurō's Rinrigaku,* 5. By the late 1990s *Climate and Culture* had gone through over fifty printings in Japan. See Befu, *Hegemony
of Homogeneity,* 51. On Heidegger's own relationship with Japanese and
Chinese thought, see May, *Heidegger's Hidden Sources*. Seven decades
later, Peter Sloterdijk would describe a similar goal—writing the spatial
companion to *Being and Time*—as a major motivation for his *Spheres* trilogy (1998–2004).

17 I have adopted Geoffrey Bownas's translation here from Watsuji, *Climate
and Culture,* 12–15; emphasis added. Note in the original Watsuji does not
use the word *funiki* (atmosphere) but *fūdo* (climate) in the final clause,

though for him the words are nearly synonymous: "Sunawachi wareware ha 'fūdo' ni oite wareware jishin o aidagara toshite no wareware jishin o miidasu no de aru." Watsuji, *Fūdo*, 8.

18 Naoki Sakai draws our attention to the distinction in modern Japanese between *shukan,* or the ontological subject recognizing its identity in distinction to others, and *shutai,* the "agent of praxis who manufactures itself for itself." As with the two Greek principles described earlier, *shukan* emphasizes self-recognition through cognition, while *shutai* shifts the conception of subjectivity toward an emphasis on interactive practices of self-formation. As Sakai argues, Watsuji's work strains to essentialize the *shutai*—the varied practices of self of those living in a place called "Japan"—in order to help shore up an all-embracing nationalist *shukan*: "What is achieved in his use of the term *shutai* is, in fact, a displacement of the practical relation by the epistemic one." Watsuji's emphasis on a uniform national atmosphere, I would add, is central to how he achieves this displacement. See Sakai, *Translation & Subjectivity,* 145 and 198–99n10.

19 As Harumi Befu notes, Watsuji's *Climate and Culture* was a major influence on the popular genre of *Nihon bunkaron* (theories of Japanese culture) emerging in the 1970s and 1980s. Befu, *Hegemony of Homogeneity,* 17.

20 Sakai, *Translation & Subjectivity,* 198–99n10. Arlie Russell Hochschild makes a similar point in the 2012 preface to her classic 1983 study of emotional labor, *The Managed Heart*: "The Japanese highly value the capacity to relate to the feelings and needs of others. So for the Japanese, emotional labor is more built in and therefore harder to see" (xi).

21 Yamamoto presents this "air" discourse as something uniquely Japanese and earlier included it alongside a host of other cultural essentialisms in his discussion of what he calls *Nihonkyō* (the Japan Religion) in his bestselling *Nihonjin to Yudayajin* (The Japanese and the Jews, 1970, published under the pseudonym Isiah Ben-Dasan). Other popular "theories of Japanese culture" often invoke the idea of *ishin denshin* (person-to-person telepathy), the idea that due to a high degree of shared assumptions Japanese tend to rely heavily on unspoken and/or implicit forms of communication. I see no reason to accept the idea there is anything exclusively *Japanese* about this practice, though I agree with Yamamoto that "air" discourse has served as a particularly powerful tool of indirect coercion in modern Japan. On *ishin denshin,* see Befu, *Hegemony of Homogeneity,* 38–39.

22 Recent titles include Kōtari Yūji, *Kūki no yomikata: Dekiru yatsu to iwaseru "shuzairyoku" kōza* (How to read the air: "Collection power" course on how to be called a can-do guy, 2008); Doi Takayoshi, *Tomodachi jigoku: "Kūki o yomu" sedai no sabaibaru* (Friendship hell: Surviving the "reading the air" generation, 2008); and Matsumoto Chitose, *Bijin ni mieru "kūki" no tsukurikata: Kirei no hiketsu 81* (Creating the "air" of a beautiful woman: 81 beauty secrets, 2012). As Doi's title indicates, in recent years there

is also a sense "reading the air" has become a more important social skill than ever before in an age where communication is often heavily mediated and identities are highly fluid.

23 This remains a problem with recent attempts to theorize atmospheric subjectivity through a Heideggerian framework, including Gumbrecht's *Atmosphere, Mood, Stimmung* (2012) and Thomas Rickert's *Ambient Rhetoric* (2013).

24 The quote is from Heidegger, *Being and Time*, 132. Here, I am in part following Sakai's critique of Watsuji, where he notes that what Watsuji "consistently evades is the undecidability of the social, inherent in the 'being in common' with others, which cannot be equated to the relational determination of an identity within the spatiality of synchronicity." Sakai, *Translation & Subjectivity*, 145.

25 Rose, *Governing the Soul*, 222.

26 Foucault, *The Birth of Biopolitics*, 260; emphasis mine. As Rose notes, with the turn to the somatic there is also a general shift from the "molar" to the "molecular," both literally with the spread of biotechnology focused on the molecular level and in the Deleuzian sense of a person understood as an assemblage of interwoven forces rather than a unified "molar" being with discreet boundaries. Rose, *The Politics of Life Itself*, 25–26.

27 Mark Driscoll explores the darker side of early Japanese biopolitics in *Absolute Erotic, Absolute Grotesque*.

28 Ruth Benedict's influential *The Chrysanthemum and the Sword* (1946) set the tone for subsequent postwar Japanese attempts to identify a uniquely "Japanese" psychology, a project useful to proponents of cultural nationalism up through the present. On the history of psychoanalysis in Japan, see Cornyetz and Vincent's introduction to *Perversion and Modern Japan*, 3–5.

29 See Koschmann, *Revolution and Subjectivity in Postwar Japan*, 171–78. The quote on Locke is from Maruyama's *Senchū to sengo no aida*, cited and translated by Koschmann on p. 178. As Koschmann traces, Maruyama's thought emerged amid a fervent postwar debate on the meaning of subjectivity (*shutai*) among Marxists, social scientists, and other intellectuals. This debate would largely end by the early 1950s with a return to more nationalist frames of reference. Two decades later, avant-garde filmmakers and theorists in the late 1960s again took up the question and produced many essays on subjectivity (*shutairon*) in the context of the political upheavals of the time. As Abé Mark Nornes notes, however, this discourse tended to lack a common conceptual framework and "would inevitably splinter into many directions at once." The debate over the properly political subject would again fall into obscurity by the mid-1970s with the turn to more autonomous conceptions of self. See Nornes, *Forest of Pressure*, 26 and 57.

30 On the postwar marketing of the "bright life" as a consumer ideal, see Partner, *Assembled in Japan*, 137–92. The Japanese student protest move-

ments of the late 1960s, while oriented toward a very different social project, nonetheless paralleled this collective emphasis in their demands for
solidarity and self-sacrifice.

31 I adopt the term "therapy culture" (*serapii bunka*) from Japanese sociologist Koike Yasushi. See Koike, *Serapii bunka no shakaigaku,* 14–15. See
also Saitō, *Shinrigakuka suru shakai.* For a critical perspective from the
United Kingdom, see Furedi, *Therapy Culture.* On micromasses, see Ivy,
"Formations of Mass Culture," 252–53. On the new forms of consumer
spirituality, see Haga, "Wakamono no taikan shikō to gendai shūkyō
būmu," 100.

32 Ueno, *<Watashi> sagashi gēmu,* 115.

33 Hosokawa, "The Walkman Effect," 165.

34 Rose, *Governing the Self,* 153.

35 Mita Munesuke dubs the mid-1970s to 1990s as the "age of fiction," which
Miyadai Shinji rephrases as the "age of self." The transition away from
grand narratives as a framework for understanding contemporary Japan
was led by Ōtsuka Eiji starting in the 1980s and revisited by Azuma Hiroki
in the new century. Azuma highlights *moe,* or "desire elements," as the
affective glue organizing anime *otaku* spectatorship. Gabriella Lukács
makes a similar point about Japanese television dramas in the 1990s, noting how as consumer tastes were rapidly diversifying, the one thing stu-
dios could find to reach across demographics was not story or message
but positive affect, "elevating the mood" of viewers regardless of a show's
plot. My reading of ambience here is largely complementary with these
historical arguments, though the ambient attunement I describe is not dependent on the presence or absence of more traditional narrative forms.
See Mita, *Social Psychology of Modern Japan,* 523; Miyadai, "Transformations of Semantics in the History of Japanese Subcultures," 233; Ōtsuka,
Monogatari shōmetsuron; Azuma, *Otaku,* 42; Lukács, *Scripted Affects,
Branded Selves,* 41.

36 We might question Miyadai's use of the term "homeostasis" here, as—
along with the general therapy culture emphasis on "balance"—it imagines self-regulation as if it were a closed system capable of being tuned up
like an engine, rather than as something integrated with more open-ended
forms of social subjectivation not necessarily tending toward equilibrium.
Miyadai, "Transformations of Semantics in the History of Japanese Subcultures," 235. For Miyadai's original argument, see Miyadai, Ishihara,
and Ōtsuka, *Sabukaruchā shinwa kaitai.*

37 Asada, "Infantile Capitalism and Japan's Postmodernism," 276.

38 Rose, *Governing the Soul,* 261.

39 Bull, *Sound Moves,* 154–57. The relationship between somatic rhythms
and everyday media is the subject of chapter 3.

40 See Allison, *Precarious Japan.*

41 As Yuriko Furuhata argues, Matsuda's "landscape theory" (*fūkeiron*) can
be understood as a prescient example of a theorist recognizing the need to

focus not just on explicit ideological debates but on how governmentality is inscribed within the urban landscape itself. Furuhata, *Cinema of Actuality*, 118.

42 Ahmed, *The Cultural Politics of Emotion, Queer Phenomenology,* and *The Promise of Happiness*; Sedgwick, *Touching Feeling*; Hochschild, *The Managed Heart*; Berlant, *The Female Complaint* and *Cruel Optimism*; Ngai, *Ugly Feelings* and *Our Aesthetic Categories*; Stewart, *Ordinary Affects*. As Rickert notes, the increasing attention to nonrepresentational elements of subjectivity is also reflected in a wide range of more recent attempts to counter the long-held bias toward language, will, and representation in models of subjectivity and social interaction: the nonhuman agency of objects and things argued for by both Bruno Latour and the object-oriented ontology thinkers, the rising attention to environmental design and ubiquitous computing, and the push in both cognitive science and affect theory for understanding the role played by preconscious affective forces.

43 Ahmed notes how feminists, for example, can come to be regarded as "killjoys" because by insisting on pointing out gender inequalities they "ruin the atmosphere" for others more comfortable with the unspoken status quo. Ahmed, *The Promise of Happiness,* 65 and 67.

44 As Sianne Ngai points out, the tone or mood overlaying a social situation can be thought of as supremely ideological, as it governs the ways people behave and interact while largely escaping conscious reflection. Following Lawrence Grossberg, Ngai defines ideology as "the materially embodied representation of an *imaginary relationship* to a holistic complex of real conditions" and notes how mood clearly shares this "virtual, diffused, but also imminent character." Ngai, *Ugly Feelings,* 47; emphasis in original.

45 Thrift, "Intensities of Feeling," 57.

46 See Guattari, *Chaosmosis*; Maurizio Lazzarato develops this argument further in *Signs and Machines*.

47 Gumbrecht calls this a "*Stimmung* that emerges from resistance to *Stimmung.*" I explore the avant-garde resistance to mood in chapter 1. Gumbrecht, *Atmosphere, Mood, Stimmung,* 129.

48 I am working here from DeNora's highly corporeal definition of agency, which includes "feeling, perception, cognition and consciousness, identity, energy, perceived situation and scene, embodied conduct and comportment." *Music in Everyday Life,* 20.

49 Böhme, "The Art of the Stage Set as a Paradigm for an Aesthetics of Atmospheres," 2–9. See also Böhme, *Atmosphäre,* translated into Japanese as *Funiki no bigaku.*

50 DeNora, *Music in Everyday Life*; McCarthy, *Ambient Television*; Bull, *Sound Moves*; Kassabian, *Ubiquitous Listening.*

51 Scarry, *Dreaming by the Book*; Fletcher, *A New Theory for American Poetry*; Ngai, *Ugly Feelings*; Gumbrecht, *Atmosphere, Mood, Stimmung.*

52 "I recommend [reading for *Stimmung*] not least of all because this is the orientation of a great number of non-professional readers (readers who are

not—and, of course, need not be—aware of the fact)." Gumbrecht, *Atmosphere, Mood, Stimmung*, 3, 5, 18.

53 Koike, *Serapii bunka no shakaigaku*, 121.

54 As Timothy Morton writes, "One function of ambience is to permeate and trouble the inside with the outside." Morton, "'Twinkle, Twinkle, Little Star' as an Ambient Poem," n.p.

55 There are of course often internal and external pressures on contemporary Japanese artists to situate themselves in relationship to this imaginary lineage, particularly when operating abroad, but this is tangential to the questions I am pursuing here. For more on the relationship between atmosphere and exoticism, see chapter 2, fn30.

56 For a wonderful study of the class politics of noise-cancelling headphones, see Hagood, "Quiet Comfort."

1. BACKGROUND MUSIC OF THE AVANT-GARDE

1 BGM is a commonly used Japanese acronym for background music (much easier to say than the fully transliterated *bakkuguraundo myūjikku*). While not frequently found in English, it is nonetheless convenient to use here as well, so I will.

2 Osaka, *Kankyō ongaku*, 90.

3 Ibid., 108.

4 Ibid., 88.

5 The misuse of sound and vibrational technology was a particular obsession of Unno, who early in his literary career worked as a government radio researcher for the Communication Ministry's Electrical Experiments Division. A staunch nationalist during the war years, Unno maintained a strong belief in science as the key to the nation's future. He was distraught by the wartime government's misuse of scientific research for political ends, however, and often aimed his fiction at a moral critique of the government's "science without conscience." Along with Edogawa Rampo and Yumeno Kyūsaku, Unno pioneered the proto–science fiction genre of the *kagaku shōsetsu* (science novel), a genre of speculative fiction warning of the dangers of scientific development without a guiding moral authority. Unno, "Jyūhachijikan no ongaku yoku"; Kawana, "Science without Conscience," 64.

6 Osaka, *Kankyō ongaku*, 96, 113.

7 For a concise history of Muzak, see Lanza, *Elevator Music*, 22–30.

8 Osaka, *Kankyō ongaku*, 219.

9 Ibid.

10 Kotler, "Atmospherics as a Marketing Tool," 50.

11 Quoted in Owen, "The Soundtrack of Your Life," n.p. For an insightful ethnographic study of background and foreground programmed music in retail space, see Sterne, "Sounds Like the Mall of America."

12 Quoted in Owen, "The Soundtrack of Your Life," n.p.

13 There is, of course, the possibility stimulus progression–style Muzak is being deployed with nostalgic, humorous, or ironic intent, though this does not seem to be the case in most places I have encountered it in Japan.

14 Osaka, *Kankyō ongaku,* 79–80.

15 Midori Yoshimoto positions the society's diverse approach to the question of environment as part of an emergent interest in creating immersive, mixed-media event spaces, an approach Japanese artists would further in the late 1960s under the banner of "intermedia." The goal of intermedia was to eliminate the frames separating established media genres and combine them into immersive experiential events. However, understanding the Environment Society as simply an early intermedia experiment risks overlooking the group's main concern: the relationship between media and the aesthetic dimensions of the urban environment. Quote from Yoshimoto, "From Space to Environment," 40 (Yoshimoto's translation).

16 Akiyama et al., "Kankyō kara X e," 65.

17 As Yoshimoto notes, the latter performance didn't go exactly to Ichiyanagi's instructions, with Tōno crawling under his chair and Ay-O falling off his. The piece literalizes Erik Satie's "furniture music," attempting to rethink the chair as a threshold of bodily instability. In this instance of "environmental music," an object usually affording bodily support tips into a precarious and uncertain balancing act. Yoshimoto, "From Space to Environment," 29, 36. A recording of Akiyama's piece is included on *Obscure Tape Music of Japan,* vol. 6, *Tape Works of Akiyama Kuniharu 1* (Omega Point Records OPA-006, 2007).

18 Osaka, *Kankyō ongaku,* 4.

19 Environmental historian Nakagawa Osamu documents the more objective, scientific understanding of the environment emerging in the 1970s and 1980s, one focused on identifying generalizable properties acting on human perception in dependable ways. Nakagawa, *Fūkeigaku,* 102.

20 Yoshimoto, "From Space to Environment," 45. For example, the expo serves as the final chapter in Havens, *Radicals and Realists,* and one of the closing scenes of the "season of image politics" in Furuhata, *Cinema of Actuality.* See also the special issue of *Review of Japanese Culture and Society* edited by Yoshimoto and dedicated to the expo.

21 Particularly the pieces emerging from the NHK Electronic Music Studio. See also Loubet, "The Beginnings of Electronic Music in Japan, with a Focus on the NHK Studio."

22 Tanaka, *Denshi ongaku in Japan,* 25–26.

23 A recording is included on *Obscure Tape Music of Japan,* vol. 5, *Toshi Ichiyanagi, Music for Tinguely* (Omega Point Records OPA-005, 2006).

24 I thank Ken Yoshida for introducing me to this essay.

25 Indeed, background listening as a practice of mood regulation is nothing new and, from a larger historical perspective, might even be considered the dominant way music has been engaged with over the centuries. Hosokawa Shūhei, building on the work of Hanns-Werner Heister, notes how

the modern idea of an autonomous musical practice based on concentrated listening has its roots in eighteenth- and nineteenth-century European moves to rationalize and objectify musical materials. This turned music audition into a specialist activity, bringing it off the street and into the concert hall and the domain of high culture. In the long history of music, concentrated listening was established as a cultural ideal only during this short period—and of course, even then the practice was restricted to privileged classes in certain parts of the world. With the emergence of mechanical reproduction, the cultural hegemony of concentrated listening gradually began to weaken. Upending the usual narrative of attentional decline, Hosokawa presents the history of recorded music not as a story of the gradual erosion of concentrated musical experience figured in the quiet and attentive concert hall but as a return to a form of listening long present in earlier times. Hosokawa, *Rekōdo no bigaku*, 115–22. On the role of architecture and musical acoustics in the culture of focused listening, see also Thompson, *The Soundscape of Modernity*.

26 Akiyama, "Dezain suru ongaku," 17.

27 Ibid.

28 Ngai is describing the "confident" tone of capitalism in Herman Melville's "Bartleby the Scrivener." Ngai, *Ugly Feelings*, 69.

29 Akiyama, "Dezain suru ongaku," 17–18.

30 "New age" music reached the Japanese market in the late 1980s and often featured Satie's softer compositions in its repertoire. Windham Hill Records, based out of Palo Alto, California, is often credited with establishing the genre. The company was founded in 1976 and grew steadily into the mid-1980s, though it was only around 1986 when they began to apply the term "new age" to their releases. While at first new age music was available only through specialty metaphysical bookstores, record stores in the United States began adding new age sections around 1985. Radio also began to take notice in the late 1980s, and new age radio programs began to appear. Stephen Hill's *Music from the Hearts of Space* (first created in 1973 at KPFA in Berkeley, California) had the greatest success, entering syndication in 1983 and being picked up by NPR and sent out to 230 national affiliates by 1986. In Japan, Kitaro (real name Takahashi Masanori) emerged as another key player in the new age scene. He achieved international notoriety following his soundtrack for NHK's long-running documentary series *Silk Road* (1980–90). Building off this success, Kitaro signed a contract for worldwide distribution with Geffen in 1986, pushing him into the forefront of the new age music scene just as it was reaching its zenith. The "world music" boom in Japan started in the mid-1980s, propelled by popular musicians like Hosono Haruomi. Gregorian chant rose to popularity after Angel Records rereleased the Benedictine Monks of Santo Domingo de Silos's 1973 recording *Chant* in 1994. The album went triple platinum in the United States and sold six million copies worldwide, becoming one of the key records of the so-called world music and new age genres. The

Gregorian chant underlying the Ichiyanagi piece echoes Erik Satie's own strong interest in early monastic music and anticipated the centrality of the style—and modal music in general—in later ambient and relaxation genres.

31 Templier, *Erik Satie,* 45.

32 Quoted in Schlomowitz, "Cage's Place in the Reception of Satie," n.p.

33 After being introduced to Satie's work by Virgil Thompson, in 1949 Cage successfully applied for a grant to go to Paris to research Satie's furniture music. From Satie, Cage developed his own theory of how music might engage with environmental sounds, becoming more fully integrated with "life" as lived in everyday environments rather than in the concert hall. "For Satie," Cage writes, "art was the art of living and through living creating artworks. Art was not separated from living or from life. In a sense, it is the same as doing the dishes." At the time, the European avant-garde did not take Satie's playful miniatures seriously, and Cage's lectures from the period see him engaged in a playful pro-Satie polemic: "Insist upon Furniture Music. Have no meetings, no get-togethers, no social affairs of any kind without Furniture Music. Don't get married without Furniture Music. Stay out of houses that don't use Furniture Music. Anyone who hasn't heard Furniture Music has no idea what true happiness is." To defend Satie against those who viewed his output as too slight to count him as a major composer, Cage often drew on an example of a short form that nonetheless was respected as a serious art: the haiku poetry of Japan. See Kostelanetz, ed., *John Cage,* 89.

34 There was scattered interest in Satie's music in Japan in the early part of the century. Koizumi Osamu published what appears to be the first Japanese essay on his work in 1923, "Kindai jiyū ongaku-ha no senkusha Sati to sono kaiki" (Satie, pioneer of the style of modern free music, and his mystique). This was followed by Sakaguchi's translation of Cocteau's writing on Satie, appearing in the literary coterie magazine *Kotoba* at the start of the Showa period (1926). Following Sakaguchi's lead, much of the early interest in Satie in Japan would come from poets arriving at Satie via Cocteau. Soprano Mitsuma Makiko gave the first Japanese performance of Satie's music in 1927, as part of a concert of modern French vocal music, and Sakaguchi and a few other writers invited her back to sing Satie's *Je te veux* in the spring of 1929. Composers Matsudaira Yoritsune and Hayasaka Fumio also introduced a few of Satie's piano pieces. In the immediate postwar period, there were a few scattered Satie concerts, including a young Takemitsu Tōru introducing the first performance of the piano version of Satie's *Parade* at the opening of an Okamoto Tarō exhibition. This was followed by the *Performance of Contemporary Works* (*Gendai sakuhin ensōkai*), held at the Ichigaya Joshigakuin, August 9, 1952. This concert claimed to introduce works by "largely unknown" European composers including Satie, Samuel Barber, Darius Milhaud, and Olivier Messiaen, as well as works by three "new" Japanese composers: Takemitsu,

Suzuki Hiroyoshi, and Yuasa Jōji. The latter three, like Akiyama, were members of Jikken Kōbō, which put on the event. In this pre–Satie boom concert, Satie is presented in the context of twelve-tone music rather than the iconoclastic *gymnopédist* image he would later acquire. See Akiyama," 'Nashi no katachi o shita ongaku' no shikō," n.p.; Cocteau, *Erikku Sati*; Miwa, "Kokutō būmu yobu"; Akiyama, *Erikku Sati oboegaki*, 498. On Satie and Ango, see Ōhara, "Bungaku to ongaku no kōsaku."

35 Takahashi, "Erikku Satie to 'Kagu no ongaku,' " n.p. Satie was already well known enough by 1968 for the *Yomiuri* newspaper to cover the Italian publication of Aldo Ciccolini's *Satie Complete Piano Works*. See "Sati no 'Piano ongaku zenshū.' "

36 The first seven concerts were held at Jean-Jean, Shibuya, beginning on September 17, 1975; subsequent concerts were held at the Nichibu kaikan (Maison Franco-Japonaise) in Ochanomizu. Other major Satie events included *The Essential Eric Satie* in 1977, part of Ichiyanagi Toshi's *Music in Museums* series; monthly Satie concerts throughout 1981 by Shimada Lily; and a 1984 reprise of the *Complete Works* by Takahashi Aki at Shibuya's Eurospace. A wide range of Satie books and recordings were also published around this time, including Nakajima Haruko's *Nemureru nashi e no fūga: Erikku Sati ron* (Fugue for a sleepy pear: On Eric Satie), a reprint of Cocteau's *Erik Satie* translated by Sakaguchi and Satō Saku, and Takahashi Aki's best-selling recording *Aki pureizu Sati: Hoshitachi no musuko* (Aki plays Satie: Son of the stars, 1985), timed to the sixtieth anniversary of Satie's passing. Kusahara Machiko recalls often hearing Satie's music piped into the crowded central shopping arcades in Shibuya, Tokyo, during the 1980s as well. See "Ishoku sakkyokuka Sati" and "Eiga to ongaku de Sati no sakuhin."

37 Alongside the music, these concerts often incorporated elements of Satie's famously idiosyncratic tastes. For example, a 1980 Satie concert at the British House in Yokohama included food and wine of only white colors, since Satie wrote in his diary he ate only white-colored foods. See "Shiroi chūshoku o tabe."

38 See Shibata, "Bunjin fū no hitogara nijimu."

39 Akiyama, *Erikku Sati oboegaki*, 498. See also Takahashi, *Parurando*, 91–94.

40 *Vexations*, a work never performed in Satie's lifetime, is the major touchstone for later composers asserting Satie's credentials as an avant-garde agitator. The piece calls for 840 repetitions of a short piano phrase and demands "serious immobilities" (*immobilités sérieuses*). The first full performance of *Vexations* in Japan took place on December 29, 1967, the second worldwide after Cage's 1963 premiere in New York. Held at the American Culture Center in Akasaka-mitsuke, Tokyo, fifteen avant-garde composers participated, including Mayuzumi Toshirō, Ichiyanagi Toshi, and Irino Yoshirō. The concert started at 11 a.m. and was scheduled to last over twenty hours. Pianist Shimada Lily later transformed *Vexations* into

an even more extreme test of endurance, performing the entire piece solo on a number of occasions.

41 Akiyama, " 'Nashi no katachi o shita ongaku' no shikō," n.p.

42 See "Sati eranda Kamiya Ikuyo-san."

43 Takahashi, "Erikku Satie to 'Kagu no ongaku,' " n.p.

44 Ibid.

45 Identifying a similar contrast, Yoshimoto notes the works presented in *From Space to Environment* "shared the industrial and hard-edge aesthetics of concurrent trends in the West such as Minimalism, Op art, light art, and kinetic-art." This emphasis on discreet lines and sharp juxtapositions was also central to the Environment Society members' work at the various Expo '70 pavilions. But it was difficult to find a hard edge over at the Pepsi Pavilion, where Nakaya Fujiko was exhibiting her first fog sculpture in collaboration with the American group Experiments in Arts and Technology (EAT). Curator Nakai Yasuyuki suggests it was the Pepsi Pavilion that most successfully carried forward the quest for dynamic environmental experience the Environment Society had sought, even though Nakaya and EAT were not associated with the group. While I agree with Nakai the Pepsi Pavilion most successfully marked the transition from the environmental aesthetics of the midsixties to the new decade of comfortable environmental design, we might also note the aesthetic differences between Nakaya's fog and the former Environment Society members' installations elsewhere on the expo grounds. The fog presents a softer and more amorphous landscape, a more permeable and ambiguous border than the one policed by Akiyama, with his concern to distinguish between art and design. Takahashi, "Erikku Satie to 'Kagu no ongaku,' " n.p.; Nakai is cited in Yoshimoto. "From Space to Environment," 44.

46 Schlomowitz, "Cage's Place in the Reception of Satie," n.p.

47 Ibid.

48 Ibid.

49 Feldman, *Give My Regards to Eighth Street,* 143.

50 With his solitary quirks, the Satie persona also served 1970s and 1980s Japan as an archetype of the contemporary intermedia celebrity. Journalists covering the Satie boom portray him as an odd but affable loner, as illustrated by his eccentric fashions (his identical velvet suits, his huge number of umbrellas), his acerbic wit (in ample evidence in his *Memoirs of an Amnesiac*), his famous friends (Cocteau, Claude Debussy, Tristan Tzara), and his Dadaist provocations (like publishing real estate advertisements for nonexistent, imaginary buildings). In his lifetime Satie often shuttled between commercial contexts (composing tunes for music hall and cabarets) and avant-garde, conceptual works. His career served as an important precedent for later Japanese musicians like Sakamoto Ryūichi, who would similarly move fluidly between art music and pop music. The Japanese fascination with Satie has yet to abate, as evidenced by a major summer 2015 exhibition at the Bunkamura museum in Shibuya, *Erikku*

Sati to sono jidai (Erik Satie and his time, July 8 to August 30, 2015). Thanks go to Anne McKnight for reminding me of the many Kitano–Satie connections in her blog post of February 15, 2012.

51 In his formulation of ambient music, Eno draws directly from Satie, as well as John Cage, British minimalist composers such as Michael Nyman and Gavin Bryars (both of whom Eno would later release on his Obscure Records label), and the studio experiments of German bands like Can.

52 Eno, "Ambient Music," n.p.

53 For what it is worth, Eno has told Japanese interviewers he was heavily influenced by "Japanese thought" at the time he was working on the *Ambient* series—particularly, the concepts of *wabi* (austere refinement and spiritual solitude) and *sabi* (quiet simplicity). Code, ed., *Unfinished,* 132.

54 Böhme, "Acoustic Atmospheres," 16. As Hosokawa writes, the Walkman became emblematic of the "autonomy" of the 1980s: "The Walkman is neither cause nor effect of that autonomy, neither evokes nor realizes it. It *is* the autonomy, or rather *autonomy-of-the-walking-self.*" Hosokawa, "The Walkman Effect," 166; emphasis in original.

55 I draw here from Eric Tamm's insightful structural analysis of Eno's ambient work. See Tamm, *Brian Eno,* 131–50.

2. THE SOUND OF EMBODIED SECURITY

1 This section of the expressway, near Sangenjaya, was recently featured in Murakami Haruki's novel *1Q84* (2009–10).

2 Soundscape researcher Barry Truax describes the "acoustic horizon" simply as "the farthest distance from which sound may be heard." See chapter 3 for further discussion. Truax, *Acoustic Communication,* 26.

3 Thibaud, "The Sonic Composition of the City," 330. This potential for blocking out the listener's surroundings has long been a point of contention surrounding portable media technology: one of Sony's original Walkman designs featured two sets of headphone jacks, with an orange button enabling the sound source to be "shared" between two listeners. Morita Akio, one of Sony's cofounders, noticed when he listened to the research models at home his wife became annoyed, as she felt shut out. So he ordered a second jack to be installed. More recently, Noah Vawter's Ambient Addition (2006) sought to address the "isolation" of the portable music player. Ambient Addition is a Walkman-style device Vawter designed at the MIT Media Lab as an attempt to reintegrate mobile headphone listeners into their surrounding environment. As the listener walks around a space, an onboard microphone records environmental noise, and an audio processor uses various techniques to soften the sounds and make them more "musical" before transmitting them to the headphones. The device gives these found sounds a sense of rhythm by repeating samples, filtering and transposing tones to approximate melodies, and filtering or masking frequencies that do not fit into the dominant musical harmonics.

Vawter hoped Ambient Addition would add a sense of curiosity and inter-
activity to a listener's relationship to their landscape. For example, they
may alter their path through space in order to explore novel sounds for
the Addition to process. According to surveys distributed to Vawter's test
subjects, however, most reported the Ambient Addition was a socially iso-
lating experience. Vawter sees this as a failure, but I would argue this partial isolation is for many listeners one of the primary appeals of ambient
listening—the way it provides a buffer between self and surroundings. See
Vawter, "Ambient Addition," 15, 90. For an early study on urban headphone listening, see Hosokawa, "The Walkman Effect."

4 For example, Truax writes disparagingly of how recorded music "is used
to fill a gap or deficiency in the environment, whether psychological or
physical. . . . If an activity is boring or frustrating, pleasant music will
make it seem easier to endure. . . . The problem, if there is one, with the
role of background sound as a surrogate in these situations is that, at the
very least, it does not change the problem or fill the deficiency—it only appears to. . . . The surrogate relationship often becomes a dependency that
prevents, or at least discourages, the person from taking any action that
will lead to a lasting solution." Truax, *Acoustic Communication,* 169–70.

5 Deleuze and Guattari, *A Thousand Plateaus,* 493.

6 Ibid. As Guattari notes elsewhere, mood arrives first and orients the
emerging subject by affectively consolidating the surrounding environment: "One says to oneself: Isn't it boring here? Isn't it nerve-racking? Isn't
the ambience great? The first given constitutes a disposition or a situation
which is that I'm here, in the room, and the enunciation takes on consis-
tency." Cited in Lazzarato, *Signs and Machines,* 218.

7 Milutis, *Ether,* 172.

8 Problems of security, of course, have been central to debates over neoliberalism and its incorporation of calculated risk into ever more areas
of everyday life. The larger issue of neoliberal (in)security is beyond the
scope of this book, though I hope to imply here some of the ways ambient
media are sensory technologies with a complex relation to larger conditions of personal and collective security, both actual and felt. For a detailed analysis of security issues with particular attention to the role of
atmosphere and affect, see Peter Sloterdijk's *Spheres* trilogy (1998–2004;
first two volumes translated as *Bubbles* and *Globes*).

9 DeNora, *Music in Everyday Life,* 67.

10 Ibid., 84–85; emphasis in original.

11 Ibid., 87–88.

12 Eno, liner notes to *Ambient 4: On Land*. Cage is again an important precursor here, with his *Imaginary Landscape* series of compositions (1939–52).

13 Quoted in Tamm, *Brian Eno,* 4.

14 Korner, "Aurora Musicalis," n.p.

15 Eno, *A Year with Swollen Appendices,* 295; quoted in Sun, *Experiments in
Musical Performance,* 85.

16 This material was republished in book form, followed by a sequel and then another discography from another publisher, each edited by Mita Itaru. Mita and Studio Voice, eds., *Anbiento myūjikku 1969–2009*; Mita, ed., *Ura anbiento myūjikku 1960–2010*; and Mita, ed., *Anbiento difinitivu 1958–2013*.

17 On Happy End and Yellow Magic Orchestra, see Bourdaghs, *Sayonara Amerika, Sayonara Nippon*, 159–94.

18 Eno began the EMI sublabel Obscure Records (1975–78) as a way to use his popularity to secure the distribution of then-unknown British composers like Gavin Bryars and Michael Nyman, as well as releasing recordings by Cage and his own early ambient experiment, *Discreet Music* (1975).

19 Hosono, *Hosono Haruomi intabyū*, 209–10.

20 Ibid., 230.

21 "Loom" features the work of YMO sound programmer Matsutake Hideki, who in the early 1970s was an apprentice to the groundbreaking Japanese electronic composer Tomita Isao. Matsutake was reportedly turned on to electronic music at the age of eighteen when he heard Wendy Carlos's *Switched-On Bach* (1968) at the American Pavilion at Expo '70. Tomita is in many ways Carlos's Japanese equivalent, producing electronic synthesizer renditions of composers like Debussy and Stravinsky.

22 Hosono, *Hosono Haruomi intabyū*, 236–38.

23 Hosono and Yoshinari, *Gijutsu no higi*, 66–67.

24 Both Eno and Hosono have lengthy résumés not just as musicians but also as record producers, where they use electronic sound technology to work at length with the spatial and textural qualities of an artist's sound. The similarities do not end there. Hosono—born ten months before Eno—followed Eno's lead in expanding his style from vocal-based pop music to more abstract instrumentals. Both describe themselves as dabblers and experimenters rather than professional musicians. And both have cultivated an androgynous celebrity image, working to undermine the machismo of the traditional rock star. Eno often performed in drag during his Roxy Music years, while Hosono plays with his gender appearance in images like the cover to the Haruomi Hosono with Friends of Earth album *S.F.X.* (Another Record Company, 1984). Nakazawa Shinichi proposes Hosono's music is about exploring femininity from the guise of a male musician. See Hosono, "Taidan: Nakazawa Shinichi," 73.

25 See Hosono, *Rekōdo purodyūsā wa sūpāman o mezasu*. On the spatialization of music production more generally, see Doyle, *Echo & Reverb*.

26 Hosono would later make a trip to Santa Fe, New Mexico, to visit a Hopi reservation for the television documentary *Subarashiki chikyū no tabi: Damatte suwatte jitto kike ~Neitibu Amerikan oto no tabi~* (Traveling the Wonderful World: Be quiet, sit down, and listen—the Native American soundquest; aired December 15, 1996).

27 Hosono, *Globule*, 175; originally in English. Cited in Thaemlitz, "Globule of Non-Standard," 97.

28 Hosono and Nakazawa, *Kankō*. On Exotic Japan, see Ivy, *Discourses of the Vanishing,* 42–48. For more on the turn to the exotic in 1980s Japan and Hosono's relationship with the more "cosmic" horizons of outer space, see Roquet, "A Blue Cat on the Galactic Railroad."

29 Hosokawa argues Hosono's solo projects in the mid-1970s sought to complicate images of exotic Asia through complex forms of mimicry and auto-orientalism. Describing Hosono's *Soy-Sauce Music* trilogy (Hosono purposefully uses the English term rather than the Japanese), Hosokawa writes that "what is central to the Trilogy is less the North American approach to exoticizing Japan and the Japanese than the Japanese way of exoticising American exoticism." See Hosokawa, "Soy Sauce Music." The trilogy includes *Tropical Dandy* (1973), *BonVoyage Co./Taian yōkō* (1976), and *Paraiso* (1978).

30 While Hosono's "globule" image was new, exoticism and atmosphere have long been close associates. David Toop traces the origins of ambient music back to Claude Debussy's visit to the Paris Exposition of 1889, where he first witnessed performances of music and dance from Java, Vietnam, Cambodia, and Japan. The more dispersed modes of attention called for in these musical styles emerged soon after in Debussy's compositions. Toop cites this as a crucial moment in the lineage of ambient listening leading up through Eno's work and on toward the present day. Debussy was of course not alone in his growing interest in an atmospheric "Asia," an aesthetic trajectory shared by many of the most influential European writers and artists of the period. Later ambient musicians in Japan, meanwhile, drew freely from the work of these European and American composers as well as from the work of pioneering Japanese electronic musicians drawing on this work, such as Tomita Isao's early synthesizer renditions of Debussy, *Snowflakes Are Dancing* (1974). This proclivity to locate ambience in a more illegible and unfamiliar foreign locale—be it the exotic East or the exotic West—is also found in ambient literature. Ann Sherif writes of Yoshimoto Banana's interest in the "supernatural potential of exoticized Asian otherworlds," pointing to the Bali setting of *Amrita* (1994). In other texts, the healing exotic is located in Europe, as in the Greek isles of Murakami Haruki's *Sputnik Sweetheart* (*Supūtoniku no koibito,* 1999) or the Francophile hotel of Kurita Yuki's *Hôtel Mole* (discussed in chapter 6). Toop, *Ocean of Sound,* 18; Sherif, "Japanese without Apology," 288. See also Clark, *Oriental Enlightenment*. On "world music" and Deep Forest, see Feld, "A Sweet Lullaby for World Music."

31 Hosono, "Taidan: Nakazawa Shinichi," 73; Hosono, *F.O.E. Manual*. On the history of the Earth image, see Garb, "The Use and Misuse of the Whole Earth Image."

32 Hosono, *Anbiento doraivā,* 18.

33 The term Hosono uses here, "oceanic feeling," is often associated with Sigmund Freud but comes from his friend and interlocutor, the religious studies scholar Romain Rolland. Freud sent a copy of his *The Future of*

an Illusion to Rolland after its publication, and Rolland responded in a letter that though he agreed with the book's comments on religion, he felt the "true source of religious sentiments" had been left out: a feeling of limitless, unbounded eternity Rolland described as the "oceanic feeling." In the opening pages of Freud's following work, *Civilization and Its Discontents,* he describes being greatly troubled by the letter and admits to being unable to discover this oceanic feeling within himself. He then attempts an explanation, describing a process where the ego begins with this feeling of wholeness, with no distinction between inside and outside, but as it matures "gradually separates off an external world from itself." What becomes the oceanic feeling for adults is a remnant of this original feeling of eternity. While this lingering feeling "might seek something like the restoration of limitless narcissism, it is ousted from its place in the foreground." Notably, Freud ends the discussion on a conciliatory note, admitting there may indeed be something more to Rolland's feeling than the "feeling of infantile helplessness" but that "for the present it is wrapped in obscurity." As William B. Parsons suggests in his study of the concept, two contrasting attitudes are proposed in Freud's reading: the oceanic feeling as "regressive and defensive," on the one hand, and "therapeutic and adaptive," on the other. As Hosono notes, the atmospheres afforded by ambient music often work toward this feeling of oceanic limitlessness, and it is not surprising debates over the social implications of the style (discussed in chapter 6) play out along similar lines to the Freud–Rolland exchange. One way of understanding the role of the "oceanic" in the 1980s is to consider the shift from Freud's earlier psychological explanation (with reference to the ego) to a more somatic understanding, in which the oceanic feeling marks a particular sensory situation rather than a problem of identity or maturity. I consider this issue further later in the book as well as in Roquet, "A Blue Cat on the Galactic Railroad." See Minato et al., "Towards a Culture of Ex-stase," 168–79; Freud, *Civilization and Its Discontents,* 15, 20–21; Parsons, *The Enigma of the Oceanic Feeling,* 109.

34 Cooper, "KALX Berkeley Interview," n.p. This new home-listening model was put forth most directly in the Warp label's highly influential *Artificial Intelligence* compilation from 1992 (the first in a series). The cover shows an android asleep in an armchair in front of a stereo system, with Kraftwerk and Pink Floyd record sleeves scattered nearby. According to Warp cofounder Steve Beckett, this design was chosen in order to signal the arrival of a new type of electronic music not intended for dancing. See Reynolds, *Generation Ecstasy,* 183.

35 Ibid.

36 Inoue uses the French spelling of "ambient" (*ambiant*) perhaps as one way to assert his work's departure from the ambient music preceding it.

37 On the influence of American pulse-pattern minimalist music on techno, see Fink, *Repeating Ourselves,* 56.

38 On the image of the otaku in the 1980s and 1990s, see Ōtsuka, *"Otaku" no seishinshi.*

39 This small image of the globe appears on all the releases of FAX's "world" sublabel, home to artists Namlook releases from outside Germany.

40 Cooper, "KALX Berkeley Interview," n.p.

41 Reynolds, "Chill." The term itself comes from Kevin Martin, who used it as the title for the fourth volume in Virgin UK's A Short History of Ambient series, *Isolationism* (AMBT4, 1994).

42 Reynolds, "Chill." See also Massumi, *The Politics of Everyday Fear,* viii.

43 Miyadai points to earlier influential manga like *Nausicaä of the Valley of the Wind* (Miyazaki Hayao, 1982–94) and *AKIRA* (Ōtomo Katsuhiro, 1982–90). For a sense of the postapocalyptic ambience of the decade, listen to Geinoh Yamashirogumi's score during the ending sequences of the *AKIRA* anime feature (1988). Later postapocalyptic styles tend to start out after everything has already been swept away (not unlike Hatakeyama's music). A prominent example in manga is Ashinano Hitoshi's *Yokohama kaidashi kikō* (Yokohama shopping log, 1994–2006), discussed in Hairston, "A Healing, Gentle Apocalypse." In music, consider Ōtomo Yoshihide's transition from his work with Ground Zero in the early and mid-1990s to the reductionist onkyō-ha styles of the late 1990s and 2000s. On stage the quiet theater movement led by Hirata Oriza in the 1990s made a similar move. Chapter 5 considers this desire to subtract in more detail.

44 The move to reintegrate electronic music with more traditional instrumentation has led some to use the term "postclassical" to describe recent ambient and minimalist approaches incorporating recognizably classical instrumentation with more contemporary electronic styles.

45 Another noteworthy album marking this shift in Japan is Onodera Yui's *Entropy* (2005).

46 Hatakeyama Chihei, interview with the author, October 14, 2013. It is difficult to imagine what Adorno would have made of ambient music given his concerns over the "deconcentration" of listening. But there is something in the darker strains of Hatakeyama's ambience that seems to echo his attempt to find a negative dialectics in sound.

47 Massumi, *The Politics of Everyday Fear,* 24.

48 Allison's *Precarious Japan* provides an overview of these issues and also, in the cumulative experience of reading the book, gives a feeling for the gloomy atmosphere I am describing here.

3. MOVING WITH THE RHYTHMS OF THE CITY

1 For the fascinating story behind the design of a station melody for Shinjuku station, see Ide, *Mienai dezain,* 8.

2 Lefebvre, *Rhythmanalysis,* 67–68.

3 Ibid., 74.

4 Ibid., 65.

5 Ibid., 89.

6 For example, Ann Adachi's touring selection of early Japanese video art, *Vital Signals* (2009), uses "Body Acts" as one of three main curatorial themes, along with "Explorations of Form" and "Collective Memory."

7 Krauss writes of "a narcissism so endemic to works of video that I find myself wanting to generalize it as *the* condition of the entire genre." Krauss, "Video," 50–52; emphasis in original.

8 Nornes, *Forest of Pressure*, xxiv, 135.

9 Ahmed, *Strange Encounters*, 83.

10 Iwabuchi, *Recentering Globalization*, 51–84.

11 Deleuze and Guattari describe how attempts to depersonalize the self and reach the level of the "cosmos" (achieving a kind of elemental mobility akin to wind and water) always bring with them the danger of dispersing oneself "too quickly," leading to a fall into an isolated vacuum, what they call a "black hole." Deleuze and Guattari, *A Thousand Plateaus*, 344.

12 See Saitō, *Hikikomori*; Fukue, "Elderly Living Alone Increasingly Dying the Same Way."

13 McCarthy, *Ambient Television*, 225–27.

14 The two most influential are *Berlin: Symphony of a Great City* (Walter Ruttmann, 1927) and *Man with a Movie Camera* (Dziga Vertov, 1929).

15 Visual music goes back to early twentieth-century painters like Hans Richter and Oskar Fischinger, who began using film to animate their abstract art practice. In the 1950s and 1960s, the Whitney brothers began introducing more psychedelic forms of sound and imagery into the genre. John Whitney later became one of the earliest proponents of computer-based visual music, the most prominent form today. On the landscape tradition in experimental film, see MacDonald, *The Garden in the Machine*.

16 See Ross, "Site et spécificité dans le cinéma élargi japonais."

17 Anna McCarthy's *Ambient Television* (2001) describes the diversification of viewing styles accompanying the spread of television screens into public space. Many writers on television have pointed out the oftentimes distracted nature of television viewing in the home—viewers are often multitasking, having simultaneous conversations, running off to the bathroom, and going off to do other activities during commercial breaks. McCarthy adds to this an awareness of all the ways television screens now serve to shape attention in public spaces as well, with televisions in bars, hospital waiting rooms, airport lounges, and restaurants. Smartphones and tablets have opened up even more opportunities for personal and portable viewing.

18 Japanese BGV producers include major labels such as Pony Canyon (home of the *Virtual Trip* series), BMG Japan, and Nihon Columbia, as well as smaller outfits like Takeo (Synforest) and Vicom (Healing Islands). A personal favorite—edging on the ambient—is Nihon Media Play's *Gensō kōjō/Industrial Romanesque* series (2006–12), featuring nighttime views of abandoned factories.

19 Eno's exhibition is referenced—often critically—in many of the essays in the ambient music special issue of the Japanese magazine *UR* (1990). While not as explicitly ambient in orientation, Nam-Jun Paik also held exhibitions in Japan a number of times in the early 1980s, culminating in the solo *Mostly Video* exhibition at the Tokyo Metropolitan Art Museum (1984).

20 For an overview of Yamaguchi's video installation work, see Yamaguchi, *Eizō kūkan sōzō*.

21 Video artist Taki Kentarō of Video Art Center Tokyo has led the push for outdoor video art installations in Japan, part of a larger explosion in projection mapping and site-specific video installations.

22 The work is included on the *Vital Signals: Early Japanese Video Art* DVD collection (Electronic Arts Intermix, 2010).

23 Traux, *Acoustic Communication*, 67.

24 Arai won the Noma Literary New Face Prize for *Vekusashion* (Vexations, 1987) and the Akutagawa Prize for *Tazunebito no jikan* (The time of missing persons, 1988). The title of the first novel is an homage to Satie's piece of the same name. The condensed milk comment is in Arai, *Kankyō bideo no jidai*, 10.

25 See, for example, the Speedometer albums *Private* (1999) and *Sense of Wander* (2002).

26 On the earlier genealogy of the term *eizō*, see Furuhata, *Cinema of Actuality*, 39.

27 This work and *Summer Afternoon* can be seen on Ise's *Late Then Never* DVD (Nibi, 2006).

28 On the turn to landscape in Japanese photography, see Sas, *Experimental Arts in Postwar Japan*, 180–200.

29 Lefebvre, *Rhythmanalysis*, 89.

30 On list making and its relation to environmental awareness, see Bogost, *Alien Phenomenology*, 35–59.

31 ARS Electronica, "ARS Electronica Festival 2010."

32 Hosono, *Anbiento doraivā*, 45. This orientational instability is reflected in Tokyo's wonderful street and subway maps, which are oriented not toward a particular cardinal direction but in whatever direction the map itself happens to be facing.

33 Michel Chion locates a shift in the balance between sound and vision with the arrival of television. Steven Shaviro provides an eloquent summary of Chion's argument: "In traditional analog cinema, the images are primary. The coherence of a film comes mostly from its mise en scène, cinematography, and editing. The soundtrack serves as a support for the images. . . . But all this changes in post-cinematic media like television and video. Sound now operates overtly instead of covertly. Instead of sound providing 'added value' to the image, now a visual element is 'nothing more than an *extra image*,' working 'to illustrate or rather decorate' whatever is spoken on the soundtrack. . . . In this way, 'television is illustrated radio'; for

'sound, mainly the sound of speech, is always foremost in television. Never offscreen, sound is always *there,* in its place, and does not need the image to be identified.'" Shaviro, *Post Cinematic Affect,* 78; Chion, *Audio-Vision,* 158.

34 DeNora, *Music in Everyday Life,* 87.

4. SOFT FASCINATIONS IN SHALLOW DEPTH

1 Jansen's brother and former Japan lead singer, David Sylvian, has long maintained ties with artists in Japan (the country), including collaborations with Sakamoto Ryūichi in the early 1980s. In recent years his Samadhisound label has often worked with Japanese ambient video and visual artists, including Ise and Takagi Masakatsu.

2 This live version is included on a Japanese DVD of the concert: Steve Jansen, *The Occurrence of Slope* (P-Vine Records, 2008).

3 The quote is from Isozaki, *Japan-ness in Architecture,* 8. For an overview and critique of this discourse in Japan in the context of Murakami Takashi's "superflat," see Lamarre, *The Anime Machine,* 111–14.

4 This was typical of the postmodern theory of the "new academicism" in the early 1980s, as well as Azuma's much later study of postmodern "database" aesthetics. See Asada Akira's best-selling *Kōzō to chikara* and *Tōsōron* and Azuma's *Otaku.*

5 As Lamarre notes, the "exploded projection can implicate a greater degree of instrumentalization and rationalization than Cartesian perspectivalism, because it operates well under conditions of movement, and it proves amenable to temporary inhabitation by a variety of modern subject effects." Lamarre, *The Anime Machine,* 113–23, 308.

6 Gibson, *The Ecological Approach to Visual Perception,* 77.

7 Lamarre argues that "it is only in relation to Western geometric perspective that orthogonal perspective has been deemed unsystematic or disorderly" and proposes the need to "acknowledge the instrumentality and rationality implicit in the distributive image." *The Anime Machine,* 120, 122, 308.

8 Rose, *The Politics of Life Itself,* 15. For a related argument about surface as the basis of self in a Japanese online context, see Nozawa, "The Gross Face and Virtual Fame."

9 Foucault, *The Birth of Biopolitics,* 260.

10 Manovich, *Software Takes Command,* 267.

11 Ibid., 281. See my earlier discussion of Eno and Hosono as producers in chapter 2.

12 Ibid., 261.

13 Brian Eno, for example, asks, "Why not regard [television] as the late 20th Century's way of making paintings?" See Eno, "My Light Years."

14 Ibid., 285.

15 See Gibson, *The Ecological Approach to Visual Perception,* 65–92.

16 Kaplan, Kaplan, and Ryan, *With People in Mind,* 18–19.

17 Kaplan, "The Restorative Benefits of Nature," 173.

18 Kaplan, Kaplan, and Ryan, *With People in Mind,* 2.

19 The term *uncanny valley* comes from robot researcher Mori Masahiro, who uses it to describe the revulsion triggered when the ability to visually perceive the difference between human and robot begins to blur. See Mori, "Bukimi no tani genshō."

20 Ishida, "STILL/ALIVE," 99.

21 On the triptych and figure/ground relations, see Deleuze, *Francis Bacon,* 62–70.

22 Takei and Keane, *Sakuteiki,* 54, 189. I know I said I would resist comparisons with earlier moments in Japanese aesthetic history, but I couldn't resist this one.

23 For example, Moriyama Daidō is a Japanese photographer well known for shooting photographs in the streets with a small point-and-shoot-style camera. For Moriyama the point-and-shoot camera, though it may not have all the manual controls and high image quality of larger models, has the crucial advantage of being unintimidating to the random passersby on the street he chooses to photograph, allowing him to capture them at their most unguarded. This style of environmental engagement has affinities with the "actualities" of the early days of filmmaking, when the camera setup was similarly self-contained and lenses were often trained on the everyday movements of humans, cars, and animals, as in the films of the Lumière brothers. My thinking in this chapter is inspired in part by Mary Ann Doane's argument this early interest in seemingly random urban events might be understood as a search for contingency in a social environment both increasingly chaotic and increasingly controlled. Furuhata notes connections between these early actualities and the late-1960s landscape theory movement in Japan. The latter's turn to "diagramming the landscape" provides an interesting contrast to the type of environmental engagement I describe here. See the documentary *Daido Moriyama: Stray Dog of Tokyo* (Fujii Kenjirō, 2001); Doane, *The Emergence of Cinematic Time*; Furuhata, *Cinema of Actuality,* 124.

24 *Journal for People* was released as a two-disc CD/DVD set by Carpark Records in 2006.

25 These works are available on Kawamura Yuki, *Slide* (DVD, Lowave, 2005). The music in these videos is by Hanno Yoshihiro.

26 *Rama* and *Aura* are available on Takagi Masakatsu, *World Is So Beautiful* (DVD, Daisyworld Discs, 2003, and Carpark Records, 2006), while *Birdland,* mentioned later, appears on *Journal for People.*

27 Included on Ise's *Late Then Never* DVD.

28 Manovich, *The Language of New Media,* 322; Bizzocchi, "Video as Ambience," n.p.

29 These videos are included as bonus material on *The Occurrence of Slope* DVD (see note 2).

5. SUBTRACTIVISM

1 Ngai, *Ugly Feelings,* 41.
2 Gumbrecht, *Atmosphere, Mood, Stimmung,* 4.
3 For example, see Lim, *Tsai Ming-liang and a Cinema of Slowness.*
4 Anderson and Richie, *The Japanese Film,* 324.
5 Oshii, for example, notes the central importance of the drifting, atmospheric, and plotless montage sequences in his anime features, like the rainy night sequence in *Ghost in the Shell* (*Kōkaku kidōtai,* 1995). For Oshii these scenes are important for depicting "not the drama itself, but the world that the characters inhabit." Quote from Jonathan Ross's interview with Oshii in episode 1 of the BBC documentary *Asian Invasion* (aired January 10, 2006).
6 Murakami's "Tony Takitani" first appeared in 1990 in the literary magazine *Bungei shunjū* and then in a longer version the following year. It was later anthologized in the 1996 Murakami collection *Rekishinton no yūrei* (The ghost of Lexington). The *New Yorker* published an English translation by Jay Rubin in 2002. The film version traveled widely and won a number of awards, including the Fipresci Prize and the Special Jury Prize at the 2005 Locarno International Film Festival, runner-up for Best Soundtrack at the Los Angeles Film Critics Association, and the Grand Prize at the Takasaki Film Festival, as well as a string of nominations, including the Grand Jury prize at Sundance. The film received positive reviews in all the major American papers, with *Variety* posting one of the few skeptical pieces. See Elley, "Review: 'Tony Takitani.'"
7 For a thorough comparison of differences between the short story and the film, see Thornbury, "History, Adaptation, Japan."
8 The 2006 DVD of the film released by Axiom in the United Kingdom includes a making-of documentary focusing on this outdoor shoot.
9 Illouz, *Saving the Modern Soul,* 82.
10 Ibid., 65. This in itself was already a step away from the "molar" model of the Cartesian self toward a more "molecular" understanding of the employee as an assemblage of traits and skills. For an insightful parallel history of management psychology in the United Kingdom, see Rose, *Governing the Soul,* 55–119.
11 Illouz, *Saving the Modern Soul,* 103.
12 Maeda, *Text and the City,* 203.
13 Kinmonth, *The Self-Made Man in Meiji Japanese Thought,* 46.
14 Maeda traces this shift toward self-improvement as an end in itself by following its emergence in popular fiction, particularly the novels of Kikuchi Kan. He demonstrates how this strand of popular literature gradually abandoned larger social themes and narrowed its focus to documenting upper-class familial concerns. This helped reimagine Meiji social imperatives through a framework of individual success, just as the private sphere was becoming increasingly visible as a topic for public discussion and government regulation. Maeda, *Text and the City,* 203.

15 Rose, *Governing the Soul*, 118.

16 Japan's first "self-development seminar" (*jikokeihatsu seminā*), based on the American self-realization model, was held in 1977. Koike, *Serapii bunka no shakaigaku*, 90. See chapter 6 for more on the emerging "healing boom."

17 This idea of the 1960s student movements being driven by unruly emotion is a common theme in Murakami's work, as in his breakthrough 1987 novel *Norwegian Wood*. The therapeutic orientation toward life is also readily evident in Murakami's own writing practice, in which he emphasizes self-discipline and parallels with his long-distance-running practice. In memoirs like *What I Talk about When I Talk about Running*, Murakami envisions writing as a potentially "toxic" practice that needs to be paired with healthy exercise—implicitly casting earlier Japanese author's tendencies toward alcoholism and suicide as (to paraphrase Tony) "just immature." For more on Murakami's role in the development of ambient literature, see the following chapter.

18 Fink, *Repeating Ourselves*, 6. Ichikawa himself started out as a director of television advertisements in the mid-1980s. An early spot won the Golden Lion at the 1985 Cannes International Advertising Festival, and this led to an invitation to direct his debut feature, *BU-SU* (1987). While their films have little in common, Ōbayashi Nobuhiko's move from television advertising to feature film directing in the late 1970s served as an important precedent for Ichikawa's later career. The slower aesthetic available in film proved appealing to others in the television industry as well, most notably Kitano Takeshi, who from the late 1980s began pairing his persona as an over-the-top television personality with a more contemplative and minimalist approach to filmmaking. Ichikawa's early films were still in a faster style, but with the part-fiction, part-documentary *Dying at a Hospital* (*Byōin de shinu koto,* 1993) and subsequent series of Ozu Yasujirō–inspired works, he began to slow everything down. At the turn of the century, Ichikawa tried, with mixed results, to eschew his restrained style for something more upbeat in films like *Tadon and Chikuwa* (*Tadon to Chikuwa,* 1998), *Tokyo Marigold* (2001), and *Ryoma's Wife, Her Husband and Her Lover* (*Ryoma to tsuma to sono otto to aijin,* 2002). In adapting Murakami's short story, however, he moved back toward the quiet style for which he was known. On Ōbayashi's career, see Roquet, "Obayashi Nobuhiko, Vagabond of Time." Abé Casio's *Beat Takeshi vs. Takeshi Kitano* is a full-length study of the relationship between Kitano's film and television personas. For more on Ichikawa's career, see the posthumous tribute volume edited by Kawade shobō shinsha, *Ichikawa Jun*.

19 Simmel, *On Individuality and Social Forms*, 336.

20 DeNora, *Music in Everyday Life*, 149–150. McGuinness and Overy gloss cosubjectivity and intersubjectivity as a difference between "communion" and "communication," hinting at the important role religious architectures once played in affording cosubjective experience. McGuiness and Overy, "Music, Consciousness, and the Brain," 245.

21 Edo (as Tokyo was known prior to 1868) was different in this respect. Comparing Edo travel guides and those from the Meiji era (1868–1912), Maeda notes a shift in focus: whereas Edo guides led visitors to places where people gathered to interact with one another in work and play, Meiji guides pointed to where the individual traveler could go on their own and see the sights. If Edo's appeal still focused on intersubjective encounters, then Meiji Tokyo offered cosubjective sights for the solitary tourist. In this Meiji model of sightseeing, however, a visitor was still attending directly to the space itself. A different relationship to the environment emerged moving into the postwar period, when Japanese cities gradually became more rationalized and anonymous through the emergence of spaces designed first around mobility and efficiency and later around the comforts of amenity culture. Maeda, *Text and the City,* 83. See also Yoshimi, "The Market of Ruins."

22 On the *Polis* urban studies website, Peter Sigrist blogs what he calls an "Embarrassing Ode to McDonald's as an Open Public Office Space." He describes spending long hours working at a McDonald's restaurant chain, despite thinking McDonald's is "completely lame." Why? He cites dependable Wi-Fi access, no pressure to buy anything, the energy of having other people around, efficiency, cleanliness, low prices, and a smoke-free environment. As Nick Kaufman points out in the comment section, "Whereas at the indie coffee shop you might feel like you are imposing or that someone is breathing down your neck, at big chains you can find anonymity [and] a lack of guilt." As Kaufman points out, the appeal of the big generic chain café or family restaurant is how it can serve as a mostly anonymous container for private use. The store design and the people who temporarily inhabit it provide a baseline energetic vibe but otherwise remain as ignorable as possible. In turn, customers can expect to be ignored themselves as long as they contribute an unobtrusive but amiable energy to the shared space. Rather than simply write off these generic containers as culturally empty "nonplaces," Sigrist proposes we might acknowledge what these spaces of anonymity afford. Standardized and generic environments allow for a specific form of public engagement—or perhaps more accurately, public disengagement. They provide a space to be with others but not have to attend to them as discreet individuals. Sigrist, "Embarrassing Ode to McDonald's as an Open Public Office Space."

23 Fukasawa, *Shisō toshite no "Mujirushi ryōhin,"* 17.

24 On discourse surrounding postmodernism in 1980s Japan, see Ivy, "Critical Texts, Mass Artifacts."

25 Saitō's argument here echoes Christopher Lasch's much earlier analysis of postmodern art and literature in *The Minimal Self* (1984). Unlike Lasch, however, Saitō (rather vaguely) asserts this apparent form of social withdrawal, at least when "used intentionally in an artistic context," also "does reality a service." He doesn't elaborate what this means but gives a clue in his description of the works of sculptor Ōmaki Shinji (1971–), which

"bring discontinuity to the experience of the observer and force a mood change." Saitō, "Floating and Disassociation," 85–87.

26 Arai, *Kankyō bideo no jidai,* 92–94. Ueno describes a similar impulse in *<Watashi> sagashi gēmu,* 86.

27 Arai, *Kankyō bideo no jidai,* 9, 84.

28 Ibid., 19–20, 95.

29 Thomas H. Davenport has pointed to an "attention crisis" emerging as a result of the rapid growth of information exposure in everyday life, particularly with the more recent rise of networked digital media. Davenport argues contemporary information societies are moving toward an "attention economy." His logic runs as follows: it is wrong to speak of an "information economy," since information is overabundant. The main resource information consumes is attention, and thus in an age oriented around information, attention becomes the true commodity. Davenport thus sees the currency of this new economy gradually shifting from money to attention. See Davenport, *The Attention Economy.*

30 Richard Lanham notes how the attention economy puts a greater emphasis on rhetorical style: "The devices that regulate attention are stylistic devices. Attracting attention is what style is all about. If attention is now at the center of the economy rather than stuff, then so is style. It moves from the periphery to the center. Style and substance switch places." Copious examples could be put forth here, but I'll stick with one clearly working with both novelty and scale: the exploding-sound (*bakuon*) film screening. Pioneered by rock critic Higuchi Yasuhito and the Baus Theatre in Kichijōji (Tokyo), the exploding-sound screening brings large rock concert speaker stacks into the movie theater and presents films with the volume turned up to eleven, often accompanied by a remixed soundtrack designed to make the added loudness more effectively visceral and pummeling. As a way to draw film viewers back into the theater, exploding sound brings scale and novelty home viewing cannot hope to compete with (of course, the novelty will eventually wear off, and hearing damage might dull *bakuon*'s volume advantage). Meanwhile, advertisers continually seek to tap preconscious forms of awareness not requiring focused attention but nonetheless influencing behavior. For example, Steve Goodman has written of "earworms," advertising jingles designed to wiggle their way into a person's unconscious without the need for them to consciously attend to the sounds themselves. See Lanham, *The Economics of Attention,* xiii–xii; Higuchi, *Eiga wa bakuon de sasayaku 99–09*; Goodman, *Sonic Warfare,* 141.

31 Manovich, *The Language of New Media,* 157, 143.

32 Ibid., 271, 128–29. The quote is from Muschamp, "Blueprint."

33 While it is beyond the scope of this chapter, the subtractivism I describe here might be productively contrasted with Koichi Iwabuchi's arguments for why Japanese consumer electronics like the Sony Walkman can pass as "culturally odorless" when exported abroad. See Iwabuchi, *Recentering Globalization,* 27–28.

34   Yoshimi links this directly back to the atmosphere of the late-1960s student protests: "Far from being postmodern, the extremely independent and provocative spirit foregrounded in Parco's advertising was an avant-garde as if it had been directly inherited from the young radicals of the '60s." Yoshimi, "The Market of Ruins," 293.

35   Ibid., 298–99.

36   Yoshimi presents this as the third major overhaul of the Tokyo landscape in the twentieth century. The first followed the Great Kanto Earthquake in 1923, which led to an urban structure based on "living in a residential suburb, commuting to a city-centre office on one of the private railway lines spreading out from central termini, and shopping in Ginza at the weekends." The second emerged during the period of rapid economic growth spurred by the massive infrastructure projects accompanying the 1964 Tokyo Olympics, like the bullet train and the Metropolitan Expressway. Unlike these first two historical moments, the 1980s transformation consisted not of large-scale construction projects but of the blending of the various urban districts into a more homogenous transnational information culture built around global capital. Once-distinct neighborhoods like Shibuya were overrun with discount national and transnational chains of the type once found only in the suburbs. Yoshimi, "The Market of Ruins," 297.

37   Tanaka, *Tezawari no media o motomete.* Cited in Yoshimi, "The Market of Ruins," 296–97.

38   Quoted in Holloway and Hones, "Muji, Materiality, and Mundane Geographies," 557.

39   Ibid., 558. As the authors go on to note, there is an inherent paradox in branding the no-style style: Muji's products claim not to attract attention to their presence, and yet this mundaneness itself "becomes the keynote of its recognizable Mujiness." See also Fukasawa, *Shisō toshite no "Mujirushi ryōhin."*

40   See the next chapter for more on the gender politics of the healing style persona.

41   There are other connections to 1980s Japanese fashion among the makers of the film as well. As noted earlier, Ichikawa first gained recognition as an award-winning creator of TV commercials in the 1980s, including many fashion ads. Hirokawa Taishi, the director of photography, first achieved recognition as an art photographer in the mid-1980s for a project in which he took a wagon full of clothing by then-prominent Japanese designers like Yamamoto, Kawakubo Rei, and Miyake Issey to rural parts of the country and asked farmers, fishermen, and other laborers to pose in the outfits while he took their photographs. See Hirokawa, *Sonomama sonomama.* For more on Japanese fashion in the 1980s, see Skov, "Fashion Trends, Japonisme, and Postmodernism."

42   As *Billboard* magazine notes in an article entitled "Sakamoto's 'Energy Flow' Enlivens Japan."

43   See Ichikawa's comments in the liner notes to the soundtrack (Commmons/Avex, 2007).

44   See Yamane for a fuller reading of the position of Tony's wife in Murakami's original story (in which she is nameless). Thornbury notes if Eiko is fifteen years younger than Tony, she was born around the time of the 1964 Tokyo Olympics. This means she grew up amid the heights of the high-growth period and, I would add, as part of the first generation to fully embrace personal mood regulation as a way of life. Yamane, "Zettai-teki kodoku no monogatari," 21; Thornbury, "History, Adaptation, Japan," 163.

45   The classic study is Mertens, *American Minimal Music.*

46   Yamane, "Zettai-teki kodoku no monogatari," 23.

47   Seo, "Namae kara no tōhi," 63.

48   It is worth noting the album version of Sakamoto's score does feature moments of hesitation mixed in with the melancholic drift; places where the melody seems to get stuck on a single note, as if the repetition was threatening to break down. Little of this made it into the film itself, however.

49   Ahmed, *The Promise of Happiness,* 135–48.

50   Discussed in Sedgwick, *Touching Feeling,* 14–15.

51   Dargis, "He's an Isolated Fellow; She's Addicted to Shopping."

52   Washida, *Mōdo no meikyū,* 8.

6. HEALING STYLE

1   *Iyashi* is a nominalization of the verb *iyasu,* meaning to heal or mend both physically and psychologically. The word in its current usage first appeared in the context of anthropologist Ueda Noriyuki's medical ethnography of a Sri Lankan village entitled "Akumabari: Iyashi no kosumorojii" (Exorcizing devils: The cosmology of healing; later published as Ueda, *Kakusei no nettowāku*). The term was picked up by a *Yomiuri shimbun* journalist covering an Ueda lecture and emerged—seven years later—as a popular expression in advertising and other media.

2   McNicol, "Designs for Life," 35.

3   The Kobe earthquake of January 17, 1995, killed, injured, and displaced thousands. As investigations progressed into the inordinate number of "earthquake-safe" buildings that had collapsed, it became clear widespread government corruption and graft had been the mainstay during the years of high economic growth. Barely two months later, doomsday cult Aum Shinrikyō committed Japan's worst terrorist attack to date, spreading toxic gas through rush-hour Tokyo commuter trains just steps away from the national legislature. Again, details of the attack showed the incident had social implications reaching well beyond the event itself. Many members of Aum were highly educated young men and women from comfortable backgrounds. That such "ordinary" Japanese youth had turned against the nation reinforced the impression Japanese society as a whole was at fault. These incidents came in the wake of intensive media cover-

age of a number of brutal homicides committed by young boys alongside less violent but more widespread instances of youth delinquency such as compensated dating (*enjo kōsai*), bullying, and chronic absenteeism from school. See Leheny, *Think Global, Fear Local*, 27–48.

4 Tanaka, *Kenkōhō to iyashi no shakaishi*, 9.

5 See Watanabe, *Ninniku kenkōhō*.

6 Tanaka, *Kenkōhō to iyashi no shakaishi*, 30. The natural healing boom built on the growing interest in personal health management. Japan's first fitness center, Nakano's Tokyo Athletic Club, started in 1969, and others soon started opening around the country following the arrival of the Big Box fitness center in Takadanobaba, Tokyo, in 1974.

7 Ibid., 32–34.

8 Rose describes this as a "sense that some, perhaps all, persons, though existentially healthy are actually asymptomatically or pre-symptomatically ill." Rose, *The Politics of Life Itself*, 19.

9 Nakamata, *Bungaku*, 32.

10 Ibid., 32–34.

11 Sherif, "Japanese without Apology," 279.

12 Literary critic Yoshida Nobuko discusses these three authors in "Banana Girls," n.p.

13 The critical establishment has also taken note: Kurita won the 2002 Subaru Literature Prize for her debut work, *Hamizabesu*, and *Onuiko Terumii* (2003), *Oteru Moru* (2005), and *Maruko no yume* (2005) have each been nominated for the Akutagawa Prize, Japan's most high-profile literary award. For a more recent Kurita novel revisiting many of the ambient strategies and healing themes discussed here, see *Tamagomachi* (2014).

14 Higashi, "Shohyō 'Oteru Moru' Kurita Yuki," 347.

15 Yoshida, "Shohyō 'Onuiko Terumii' Kurita Yuki," 291; Kakuta, *Yotte iitai yoru mo aru*, 102.

16 Kurita, *Hamizabesu*, 203. Nakamata also connects an easy-to-read style with the healing quality of Murakami Haruki's novels. Nakamata, *Bungaku*, 32.

17 Kurita, *Hamizabesu*, 204.

18 Scarry, *Dreaming by the Book*, 9.

19 Deleuze, *Cinema 2*, 12.

20 Scarry, *Dreaming by the Book*, 25.

21 Ibid., 12.

22 Smith, *Film Structure and the Emotion System*, 149–51. See note 2 of the introduction.

23 The spiritual retreat is among the Sri Lankan healing traditions described in Ueda, *Kakusei no nettowāku*.

24 The small pocket-size Japanese paperback format (*bunkobon*) was first produced by Iwanami in the 1920s.

25 Nakamata, *Bungaku*, 29. Murakami explicitly invokes the camera as narrator in *Afutā dāku* (2004, translated by Jay Rubin as *After Dark*, 2007).

26 Deleuze, *Cinema 2*, 3. Deleuze describes how with such an empty subjectivity "the connection of the parts of space is not given, because it can come about only from the subjective point of view of a character who is, nevertheless, absent, or has even disappeared, not simply out of the frame, but passed into the void." Deleuze, *Cinema 2*, 8. Gumbrecht similarly notes how a literary atmosphere "enables the reader to inhabit worlds of sensation—worlds that feel like physical environments." Gumbrecht, *Atmosphere, Mood, Stimmung*, 75.

27 Kakuta, *Yotte iitai yoru mo aru*, 102. On the writerly/readerly distinction, see Barthes, *S/Z*, 5.

28 Deleuze, *Cinema 2*, 7.

29 Gumbrecht, *Atmosphere, Mood, Stimmung*, 75.

30 Carroll, "Film, Emotion, and Genre," 34.

31 Kakuta, *Yotte iitai yoru mo aru*, 103.

32 Ibid. Note the parallel here with the flexible controls of neoliberal governmentality Foucault points out: as long as the overall system continues to function, a high degree of freedom can be tolerated at the local level.

33 Quoted in Kuroko, " 'Iyashi-kyō' ni kogareru wakamonotachi," 158.

34 Ibid., 160–61. Notably, gustatory concerns seem to be a common feature of the debate. Murakami's characters relish their meals as much as Yoshimoto enjoys her cake. In both cases, advocates of a literature of critique cannot seem to stomach bringing fiction down to the level of more proximate (and supposedly less rational) senses like taste and touch.

35 Sherif, "Japanese without Apology," 299–300.

36 Morioka, *Mutsū bunmeiron*; Asada, "Infantile Capitalism and Japan's Postmodernism;" Yoda, "The Rise and Fall of Maternal Society," 884.

37 Lasch, *The Minimal Self*, 19.

38 Ibid., 58.

39 Jameson, *Postmodernism, or, the Cultural Logic of Late Capitalism*, 10.

40 Oguma and Ueno, *<Iyashi> no nashonarizumu*; Yagi, *<Iyashi> toshite no sabetsu*. For a critique of the influence of therapy culture on education in the United Kingdom, see Furedi, *Therapy Culture*. For a recent argument similar to Yagi's but in an Anglophone context, see Ahmed, *Willful Subjects*.

41 Ahmed, *The Cultural Politics of Emotion*, 153.

42 For example, Elizabeth Le Guin writes of using relaxation music as a retreat from the stresses and pressures of a patriarchal society—even as she simultaneously recognizes the music itself does nothing directly to remedy the situation. Le Guin, "Uneasy Listening."

43 The blanket dismissal of "trigger warnings" by some self-identified leftists during recent debates in the English-language academy falls prey to a similar problem: by diagnosing any and all content warnings as capitulation to an oversensitive therapy culture, the diversity of possible student responses to course content is erased in favor of an idealized and unemotional critical subject. On the lure of the strong critical persona for the

reader, see Bull, *Anti-Nietzsche*. Sedgwick's essay on paranoid reading in *Touching Feeling* (123–52) raises similar points. For an excellent analysis of the figure of the oversensitive student and its complex relationship to neoliberalism, see Ahmed, "Against Students."

44 Illouz, *Saving the Modern Soul*, 19.
45 Ibid., 20.
46 Clammer, *Contemporary Urban Japan*, 9.
47 See McGee, *Self-Help, Inc.*
48 "Black corporation" (*burakku kigyō*) is a Japanese term referring to a company engaged in exploitative labor practices, often related to forced overtime, power harassment, and poor working conditions. The term first emerged in the IT industry around the turn of the century. See Mie, "Black kigyo."
49 Kurita, "Kurita Yuki."
50 Higashi, "Shohyō 'Oteru Moru' Kurita Yuki," 347.
51 See Matsuura, "Dai 26-kai Subaru bungakushō jushōsha intabyū," 186. For the classic study of emotional labor, see Hochschild, *The Managed Heart*.

CONCLUSION

1 Rose, *Governing the Self,* 260.
2 For one version of this story, see Toop, *Ocean of Sound,* 139.
3 Hosono and Yoshinari, *Gijutsu no higi,* 66–67.
4 Code, ed. *Unfinished,* 31–33.
5 Arai, *Kankyō bideo no jidai,* 88.
6 Matsuura, "Dai 26-kai Subaru bungakushō jushōsha intabyū," 186.
7 Hosokawa traces the emergence of *weak listening* through Muzak, John Cage, and Brian Eno. Hosokawa, *Rekōdo no bigaku,* 303–38.
8 See Washida, *<Yowasa> no chikara.*
9 Ahmed, *The Cultural Politics of Emotion,* 148; emphasis in original.
10 See Irigaray, *The Forgetting of Air in Martin Heidegger.*

BIBLIOGRAPHY

Abé Casio. *Beat Takeshi vs. Takeshi Kitano.* Translated by William O. Gardner and Takeo Hori. New York: Kaya, 2004.

Adorno, Theodor W. *Minima Moralia: Reflections from Damaged Life.* New York: Verso, 1978.

Ahmed, Sara. "Against Students." http://feministkilljoys.com/2015/06/25/against-students/.

———. *The Cultural Politics of Emotion.* New York: Routledge, 2004.

———. *The Promise of Happiness.* Durham, N.C.: Duke University Press, 2010.

———. *Queer Phenomenology: Orientations, Objects, Others.* Durham, N.C.: Duke University Press, 2006.

———. *Strange Encounters: Embodied Others in Post-coloniality.* New York: Routledge, 2000.

———. *Willful Subjects.* Durham, N.C.: Duke University Press, 2014.

Akiyama Kuniharu. "Dezain suru ongaku"(Music that designs). *Dezain hihyō* 1, no. 1 (November 1966): 15–19.

———. *Erikku Sati oboegaki* (Erik Satie memorandum). Tokyo: Seidosha, 1990.

———. " 'Nashi no katachi o shita ongaku' no shikō" (The aim of "music in the shape of a pear"). *Yomiuri shimbun,* December 27, 1977.

Akiyama Kuniharu, Isozaki Arata, Tōno Yoshiaki, Tōmatsu Shōmei, Fukuda Shigeo, and Yoshimura Masunobu. "Kankyō kara X e: 'Kūkan kara kankyō e' ten kara 1 nen" (From environment to X: One year after the "From space to environment" exhibition). *Bijutsu techō* 291 (December 1967): 56–68.

Akiyama Teruo, ed. *Ongaku no techō: Sati* (Music notebook: Satie). Seidosha, 1981.

Allison, Anne. *Precarious Japan.* Durham, N.C.: Duke University Press, 2013.

Anderson, Joseph L., and Donald Richie. *The Japanese Film: Art and Industry.* New York: Grove Press, 1959.

Appleton, Jay. *The Experience of Landscape.* London: Wiley, 1975.

Arai Man. *Kankyō bideo no jidai* (The age of ambient video). Tokyo: Elans Books, 1990.

———. *Tazunebito no jikan* (The time of missing persons). Tokyo: Bungei shunjū, 1988.

———. *Vekusashion* (Vexations). Tokyo: Bungei shunjū, 1987.

ARS Electronica. "ARS Electronica Festival 2010: Prix Forum Digital Musics and Sound Art." Vimeo video, 1:32:13. http://vimeo.com/15351256.

Asada Akira. "Infantile Capitalism and Japan's Postmodernism: A Fairy Tale." In *Postmodernism and Japan,* edited by Masao Miyoshi and Harry D. Harootunian, 273–78. Durham, N.C.: Duke University Press, 1989.

————. *Kōzō to chikara: Kigōron o koete* (Structure and power: Beyond semiotics). Tokyo: Keisō shobō, 1983.

————. *Tōsōron: Sukizo-kizzu no bōken* (On escape: Adventures of the schizokids). Tokyo: Chikuma shobō, 1984.

Ashinano Hitoshi. *Yokohama kaidashi kikō* (Yokohama shopping log). 14 vols. Tokyo: Kōdansha, 1994–2006.

Azuma Hiroki. *Otaku: Japan's Database Animals.* Translated by Jonathan Abel and Shion Kono. Minneapolis: University of Minnesota Press, 2009.

Barthes, Roland. *S/Z.* Translated by Richard Miller. New York: Hill and Wang, 1974.

Befu, Harumi. *Hegemony of Homogeneity: An Anthropological Analysis of "Nihonjinron."* Melbourne: Trans Pacific Press, 2001.

Benedict, Ruth. *The Chrysanthemum and the Sword: Patterns of Japanese Culture.* Boston: Houghton Mifflin, 1946.

Berlant, Lauren. *Cruel Optimism.* Durham, N.C.: Duke University Press, 2011.

————. *The Female Complaint: The Unfinished Business of Sentimentality in American Culture.* Durham, N.C.: Duke University Press, 2008.

Bizzocchi, Jim. "Video as Ambience: Reception and Aesthetics of Flat-Screen Video Display." *Journal of Moving Image Studies* 4, no. 1 (Spring 2005). http://www.avila.edu/journal/.

Bogost, Ian. *Alien Phenomenology, or What It's Like to Be a Thing.* Minneapolis: University of Minnesota Press, 2012.

Böhme, Gernot. "Acoustic Atmospheres: A Contribution to the Study of Ecological Aesthetics." *Soundscape: The Journal of Acoustic Ecology* 1, no. 1 (Spring 2000): 14–18.

————. "The Art of the Stage Set as a Paradigm for an Aesthetics of Atmospheres." Centre for Research on Sonic Space & Urban Environment. http://www.cresson.archi.fr/PUBLI/pubCOLLOQUE/AMB8-confGBohme-eng.pdf.

————. *Atmosphäre: Essays zur neuen Ästhetik* (Atmosphere: Essays on the new aesthetics). Frankfurt am Main: Suhrkamp, 1995.

————. *Funiki no bigaku: Atarashii genshōgaku no chōsen* (The aesthetics of atmosphere: The challenge of a new phenomenology). Translated by Kajitani Shinji, Saitō Shō, and Nomura Fumihiro. Kyoto: Kōyō shobō, 2006.

Borovoy, Amy. "Japan as Mirror: Neoliberalism's Promise and Costs." In *Ethnographies of Neoliberalism,* edited by Carol J. Greenhouse, 60–75. Philadelphia: University of Pennsylvania Press, 2010.

Bourdaghs, Michael. *Sayonara Amerika, Sayonara Nippon: A Geopolitical Prehistory of J-Pop.* New York: Columbia University Press, 2012.

Bull, Malcolm. *Anti-Nietzsche.* New York: Verso, 2011.

Bull, Michael. *Sound Moves: iPod Culture and Urban Experience.* London: Routledge, 2007.

Carroll, Noël. "Film, Emotion, and Genre." In *Passionate Views: Film, Cognition, and Emotion,* edited by Carl Plantinga and Greg M. Smith, 21–47. Baltimore, Md.: Johns Hopkins University Press, 1999.

Chion, Michel. *Audio-Vision: Sound on Screen.* Translated by Claudia Gorbman. New York: Columbia University Press, 1994.

Clammer, John. *Contemporary Urban Japan: A Sociology of Consumption.* Oxford: Blackwell, 1997.

Clark, J. J. *Oriental Enlightenment: The Encounter between Asian and Western Thought.* New York: Routledge, 1997.

Cocteau, Jean. *Erikku Sati* (Erik Satie). Translated by Sakaguchi Ango and Satō Saku. Kyō no ongaku series. Tokyo: Shinyasōsho, 1977.

Code, ed. *Unfinished.* Tokyo: Agle, 2000.

Cooper, Sean. "KALX Berkeley Interview." Interview with Tetsu Inoue. http://music.hyperreal.org/artists/tetsu/press/inouevw.

Cornyetz, Nina, and J. Keith Vincent, eds. *Perversion and Modern Japan: Psychoanalysis, Literature, Culture.* New York: Routledge, 2010.

Dargis, Manohla. "He's an Isolated Fellow; She's Addicted to Shopping." *New York Times,* July 29, 2005.

Davenport, Thomas H. *The Attention Economy: Understanding the New Currency of Business.* Boston: Harvard Business Press, 2001.

Deleuze, Gilles. *Cinema 2: The Time Image.* Translated by Hugh Tomlinson and Barbara Habberjam. Minneapolis: University of Minnesota Press, 1989.

———. *Francis Bacon: The Logic of Sensation.* Translated by Daniel W. Smith. Minneapolis: University of Minnesota Press, 2004.

Deleuze, Gilles, and Félix Guattari. *A Thousand Plateaus: Capitalism and Schizophrenia.* Translated by Brian Massumi. Minneapolis: University of Minnesota Press, 1987.

DeNora, Tia. *Music in Everyday Life.* Cambridge: Cambridge University Press, 2000.

Doane, Mary Ann. *The Emergence of Cinematic Time: Modernity, Contingency, the Archive.* Cambridge, Mass.: Harvard University Press, 2002.

Doi Takayoshi. *Tomodachi jigoku: "Kūki o yomu" sedai no sabaibaru* (Friendship hell: Surviving the "reading the air" generation). Tokyo: Tokuma shoten, 2008.

Doyle, Peter. *Echo & Reverb: Fabricating Space in Popular Music Recording 1900–1960.* Middletown, Conn.: Wesleyan University Press, 2005.

Driscoll, Mark. *Absolute Erotic, Absolute Grotesque: The Living, Dead, and Undead in Japan's Imperialism: 1895–1945.* Durham, N.C.: Duke University Press, 2010.

"Eiga to ongaku de Sati no sakuhin" (Satie's works through film and music). *Asahi shinbun,* January 11, 1977.

Ekman, Ulrik, ed. *Throughout: Art and Culture Emerging with Ubiquitous Computing.* Cambridge, Mass.: MIT Press, 2013.

Elley, Derek. "Review: 'Tony Takitani.'" *Variety,* August 17, 2004.

Eno, Brian. "Ambient Music." Liner notes. *Ambient 1: Music for Airports.* EG, record, 1978.

———. Liner notes. *Ambient 4: On Land.* EG, record, 1982 (revised 1986).

———. "My Light Years." In *77 Million Paintings* liner notes. All Saints Records, 2006.

———. *A Year with Swollen Appendices*. London: Faber and Faber, 1996.

Feld, Steven. "A Sweet Lullaby for World Music." *Public Culture* 12, no. 1 (2000): 145–71.

Feldman, Morton. *Give My Regards to Eighth Street: Collected Writings of Morton Feldman*. Cambridge, Mass.: Exact Change, 2000.

Fink, Robert. *Repeating Ourselves: American Minimal Music as Cultural Practice*. Berkeley: University of California Press, 2005.

Fletcher, Angus. *A New Theory for American Poetry: Democracy, the Environment, and the Future of Imagination*. Cambridge, Mass.: Harvard University Press, 2004.

Foucault, Michel. *The Birth of Biopolitics: Lectures at the Collège de France 1978–1979*. Translated by Graham Burchell. New York: Picador, 2008.

———. *Ethics: Subjectivity and Truth*. Edited by Paul Rabinow. New York: The New Press, 1997.

———. *The Hermeneutics of the Subject: Lectures at the Collège de France 1981–1981*. Translated by Graham Burchell. New York: Picador, 2005.

Freud, Sigmund. *Civilization and Its Discontents*. Translated by James Strachey. New York: W. W. Norton, 1961.

———. *The Future of an Illusion*. Translated by James Strachey. New York: W. W. Norton, 1961.

Fukasawa Megumi. *Shisō toshite no "Mujirushi ryōhin": Jidai to shōhi to Nihon to* ("Mujirushi ryōhin" as a way of thinking: With the era, with consumption, with Japan). Tokyo: Chikura, 2011.

Fukue Natsuko. "Elderly Living Alone Increasingly Dying the Same Way." *Japan Times,* July 21, 2010.

"Funiki" (Atmosphere). *Seisenban Nihonkokugo daijiten*. Tokyo: Shōgakukan, 2006.

Furedi, Frank. *Therapy Culture: Cultivating Vulnerability in an Uncertain Age*. New York: Routledge, 2004.

Furuhata, Yuriko. *Cinema of Actuality: Japanese Avant-Garde Filmmaking in the Season of Image Politics*. Durham, N.C.: Duke University Press, 2013.

Garb, Yaakov J. "The Use and Misuse of the Whole Earth Image." *Whole Earth Review*, 1985, 18–25.

Gibson, James J. *The Ecological Approach to Visual Perception*. Boston: Houghton Mifflin, 1979.

Goodman, Steve. *Sonic Warfare: Sound, Affect, and the Ecology of Fear*. Cambridge, Mass.: MIT Press, 2010.

Guattari, Félix. *Chaosmosis: An Ethico-aesthetic Paradigm*. Bloomington: Indiana University Press, 1995.

Gumbrecht, Hans Ulrich. *Atmosphere, Mood, Stimmung: On a Hidden Potential of Literature*. Translated by Eric Butler. Stanford: Stanford University Press, 2012.

Haga Manabu. "Wakamono no taikan shikō to gendai shūkyō būmu: Sono riaritī kankaku to aidentiti no isō" (The sensory orientation of youth and the contemporary religion boom: Its feeling of reality and the topology of identity). *Tokyo gakugei daigaku kiyō 3 bumon shakaikagaku* 43 (1992): 100.

Hagood, Mack. "Quiet Comfort: Noise, Otherness, and the Mobile Production of Personal Space." *American Quarterly* 63, no. 3 (September 2011): 573–89.

Hairston, Marc. "A Healing, Gentle Apocalypse: Yokohama kaidashi kikō." *Mechademia* 3 (2008): 256–58.

Hanebayashi Yuzu. *Iyashi-kei josei ni naru hinto* (Hints on becoming a healing style woman). Tokyo: Seishun shuppansha, 2005.

Havens, Thomas R. *Radicals and Realists in the Japanese Nonverbal Arts: The Avant-garde Rejection of Modernism.* Honolulu: University of Hawaii Press, 2006.

Hayashi, Sharon. "From Exploitation to Playful Exploits: The Rise of Collectives and the Redefinition of Labor, Life, and Representation in Neoliberal Japan." In *Neoliberalism and Global Cinema: Capital, Culture, and Marxist Critique*, edited by Jyostna Kapur and Keith B. Wagner, 180–96. New York: Routledge, 2011.

Heidegger, Martin. *Being and Time.* Translated by Joan Stambaugh. Albany: State University of New York Press, 2010.

Higashi Naoko. "Shohyō 'Oteru moru' Kurita Yuki: Toshi no soko no yōchū no nemuri" (Book review of Kurita Yuki's *Oteru moru*: A larva sleeps at the bottom of the city). *Bungakukai* 59, no. 6 (2005): 346–48.

Higuchi Yasuhito. *Eiga wa bakuon de sasayaku 99–09* (Film whispers with an exploding sound 99–09). Tokyo: Boid, 2010.

Hirokawa Taishi. *Sonomama sonomama* (As it is, as it is). Tokyo: Ryūkō tsūshin, 1987.

Hochschild, Arlie Russell. *The Managed Heart: Commercialization of Human Feeling.* Berkeley: University of California Press, 1983.

Holloway, Julian, and Sheila Hones. "Muji, Materiality, and Mundane Geographies." *Environment and Planning A* 39, no. 3 (2007): 555–69.

Hosokawa Shūhei. *Rekōdo no bigaku* (Aesthetics of the record). Tokyo: Keisō shobō, 1990.

———. "Soy Sauce Music: Haruomi Hosono and Japanese Self-Orientalism." In *Widening the Horizon: Exoticism in Post-war Popular Music,* edited by Philip Hayward, 114–144. Sydney, Australia: John Libbey and Company, 1999.

———. "The Walkman Effect." *Popular Music* 4 (1984): 165–80.

Hosono Haruomi. *Anbiento doraivā* (The ambient driver). Tokyo: Māburutoron/Chūō kōron shinsha, 2006.

———. *F.O.E. Manual.* Tokyo: Fusōsha, 1986.

———. *Globule.* Tokyo: Non-Standard Books, 1984.

———. *Hosono Haruomi intabyū: The Endless Talking* (Hosono Haruomi interviews: The endless talking). Tokyo: Chikuma shobō, 2005.

————. *Rekōdo purodyūsā wa sūpāman o mezasu* (A record producer aims to be Superman). Tokyo: Tokuma shoten, 1984.

————. "Taidan: Nakazawa Shinichi—Yutaka ni torikomu 'joseisei'" (Discussion: Nakazawa Shinichi—A richly absorbed "femininity"). *Studio Voice* 383 (September 2008): 72–73.

Hosono Haruomi and Nakazawa Shinichi. *Kankō: Nihon reichi junrei* (Sightseeing: Pilgramage to the sacred places of Japan). Tokyo: Chikuma bunko, 1990.

Hosono Haruomi and Yoshinari Mayumi. *Gijutsu no higi* (The secret ceremony of technique). Shūkanbon/The Weekly Fluctuant series 15. Tokyo: Asahi, 1984.

Ichikawa Jun. Liner notes to Sakamoto Ryūichi, *Tony Takitani.* Commmons/Avex, CD, 2007.

Ide Hiroaki. *Mienai dezain: Saundo supēsu compōzā no shigoto* (Invisible design: The work of the sound space composer). Tokyo: Yamaha myūjikku media, 2009.

Illouz, Eva. *Saving the Modern Soul: Therapy, Emotions, and the Culture of Self-Help.* Berkeley: University of California Press, 2008.

Irigaray, Luce. *The Forgetting of Air in Martin Heidegger.* Translated by Mary Beth Mader. Austin: University of Texas Press, 1999.

Ishida Tetsurō. "*STILL/ALIVE*: Life, Time, and Possibility Captured in the Present Moment." *Sutiru/araivu: Nihon no shinshin sakka Vol. 6.* Tokyo: Tōkyōto shashin bijutsukan, 2007: 96–105.

"Ishoku sakkyokuka Sati" (The unique composer Satie). *Asahi shinbun,* September 16, 1975.

Isozaki Akira. *Japan-ness in Architecture.* Translated by Sabu Kohso. Cambridge, Mass.: MIT Press, 2006.

Ivy, Marilyn. "Critical Texts, Mass Artifacts: The Consumption of Knowledge in Postmodern Japan." In *Postmodernism and Japan,* edited by Masao Miyoshi and Harry D. Harootunian, 21–46. Durham, N.C.: Duke University Press, 1989.

————. *Discourses of the Vanishing: Modernity, Phantasm, Japan.* Chicago: University of Chicago Press, 1995.

————. "Formations of Mass Culture." In *Postwar Japan as History,* edited by Andrew Gordon, 239–58. Berkeley: University of California Press, 1993.

Iwabuchi, Koichi. *Recentering Globalization: Popular Culture and Japanese Transnationalism.* Durham, N.C.: Duke University Press, 2002.

Jameson, Frederic. *Postmodernism, or, the Cultural Logic of Late Capitalism.* Durham, N.C.: Duke University Press, 1991.

Kakuta Mitsuyo. *Yotte iitai yoru mo aru* (There are also nights when you want to drink and confess). Tokyo: Ōta shuppan, 2005.

Kaplan, Stephen. "The Restorative Benefits of Nature: Toward an Integrative Framework." *Journal of Environmental Psychology* 15 (1995): 169–82.

Kaplan, Stephen, Rachel Kaplan, and Robert L. Ryan. *With People in Mind:*

Design and Management of Everyday Nature. Washington, D.C.: Island Press, 1998.

Kassabian, Anahid. *Ubiquitous Listening: Affect, Attention, and Distributed Subjectivity*. Berkeley: University of California Press, 2013.

Kawade shobō shinsha, ed. *Ichikawa Jun*. Tokyo: Kawade shobō shinsha, 2009.

Kawana, Sari. "Science without Conscience: Unno Jūza and *Tenkō* of Convenience." In *Converting Cultures: Religion, Ideology, and Transformations of Modernity*, edited by Dennis C. Washburn and A. Kevin Reinhart, 183–208. Boston: Brill, 2007.

Kawasaki Kōji. *Nihon no denshi ongaku* (Japanese electronic music). Rev. ed. Tokyo: Aiikusha, 2009.

Kinmonth, Earl H. *The Self-Made Man in Meiji Japanese Thought: From Samurai to Salaryman*. Berkeley: University of California Press, 1981.

Koike Yasushi. *Serapii bunka no shakaigaku: Nettowāku bijinesu, jikokeihatsu, torauma* (The sociology of therapy culture: Network businesses, self-development, trauma). Tokyo: Keisō Shobō, 2007.

Koizumi Osamu. "Kindai jiyū ongaku-ha no senkusha Sati to sono kaiki" (Modern free music school pioneer Satie and his era). *Shi to ongaku*, July 1923.

Korner, Anthony. "Aurora Musicalis." Interview with Brian Eno. *Artforum*, summer 1996.

Koschmann, J. Victor. *Revolution and Subjectivity in Postwar Japan*. Chicago: University of Chicago Press, 1996.

Kostelanetz, Richard, ed. *John Cage*. New York: Praeger, 1970.

Kōtari Yūji. *Kūki no yomikata: Dekiru yatsu to iwaseru "shuzairyoku" kōza* (How to read the air: "Collection power" course on how to be called a can-do guy). Tokyo: Shōgakukan, 2008.

Kotler, Philip. "Atmospherics as a Marketing Tool." *Journal of Retailing* 49, no. 4 (Winter 1973–74): 48–64.

Krauss, Rosalind. "Video: The Aesthetics of Narcissism." *October* 1 (Spring 1976): 50–64.

Kurita Yuki. *Hamizabesu* (Hamizabeth). Tokyo: Shūeisha, 2003.

———. "Kurita Yuki." Interview with Nakazawa Akiko. Yahoo! Japan. Accessed November 22, 2005. http://books.yahoo.co.jp/interview/detail/31614071/01.html. Site discontinued.

———. *Maruko no yume* (Maruko's dream). Tokyo: Shūeisha, 2005.

———. *Onuiko Terumii* (The seamstress Terumii). Tokyo: Shūeisha, 2004.

———. *Oteru moru* (Hôtel Mole). Tokyo: Shūeisha, 2005.

———. *Tamagomachi* (Eggtown). Tokyo: Popura bunko, 2014.

Kuroko Kazuo. " 'Iyashi-kyō' ni kogareru wakamonotachi: Yoshimoto Banana no bungaku wa 'kyōsai' no kanō ni suru ka?" (The young people yearning for a "healing religion:" Can Yoshimoto Banana's literature provide "salvation?"). *Daihōrin* 69, no. 6 (2002).

Lamarre, Thomas. *The Anime Machine: A Media Theory of Animation*. Minneapolis: University of Minnesota Press, 2009.

Lanham, Richard A. *The Economics of Attention: Style and Substance in the Age of Information*. Chicago: University of Chicago Press, 2006.

Lanza, Joseph. *Elevator Music: A Surreal History of Muzak, Easy-Listening, and Other Moodsong*. New York: St. Martin's Press, 1994.

Lasch, Christopher. *The Minimal Self: Psychic Survival in Troubled Times*. New York: W. W. Norton, 1984.

Lazzarato, Maurizio. *Signs and Machines: Capitalism and the Production of Subjectivity*. Translated by Joshua David Jordan. Los Angeles: Semiotext(e), 2014.

Le Guin, Elisabeth. "Uneasy Listening." *repercussions* 3, no. 1 (1994): 5–21.

Lefebvre, Henri. *Rhythmanalysis: Space, Time, and Everyday Life*. Translated by Stuart Elden and Gerald Moore. London: Continuum, 2004.

Leheny, David Richard. *Think Global, Fear Local: Sex, Violence, and Anxiety in Contemporary Japan*. Ithaca, N.Y.: Cornell University Press, 2006.

Lemke, Thomas. "The Birth of Biopolitics: Michel Foucault's Lecture at the Collège de France on Neo-liberal Governmentality." *Economy and Society* 30, no. 2 (2001): 190–207.

Lim, Song Hwee. *Tsai Ming-liang and a Cinema of Slowness*. Honolulu: University of Hawai'i Press, 2014.

Loubet, Emmanuelle. "The Beginnings of Electronic Music in Japan, with a Focus on the NHK Studio: The 1970s." *Computer Music Journal* 22, no. 1 (Spring 1998): 49–55.

Lukács, Gabriella. *Scripted Affects, Branded Selves: Television, Subjectivity, and Capitalism in 1990s Japan*. Durham, N.C.: Duke University Press, 2010.

MacDonald, Scott. *The Garden in the Machine: A Field Guide to Independent Films about Place*. Berkeley: University of California Press, 2001.

Maeda Ai. *Text and the City*. Edited by James A. Fujii. Durham, N.C.: Duke University Press, 2004.

Manovich, Lev. *The Language of New Media*. Cambridge, Mass.: MIT Press, 2002.

———. *Software Takes Command*. New York: Bloomsbury, 2013.

Maruyama Masao. *Senchū to sengo no aida: 1936–1957* (During and after the war: 1936–1957). Tokyo: Misuzu shobō, 1976.

Massumi, Brian, ed. *The Politics of Everyday Fear*. Minneapolis: University of Minnesota Press, 1993.

Matsumoto Chitose. *Bijin ni mieru "kūki" no tsukurikata: Kirei no hiketsu 81* (Creating the "air" of a beautiful woman: 81 beauty secrets). Tokyo: Kōdansha, 2012.

Matsuura Izumi. "Dai 26-kai Subaru bungakushō jushōsha intabyū: Kurita Yuki" (The 26th Subaru literature prize winner interview: Kurita Yuki). *Subaru* 24, no. 11 (2002): 186.

May, Reinhard. *Heidegger's Hidden Sources: East-Asian Influences on His Work*. Translated by Graham Parkes. New York: Routledge, 1996.

McCarthy, Anna. *Ambient Television: Visual Culture and Public Space.* Durham, N.C.: Duke University Press, 2001.

McGee, Micki. *Self-Help, Inc.: Makeover Culture in American Life.* Oxford: Oxford University Press, 2005.

McGuiness, Andy, and Katie Overy. "Music, Consciousness, and the Brain: Music as Shared Experience of an Embodied Present." In *Music and Consciousness: Philosophical, Psychological, and Cultural Perspectives,* edited by David Clarke and Eric F. Clarke, 245–62. Oxford: Oxford University Press, 2011.

McLuhan, Marshall. *Understanding Media: The Extensions of Man.* New York: McGraw-Hill, 1964.

McNicol, Tony. "Designs for Life: Toy Story." *Japan Journal,* April 2006, 34–35.

Mertens, Wim. *American Minimal Music: La Monte Young, Terry Riley, Steve Reich, Phillip Glass.* Translated by J. Hautekiet. London: Kahn & Averill, 1983.

Mie, Ayako. "Black Kigyo: Unpaid Overtime Excesses Hit Young." *Japan Times,* June 25, 2013.

Milutis, Joe. *Ether: The Nothing That Connects Everything.* Minneapolis: University of Minnesota Press, 2006.

Minato Chihiro, Nakazawa Shinichi, Hosono Haruomi, and Itō Toshimaru. "Towards a Culture of Ex-stase: The Appearance of Intensive Expanse in the Digital Realm." Panel discussion at the NTT InterCommunications Center, Tokyo. *InterCommunication* 26 (Autumn 1998): 168–79.

Mita Itaru, ed. *Anbiento difinitivu 1958–2013* (Ambient definitive 1958-2013). Ele-king Books series. Tokyo: P-Vine, 2013.

———. *Ura anbiento myūjikku 1960–2010* (Ambient music part 2: 1960-2010). Tokyo: Infas Publishing, 2010.

Mita Itaru and Studio Voice, eds. *Anbiento myūjikku 1969–2009* (Ambient music 1969-2009). Tokyo: Infas Publishing, 2009.

Mita Munesuke. *Social Psychology of Modern Japan.* Translated by Stephen Suloway. London: Kegan Paul International, 1992.

Miwa Hidehiko. "Kokutō būmu yobu: Futsu shuppankai no keikō" (Hailing the Cocteau boom: A trend in French publishing). *Yomiuri shinbun,* September 3, 1973.

Miyadai Shinji. *Owari naki nichijō o ikiro: Ōmu kanzen kokufuku manyuaru* (Live the endless everyday: Complete manual for overcoming Aum). Tokyo: Chikuma shobō, 1995.

———. "Transformations of Semantics in the History of Japanese Subcultures." Translated by Shion Kono. *Mechademia* 6 (2011): 231–58.

Miyadai Shinji, Ishihara Hideki, and Ōtsuka Mieko. *Sabukaruchā shinwa kaitai: Shōjo, ongaku, manga, sei no henyō to genzai* (Dismantling subculture mythology: The transfiguration and the present of shōjo, music, manga, and sex). Expanded ed. Tokyo: Chikuma shobō, 2007.

Mori Masahiro. "Bukimi no tani genshō" (The uncanny valley phenomenon). *Energy* 7, no. 4 (1970): 33–35.

Morioka Masahiro. *Mutsū bunmeiron* (Painless civilization). Tokyo: Toransubyū, 2003.

Morris-Suzuki, Tessa. *Beyond Computopia: Information, Automation, and Democracy in Japan.* London: Kegan Paul International, 1988.

Morton, Timothy. *Ecology without Nature: Rethinking Environmental Aesthetics.* Cambridge, Mass.: Harvard University Press, 2007.

———. "'Twinkle, Twinkle, Little Star' as an Ambient Poem: A Study of a Dialectical Image; with Some Remarks on Coleridge and Wordsworth." In *Romanticism and Ecology.* Edited by James McKusick. 2001. http://www.rc.umd.edu/praxis/ecology/.

Murakami Haruki. *After Dark.* Translated by Jay Rubin. New York: Alfred A. Knopf, 2007.

———. *IQ84.* Translated by Jay Rubin and Philip Gabriel. New York: Alfred A. Knopf, 2011.

———. *Kaze no uta o kike* (Hear the wind sing). Tokyo: Kōdansha, 1982.

———. *Norwegian Wood.* Translated by Jay Rubin. New York: Vintage International, 2000.

———. *Rekishinton no yūrei* (The ghost of Lexington). Tokyo: Bungei shunjū, 1996.

———. *Sputnik Sweetheart.* Translated by Philip Gabriel. New York: Alfred A. Knopf, 2001.

———. "Tony Takitani." Translated by Jay Rubin. *New Yorker,* April 15, 2002, 74–81.

———. *What I Talk about When I Talk about Running: A Memoir.* Translated by Philip Gabriel. New York: Alfred A. Knopf, 2008.

Muschamp, Herbert. "Blueprint: The Shock of the Familiar." *New York Times Magazine,* December 13, 1998.

Nakagawa Osamu. *Fūkeigaku: Fūkei to keikan o meguru rekishi to genzai* (Landscape studies: The history and present of landscape and scenery). Tokyo: Kyōritsu shuppan, 2008.

Nakajima Haruko. *Nemureru nashi e no fūga: Erikku Sati ron* (Fugue for a sleepy pear: On Eric Satie). Kyō no ongaku (Today's music) series. Tokyo: Shinyasōsho, 1977.

Nakajima Yoshimichi. *Urusai Nihon no Watashi: "Otozuke shakai" to no hateshinaki tatakai (Japan, the noisy, and myself: The endless battle with the "pickled sound society").* Tokyo: Yōsensha, 1992.

Nakamata Akio. *Bungaku: Posuto-Murakami no Nihon bungaku* (Literature: Japanese literature after the Murakami revolution). Tokyo: Asahi, 2002.

Newton, Isaac. *Opticks: Or, A Treatise on the Reflexions, Refractions, Inflexions and Colours of Light.* London: Smith and Walford, 1704.

Ngai, Sianne. *Our Aesthetic Categories: Zany, Cute, Interesting.* Cambridge, Mass.: Harvard University Press, 2012.

———. *Ugly Feelings.* Cambridge, Mass.: Harvard University Press, 2005.

Nornes, Abé Mark. *Forest of Pressure: Ogawa Shinsuke and Postwar Japanese Documentary.* Minneapolis: University of Minnesota Press, 2007.

Nozawa, Shunsuke. "The Gross Face and Virtual Fame: Semiotic Mediation in Japanese Virtual Communication." *First Monday* 17, no. 3 (March 2012). http://firstmonday.org/ojs/index.php/fm/article/view/3535/3168.

Oguma Eiji and Ueno Yōko. *<Iyashi> no nashonarizumu: Kusa no ne hoshu undō no jisshō kenkyū* (The nationalism of "healing": An empirical study of the grassroots conservative moment). Tokyo: Keiō gijuku daigaku shuppankai, 2003.

Ōhara Yūji. "Bungaku to ongaku no kōsaku: Shuppatsuki ni okeru Sakaguchi Ango" (Interplay between literature and music: Early days of Sakaguchi Ango). *Jinbun shakai kagaku kenkyū* 20 (March 2010): 1–16.

Osaka Ryōji. *Kankyō ongaku: Kaiteki na seikatsu kūkan o tsukuru* (Environmental music: Making a comfortable living space). Tokyo: Dainihon tosho, 1992.

Ōtsuka Eiji. *Monogatari shōmetsuron: Kyarakutāka suru "watashi," ideorogiika suru "monogatari"* (On the disappearance of narrative: "I" becomes a character, "narrative" becomes ideology). Tokyo: Kadokawa, 2004.

———. *"Otaku" no seishinshi: 1980-nendai ron* (A history of the "otaku" mind: On the 1980s). Tokyo: Kōdansha gendai shinsho, 2004.

Owen, David. "The Soundtrack of Your Life." *New Yorker,* April 10, 2006.

Parsons, William B. *The Enigma of the Oceanic Feeling: Revisioning the Psychoanalytic Theory of Mysticism.* New York: Oxford University Press, 1999.

Partner, Simon. *Assembled in Japan: Electrical Goods and the Making of the Japanese Consumer.* Berkeley: University of California Press, 1999.

Pinkus, Karen. "Ambiguity, Ambience, Ambivalence, and the Environment." *Common Knowledge* 19, no. 1 (Winter 2013): 88–95.

Reynolds, Simon. "Chill: The New Ambient—Music of the Fears." *ArtForum,* January 1995, 60–62.

———. *Generation Ecstasy: Into the World of Techno and Rave Culture.* New York: Routledge, 1999.

Rickert, Thomas. *Ambient Rhetoric: The Attunements of Rhetorical Being.* Pittsburgh: University of Pittsburgh Press, 2013.

Roquet, Paul. "A Blue Cat on the Galactic Railroad: Anime and Cosmic Subjectivity." *Representations* 128 (Fall 2014): 124–58.

———. "Obayashi Nobuhiko, Vagabond of Time." *Midnight Eye,* November 10, 2009. http://www.midnighteye.com/features/nobuhiko-obayashi -vagabond-of-time/.

Rose, Nikolas. *Governing the Soul: The Shaping of the Private Self.* 2nd ed. London: Free Association Books, 1999.

———. *The Politics of Life Itself: Biomedicine, Power, and Subjectivity in the Twenty-First Century.* Princeton, N.J.: Princeton University Press, 2007.

Ross, Julian. "Site et spécificité dans le cinéma élargi japonais: L'essor de l'intermedia à la fin des années 1960" (Site and specificity in Japanese expanded cinema: Intermedia and its development in the late

1960s). *Décadrages,* March 2013, 81–95. http://www.decadrages.ch/site-and-specificity-japanese-expanded-cinema-intermedia-and-its-development-late-60s-julian-ross.

Saitō Tamaki. "Floating and Disassociation." *ART iT* 18 (Winter/Spring 2008): 84–89.

———. *Hikikomori: Adolescence without End.* Translated by Jeffrey Angles. Minneapolis: University of Minnesota Press, 2013.

———. *Shinrigakuka suru shakai: Iyashitai no wa "torauma" ka "nō" ka* (The psychologizing society: Do we want to heal "trauma" or "the brain?"). Tokyo: Kawade shobō shinsha, 2009.

Sakai, Naoki. *Translation & Subjectivity: On "Japan" and Cultural Nationalism.* Minneapolis: University of Minnesota Press, 1997.

"Sakamoto's 'Energy Flow' Enlivens Japan." *Billboard,* July 2, 1999.

Sas, Miryam. *Experimental Arts in Postwar Japan: Moments of Encounter, Engagement, and Imagined Return.* Cambridge, Mass.: Harvard University East Asia Center, 2011.

"Sati eranda Kamiya Ikuyo-san" (Kamiya Ikuyo who chose Satie). *Yomiuri shinbun,* September 11, 1985.

"Sati no 'Piano ongaku zenshū'" (Satie's "Complete Piano Music"). *Yomiuri shinbun,* March 14, 1968.

Satie, Erik. *Memoirs of an Amnesiac: To Be Read Far from the Herd and the Mummified Dead, Those Great Scourges of Humanity.* London: M. Paddison, 1981.

Scarry, Elaine. *Dreaming by the Book.* Princeton, N.J.: Princeton University Press, 1999.

Schlomowitz, Matthew. "Cage's Place in the Reception of Satie." 1999. http://www.shlom.com/?p=cagesatie.

Sedgwick, Eve Kosofsky. *Touching Feeling: Affect, Pedagogy, Performativity.* Durham, N.C.: Duke University Press, 2003.

Seo Inwoo. "Namae kara no tōhi: 'Koyūmei' no aregorii toshite yomu 'Tony Takitani'" (Escape from the name: "Tony Takitani" as an allegory of the "proper noun"). In *Kyūdainichibun* 10 (October 2007): 52–64.

Shamberg, Michael. *Guerilla Television.* New York: Raindance, 1971.

Shaviro, Steven. *Post Cinematic Affect.* Winchester, U.K.: Zero Books, 2010.

Sherif, Ann. "Japanese without Apology: Yoshimoto Banana and Healing." In *Ōe and Beyond: Fiction in Contemporary Japan,* edited by Phillip Gabriel and Stephen Snyder, 278–301. Honolulu: University of Hawai'i Press, 1999.

Shibata Namio. "Bunjin fū no hitogara nijimu: Barubie no Sati sakuhin ensō" (A personality steeped in literati style: Barbier performs Satie's works). *Asahi shinbun,* December 28, 1977.

"Shiroi chūshoku o tabe: Sati no rendankyoku" (Eat a white lunch: Satie's piano duets). *Asahi shinbun,* September 26, 1980.

Sigrist, Peter. "Embarrassing Ode to McDonald's as an Open Public Office Space." *Polis.* http://www.thepolisblog.org/2011/06/embarrassing-ode-to-mcdonalds-as-open.html.

Simmel, Georg. *On Individuality and Social Forms: Selected Writings.* Chicago: University of Chicago Press, 1971.

Skov. "Fashion Trends, Japonisme, and Postmodernism." *Theory, Culture, and Society* 13, no. 3 (August 1996): 129–51.

Sloterdijk, Peter. *Bubbles.* Vol. 1, *Spheres.* Translated by Weiland Hoban. Los Angeles: Semiotext(e), 2011.

———. *Globes.* Vol. 2, *Spheres.* Translated by Weiland Hoban. Los Angeles: Semiotext(e), 2014.

Smith, Greg M. *Film Structure and the Emotion System.* Cambridge: Cambridge University Press, 2003.

Spitzer, Leo. "Milieu and Ambiance: An Essay in Historical Semantics." *Philosophy and Phenomenological Research* 3, no. 1 (September 1942): 1–42.

Sterne, Jonathan. "Sounds Like the Mall of America: Programmed Music and the Architectonics of Commercial Space." *Ethnomusicology* 41, no. 1 (Winter 1997): 22–50.

Stewart, Kathleen. *Ordinary Affects.* Durham, N.C.: Duke University Press, 2007.

Studio Voice 392. Ambient & Chill Out special issue (August 2008).

Sun, Cecilia Jian-Xuan. "Experiments in Musical Performance: Historiography, Politics, and the Post-Cagian Avant-garde." Ph.D. diss., University of California, Los Angeles, 2004.

Takahashi Aki. "Erikku Satie to 'Kagu no ongaku'" (Erik Satie and "furnishing music"). *Ansanburu.* 1999. Accessed March 17, 2010. http://members.jcom.home.ne.jp/akitakahashi/akinote3.html. Site discontinued.

———. *Parurando: Watashi no piano jinsei* (Parlando: My life as a pianist). Tokyo: Shunjūsha, 2013.

Takei, Jirō, and Mark P. Keane. *Sakuteiki: Visions of the Japanese Garden.* Boston: Periplus Editions, 2001.

Tamm, Eric. *Brian Eno: His Music and the Vertical Color of Sound.* Boston: Faber and Faber, 1989.

Tanaka Naoki. *Tezawari no media o motomete: Shōhi shakai no genzai* (Pursue a tactile media: Contemporary consumer society). Tokyo: Mainichi shinbunsha, 1986.

Tanaka Satoshi. *Kenkōhō to iyashi no shakaishi* (A social history of health techniques and healing). Tokyo: Seikyūsha, 1996.

Tanaka Yūji. *Denshi ongaku in Japan* (Electronic music in Japan). Tokyo: Asupekuto, 2001.

Templier, Pierre-Daniel. *Erik Satie.* Translated by Elena L. French and David S. French. Cambridge, Mass.: MIT Press, 1969.

Thaemlitz, Terre. "Globule of Non-Standard: An Attempted Carification of Globular Identity Politics in Japanese Electronic 'Sightseeing Music.'" *Organized Sound* 8, no. 1 (2003): 97–107.

Thibaud, Jean-Paul. "The Sonic Composition of the City." In *The Auditory Culture Reader,* edited by Michael Bull and Les Back, 329–41. Oxford: Berg, 2003.

Thompson, Emily Ann. *The Soundscape of Modernity: Architectural Acoustics and the Culture of Listening in America, 1900–1933.* Cambridge, Mass.: MIT Press, 2002.

Thornbury, Barbara. "History, Adaptation, Japan: Haruki Murakami's 'Tony Takitani' and Jun Ichikawa's *Tony Takitani*." *Journal of Adaptation in Film & Performance* 4, no. 2 (2011): 159–71.

Thrift, Nigel. "Intensities of Feeling: Towards a Spatial Politics of Affect." *Geografiska Annaler* 86B, no. 1 (2004): 57–78.

Toop, David. *Ocean of Sound: Aether Talk, Ambient Sound, and Imaginary Worlds.* London: Serpent's Tail, 1995.

Truax, Barry. *Acoustic Communication.* Norwood, N.J.: Ablex, 1984.

Ueda Noriyuki. *Kakusei no nettowāku* (Network of awakening). Tokyo: Katatsumurisha, 1990.

Ueno Chizuko. *<Watashi> sagashi gēmu: Yokubō shimin shakairon* (The game of searching for "me": On a society of desiring private citizens). Tokyo: Chikuma shobō, 1987.

Unno Jūza. "Jūhachijikan no ongaku yoku" (The music bath at 1800 hours). In *Unno Jūza zenshū*, vol. 4. Tokyo: Sanichi shobō, 1988.

UR. Ambient Music special issue. December 1990.

Vawter, Noah. "Ambient Addition: How to Turn Urban Noise into Music." Master's thesis, Massachusetts Institute of Technology, 2006.

Washida Kiyokazu. *Mōdo no meikyū* (The labyrinth of fashion). Tokyo: Chikuma shobō, 1996.

———. *<Yowasa> no chikara: hosupitaburu na kōkei* (The power of "weakness": Scenes of hospitality). Tokyo: Kōdansha, 2001.

Watanabe Tadashi. *Ninniku kenkōhō: Naze kiku, nan ni kiku, dō taberu* (Garlic healing methods: Why it works, what it works for, how to eat it). Tokyo: Kōbunsha, 1974.

Watsuji Tetsurō. *Climate and Culture: A Philosophical Study.* Translated by Geoffrey Bownas. New York: Greenwood Press, 1988.

———. *Fūdo: Ningengakuteki kōsatsu* (Climate: An anthropological inquiry). Tokyo: Iwanami shoten, 1935.

———. *Watsuji Tetsurō's Rinrigaku: Ethics in Japan.* Translated by Robert E. Carter. Albany: State University of New York Press, 1996.

Yagi Kōsuke. *<Iyashi> toshite no sabetsu: Hito shakai no shintai to kankei no shakaigaku* ("Healing" as discrimination: Sociology of human society's relationship to the body). Tokyo: Hihyōsha, 2004.

Yamaguchi Katsuhiro. *Eizō kūkan sōzō* (Image space creation). Tokyo: Bijutsu shuppansha, 1987.

Yamamoto Shichihei. *"Kūki" no kenkyū* (Research on "air"). Tokyo: Bungei shunjū, 1977.

———. *Nihonjin to Yudayajin* (The Japanese and the Jews). Tokyo: Kadokawa shoten, 1971.

Yamane Yumie. "Zettai-teki kodoku no monogatari: Murakami Haruki 'Tonii Takitani' 'Kōriotoko' ni okeru jendā ishiki" (A story of absolute isolation:

Gender consciousness in Murkami Haruki's "Tony Takitani" and "The Ice Man"). *Kokubun gakkō* 205 (March 2010): 19–33.

Yoda, Tomiko. "The Rise and Fall of Maternal Society: Gender, Labor, and Capital in Contemporary Japan." *South Atlantic Quarterly* 99, no. 4 (Fall 2000): 865–902.

Yoshida Nobuko. "Banana Girls: Three Storytellers Carry on Yoshimoto Banana's Tales of Healing and Renewal." Japanese Fiction Project: Emerging Writers in Translation. Accessed October 12, 2006. http://www.j-lit.or.jp/e/programs/%20newtrends/nobuko_yoshimoto.en.html. Site discontinued.

———. "Shohyō 'Onuiko Terumii' Kurita Yuki: Tarareba no nai sekai" (Book review of Kurita Yuki's *Terumii the seamstress*: A world with no "what-ifs"). *Bungakukai* 58, no. 8 (2004): 291–93.

Yoshimi Shunya. "The Market of Ruins, or the Destruction of the Cultural City." Translated by Jo Lumley. *Japan Forum* 23, no. 2 (2011): 287–300.

Yoshimoto Banana. *Amrita*. Translated by Russell F. Wasden. New York: Grove Press, 1997.

———. *Kitchen*. Translated by Megan Backus. New York: Grove Press, 1993.

Yoshimoto, Midori. "From Space to Environment: The Origins of *Kankyo* and the Emergence of Intermedia Art in Japan." *Art Journal,* September 22, 2008, 24–45.

Yoshimoto, Midori, ed. *Expo '70 and Japanese Art: Dissonant Voices.* Special issue, *Review of Japanese Culture and Society* 23 (2011).

FILM AND VIDEOGRAPHY

Akarui mirai (Bright future) (Kurosawa Kiyoshi, Japan, 2003).

Apoptosis (Tsuchiya Takafumi, Japan, 2008).

Aura (Takagi Masakatsu, Japan, 2003).

Berlin: Die Sinfonie der Grosstadt (Berlin: Symphony of a great city) (Walter Ruttmann, Germany, 1927).

Birdland (Takagi Masakatsu, Japan, 2001–2).

BU-SU (Ichikawa Jun, Japan, 1987).

Byōin de shinu koto (Dying at a hospital) (Ichikawa Jun, Japan, 1993).

Chelovek s kinoapparatom (Man with a movie camera) (Dziga Vertov, USSR, 1929).

Daidō Moriyama (Stray Dog of Tokyo) (Fujii Kenjirō, Japan, 2001).

Empire (Andy Warhol, USA, 1964).

Entr'acte (Rene Clair, France, 1924).

Friends of Minamata Victims: A Video Diary (Nakaya Fujiko, Japan, 1971–72).

Future Garden (Yamaguchi Katsuhiro, Japan, 1983).

Galaxy Garden (Yamaguchi Katsuhiro, Japan, 1986).

Gensō kōjō (Industrial romanesque) (Nihon Media Play series, Japan, 2006–12).

Hatsu-yume/First Dream (Bill Viola, Japan, 1981).

Hitsuji ga suki: Nihon no hitsuji bokujō (I like sheep: Japanese sheep ranches) (Synforest, Japan, 2009).

Jellyfish: Healing Kurage (Kikkawa Hiroshi and Kodama Yūichi, Japan, 2006).

Jour de reve (Kawamura Yuki, France, 2005).

Kick the World (Kawanaka Nobuhiro, Japan, 1974).

Kiri (Mist, Hagiwara Sakumi, Japan, 1972).

Kōkaku kidōtai (Ghost in the Shell) (Oshii Mamoru, Japan, 1995).

Le feu follet (Will o' the wisp/The fire within) (Louie Malle, France, 1963).

Light Park #2 (Takagi Masakatsu, Japan, 2001–2).

Mabataki no kazu (Number of blinks) (Ise Shōko, Japan, 2003).

Mercuric Dance (Arai Tadayoshi, Japan, 1984).

Noema (Ise Shōko, Japan, 2008).

Paradise View (Takamine Gō, Japan, 1985).

+Intersection (Ise Shōko, Japan, 2002).

Port (Kawamura Yuki, France, 2005).

Rama (Takagi Masakatsu, Japan, 2002).

rheo: 5 horizons (Kurokawa Ryōichi, Japan, 2010).

Ryoma to tsuma to sono otto to aijin (Ryoma's wife, her husband, and her lover) (Ichikawa Jun, Japan, 2002).

The Silk Road (NHK television series, Japan, 1980–84 and 1988–89).

Slide (Kawamura Yuki, France, 2005).
Sono otoko, kyōbō ni tsuki (Violent cop) (Kitano Takeshi, Japan, 1989).
Summer Afternoon (Ise Shōko, Japan, 2008).
Swimming in Qualia (Ise Shōko, Japan, 2007).
Tadon to Chikuwa (Tadon and Chikuwa) (Ichikawa Jun, Japan, 1998).
The Third Man (Carol Reed, UK, 1949).
Thursday Afternoon (Brian Eno, USA/Japan, 1984).
Tokyo Marigold (Ichikawa Jun, Japan, 2001).
Tony Takitani (Ichikawa Jun, Japan, 2004).
Ugetsu monogatari/Ugetsu (Mizoguchi Kenji, Japan, 1953).

DISCOGRAPHY

Akiyama Kuniharu. *Obscure Tape Music of Japan*. Vol. 6, *Tape Works of Aki-yama Kuniharu 1*. Omega Point, 2007.
Benedictine Monks of Santo Domingo de Silos. *Chant*. Angel, 1994.
Caelum. *Weather Report*. Around the Records, 2008.
Carlos, Wendy. *Switched-On Bach*. Columbia, 1968.
Davis, Miles. *Kind of Blue*. Columbia, 1959.
Deep Forest. *Deep Forest*. Columbia, 1992.
Enigma. *MCMXC a.D.* Virgin, 1990.
Eno, Brian. *Ambient 1: Music for Airports*. EG, 1978.
——. *Ambient 4: On Land*. EG, 1982.
——. *Discreet Music*. Obscure Music, 1975.
HAT. *Tokyo Frankfurt New York*. Daisyworld, 1996.
Hatakeyama Chihei. *Minima Moralia*. Kranky, 2006.
Hosono Haruomi. *BonVoyage Co./Taian yōkō*. Panam, 1976.
——. *Coincidental Music*. Monad, 1985.
——. *The Endless Talking*. Monad, 1985.
——. *Mercuric Dance*. Monad, 1985.
——. *Paradise View*. Monad, 1985.
——. *Paraiso*. Alfa, 1978.
——. *Tropical Dandy*. Panam, 1976.
Hosono Haruomi and Yokoo Tadanori. *Cochin Moon*. King, 1978.
Hosono Haruomi with Friends of Earth. *S.F.X.* Teichiku/Non Standard, 1984.
Ichiyanagi Toshi. *Obscure Tape Music of Japan*. Vol. 5, *Toshi Ichiyanagi, Music for Tinguely*. Omega Point, 2006.
Inoue, Tetsu. *Ambiant Otaku*. FAX +49–69/450464, 1994.
——. *Fragment Dots*. Tzadik, 2000.
——. *Slow and Low*. FAX +49–69/450464, 1995.
——. *World Receiver*. Instinct Ambient, 1996.
Inoue, Tetsu, and Pete Namlook. *2350 Broadway*. FAX +49–69/4504643, three volumes, 1993–96.
Jansen, Steve. *Swimming in Qualia (Ascent)*. Samadhisound, 2008.
Kitaro. *Silk Road*. 2 volumes. Pony Canyon, 1980.
KLF. *Chill Out*. KLF Communications, 1990.
Onodera Yui. *Entropy*. Critical Path, 2005.
Sakamoto Ryūichi. "Energy Flow." *BTTB*. Sony Classical, 1999.
——. *Tony Takitani*. Commmons/Avex, 2007.
Speedometer. *Private*. Flavour of Sound, 1999.
——. *Sense of Wander*. Roots, 2002.

Takahashi Aki. *Aki pureizu Sati: Hoshitachi no musuko* (Aki plays Satie: Son of the stars). EMI, 1985.

Tomita Isao. *Snowflakes are Dancing*. RCA Red Seal, 1974.

Various Artists. *Ambient 4: Isolationism*. Virgin, 1994.

Various Artists. *Artificial Intelligence*. Warp, 1992.

Yellow Magic Orchestra. *BGM*. Alfa, 1981.

INDEX

Paul Roquet is a postdoctoral fellow in global media and film studies at Brown University.